Property Disobedience as Protest

DEMOCRACY, CITIZENSHIP,
AND CONSTITUTIONALISM

Jeffrey Green, Series Editor

PROPERTY DISOBEDIENCE AS PROTEST

Rethinking Political Nonviolence

William E. Scheuerman

PENN

UNIVERSITY OF PENNSYLVANIA PRESS

PHILADELPHIA

Published by
University of Pennsylvania Press
Philadelphia, Pennsylvania 19104–4112 USA
www.pennpress.org

EU Authorized Representative:
Easy Access System Europe - Mustamäe tee 50,
10621 Tallinn, Estonia, gpsr.requests@easproject.com.

Printed in the United States of America on acid-free paper
10 9 8 7 6 5 4 3 2 1

A Cataloging-in-Publication record is
available from the Library of Congress

Hardback ISBN 978-1-5128-2867-2
eBook ISBN 978-1-5128-2868-9

CONTENTS

Introduction. Protest and Property Damage   1

Chapter 1. Why Property Disobedience?   7

Chapter 2. Violence and Property   28

Chapter 3. Symbolic Property Disobedience   53

Chapter 4. Disruptive Property Disobedience   78

Chapter 5. Property Seizures   106

Chapter 6. Revisiting Property   146

Chapter 7. Goodbye to Nonviolence?   167

Notes   185

Index   223

Acknowledgments   231

INTRODUCTION

Protest and Property Damage

Commenting on campus protests opposing Israel's war in response to the October 2023 Hamas terrorist attack, then–President Joseph Biden on May 2, 2024 reiterated conventional wisdom about non-violent versus violent protests. While noting that "peaceful protest is in the best tradition of how Americans respond to consequential issues," Biden observed that we also remain committed to the rule of law, underscoring that "violent protest is not protected; peaceful protest is. It's against the law when violence occurs. Vandalism, trespassing, breaking windows, shutting down campuses, forcing the cancellation of classes and graduations—none of this is a peaceful protest. . . . Threatening people, intimidating people, instilling fear in people is not peaceful protest. It's against the law. . . . There should be no place on any campus, no place in America for antisemitism or threats of violence against Jewish students."[1] Donald Trump had already gone further, a week earlier characterizing the campus upheavals as unruly, destructive riots. In contrast to Biden, who not only recognized the virtues of peaceful dissent but acknowledged that most campus protest tactics likely fell under its rubric, Trump seemed to label *all* participants violent antisemites. A 2017 white supremacist rally in Charlottesville, Virginia, Trump claimed, was a "little peanut and . . . nothing compared" to what was transpiring on college campuses.[2]

About forty people were injured in Charlottesville when a neo-Nazi drove a car into a crowd of opponents. At the time, President Trump was widely criticized for remarks suggesting equivalency between violent far-right extremists and peaceful counter-protestors. Trump's comments were emblematic of a longstanding tendency to demonize protestors whose positions he rejects while looking the other way at destructive and sometimes violent acts by allies and sympathizers.

To be sure, Biden's familiar liberal and Trump's authoritarian-populist assessments differ in morally and politically consequential ways. Nonetheless, both suggested that a wide range of protest activities—including property damage, trespassing, and vandalism—deserved to be described as violent, or at least: *prospectively* violent intimidation. Both presupposed broad ideas of violence as encompassing destructive harms to persons as well as property. Neither seemed interested in empirical evidence demonstrating that violence had in fact been marginal to the protests.[3] Invoking the venerable ideal of the rule of law, Biden's more nuanced remarks still downplayed the fact that the "best tradition" of American protest encompasses illegal but politically motivated acts, including those usually characterized as *nonviolent civil disobedience*. His audience might easily have forgotten that one of its greatest practitioners, Dr. Martin Luther King Jr., is honored on a national holiday every third Monday in January.

Countless other major political figures, pundits, and media commentators similarly frame politically motivated property harms as political violence, a familiar pattern that typically functions to place them beyond the pale of acceptable dissent. Since empirical research shows that public opinion generally responds negatively to violent protest, the consequences can prove disastrous for political movements.[4]

This volume pushes back against these and related conflations of politically motivated violations of property rights with violence. It does so not because this author thinks we should celebrate smashing windows, tearing down statues, sabotaging pipelines, occupying land or buildings, or looting. Nor do I believe that physical intimidation or "threats of violence" are acceptable in democracies. But indiscriminately clumping property damage with political acts destructive of and harmful to persons is conceptually confusing and politically misleading. As a kid growing up in upstate New York with an interest in history, my teachers taught me to celebrate the Boston Tea Party. So why do so most of us now brand parallel acts of political vandalism violent and condemn them? When, if ever, are politically motivated property harms justifiable? What standards should we expect those pursuing them to meet, under imperfect yet identifiably democratic conditions? Are there nonviolent as well as violent varieties of what I will describe as *property disobedience*?

What follows is a work of empirically informed, normative political theory. Lawyers explore the binding rules and standards regulating protest politics. Historians and social scientists seek to understand the roots of political protest and identify general patterns and their probable causes. Although I rely on their research, mine is an evaluative endeavor focused chiefly on the question of how democracy—and the core ideal of political equality—potentially permits some but not all politically based property harms. I do not intend to moralize from my perch in the ivory tower. Rather, the approach employed here accords roughly with a vision of political theory as "democratic underlaboring," that is, an identifiably scholarly and theoretical inquiry but one aimed at raising the quality of political discussion within democratic contexts, while not claiming any privileged epistemological (or political) standpoint.[5] In this vein, I focus on real-life cases and examples from social movements, taking seriously what participants in and defenders of property disobedience, as well as their critics, have had to say, with special attention to democracy's core premises. Surveying property disobedience and the debates it generates, in conjunction with some basic normative intuitions derived from widely shared ideas of democracy and political equality, should provide us with useful evaluative standards.

This study grows out of my previous writings on nonviolent civil disobedience, whose major theorists and iconic practitioners usually looked askance at property harm. They worried that it too often counterproductively detracted from otherwise predominantly nonviolent political efforts.[6] Much can be said in defense of this position. Nonetheless, when we rethink the conventional account of property disobedience as a priori violent, matters get more complicated. It then becomes difficult to see why it always must be viewed as politically out of bounds. Civil disobedience involves politically motivated illegalities, but judges, juries, and government officials sometimes rightly demarcate it from opportunistic, self-serving criminality; protest participants may be penalized less severely than ordinary lawbreakers. This makes sense: it is one thing to occupy a lunch counter to demand a free lunch because you forgot your wallet; it is quite another to do so because you oppose racial segregation. Similarly, I argue that citizens and state officials need to distinguish property disobedience from run-of-the-mill criminality, recognizing that while illegal it often rests on political motives that deserve a proper hearing in a pluralistic democracy.

Is it unrealistic to expect officials—and especially those responsible for enforcing and upholding the law—to start viewing some cases of property disobedience more favorably? Most likely, given the present political climate. But historical examples provide some reason for hope. Although heavily regulated, picket lines (by striking workers, for example) are now basically legal in the United States and constitute a familiar feature of the political landscape.

Prior to the New Deal, however, they were illegal; the Supreme Court equated them with violent intimidation.[7]

Unfortunately, governments are promulgating statutes that invite officials to sanction even basically peaceful protests, effectively foreclosing avenues for identifiably constructive expressions of political dissent.[8] Others—including the US government—are claiming far-reaching authority based on existing statutes and constitutional norms to pursue unusual and perhaps unprecedented repression.[9] This trend has hit property disobedients hard.[10] Democracy is under attack in the United States and around the world. To resist that attack we need to counter the ongoing, sometimes draconian criminalization of peaceful protest. In the process, we need to leave more political space for basically nonviolent protests that involve damage to property.

Chapter 1 defines and also positions property disobedience within general debates about politically motivated lawbreaking, including nonviolent civil disobedience. Engaging King's thoughtful reflections on property harms amid riots that severely impacted US cities in the mid- and late 1960s, I explore why the topic again seems timely. At various junctures in the volume, I return to King's ideas for political inspiration and theoretical clarification.

In scholarly discussions of disobedience, protest, and resistance, we presently find two competing theoretical and political "camps." On the one hand, defenders of strictly nonviolent civil disobedience typically associate property damage with violence and consider it out of bounds. On the other hand, a growing range of voices defends militant or uncivil disobedience and resistance. The latter group often condones limited political violence, under whose rubric they place property harms. Unfortunately, neither camp treats property damage as a distinctive matter worthy of special investigation. Nor do they push back strongly enough against the commonplace view of protests involving property damage as inherently violent.

Chapter 2 defends a sharp conceptual distinction between violence and property harms, arguing that the latter are sometimes closely related to the former but there is no reason to conflate them. When property disobedience fails to result in—or cannot be meaningfully related to—concrete injuries or harms to persons, it does not make sense to view it as violent. The key takeaway is that some property disobedience remains in principle congruent with political nonviolence vis-à-vis persons, which I defend as a sine qua non of democracy.

The proceeding three chapters turn to property disobedience's ideal-typical varieties. Chapter 3 considers *symbolic property disobedience* by focusing on recent controversies about Black Lives Matter (BLM) protests that resulted in damages to or removals of Confederate and other racist monuments and statues. Once we recognize that defacing or tearing down commemorative artifacts is fundamentally different from violent acts harmful to and destructive of persons, many of these protests appear basically akin to nonviolent civil disobedience. Describing them as such should have significant moral, legal, and political consequences.

Chapter 4 addresses *disruptive property damage*, with close attention to illuminating examples of radical labor unionists and environmental militants who have embraced sabotage as a tactic. Although in principle potentially nonviolent, sabotage encourages a martial mindset and paramilitary orientation inconsistent with democracy. As calls for sabotage become fashionable among some green militants, they would do well to reflect on and circumvent its familiar dangers.

Chapter 5 explores *property seizures*, which take three main types: (1) *reclamations* or *repossessions*, (2) *repurposings* or *reusages* (usually of buildings or land), and (3) *takings* or *usages* (of consumer goods). More clearly than other modes of property disobedience, seizures pose fundamental questions about property and its different types. By attending to a range of recent and historical examples, this chapter begins to address them. Crucially, I reject the commonplace view that property disobedience entails a violent assault on property qua property. If we stop and listen to what squatters who reuse land or buildings have to say, for example, this does not make sense: they criticize existing property relations while articulating their own sometimes plausible ideas about property. Property disobedience usefully thematizes the messy relationship between many widely held intuitions about property and their real-world instantiations; the two are frequently in tension.

Chapter 6 systematically addresses key questions about property. Property disobedience not only presupposes distinguishing between and among public and private property but also the latter's different subtypes (for example, sole proprietorships, partnerships, and corporations), something I briefly try to unpack and explore. Some acts of property disobedience are best viewed as seeking to realize the social and economic preconditions of a reformed, more egalitarian democratic community. Others are suitably controversial and may pose threats to democracy's underlying normative and political principles.

Finally, Chapter 7 responds to a growing number of voices for whom my attempt to update political nonviolence is likely to represent a rearguard action oblivious to the harsh dictates of our violent political universe. To be sure, the worldwide authoritarian resurgence poses far-reaching challenges to my defense of a nuanced but identifiably nonviolent vision of political protest. Like many now condoning violent protest, I aim to provide space for carefully selected property harms. In contrast, however, my efforts remain part of a concerted attempt to update and defend political nonviolence, something they increasingly appear to reject. Whether I succeed in doing so will ultimately have to be determined by you, the reader.

CHAPTER 1

Why Property Disobedience?

Can politically motivated property damage be justified? If so, what conditions should we expect those engaging in it to meet? What role, if any, can property harms play as normatively admissible political lawbreaking? Can we delineate its justifiable from unjustifiable renditions?

These—and related—questions are hardly of mere academic interest. Within recent years *property disobedience* has constituted a prominent feature of a wide range of political protests:

1. Beginning on November 8, 2016 and extending into the spring of 2017, Iowa-based environmental and Catholic Worker activists Ruby Katherine Montoya and Jessica Recznicek secretly punctured holes in and engaged in arson attacks on the Dakota Access Pipeline, which they viewed as posing serious contamination risks to local water supplies.[1] Montoya and Recznicek embraced sabotage, they claimed, only after pursuing possible legal avenues for redress and participating in conventional protests. Inspired by the radical Catholic peace activists Daniel Berrigan and the Plowshares Eight, and in solidarity with Indigenous protestors who deemed the proposed pipeline a violation of treaty rights that posed environmental threats, they insisted that they had conscientiously sought to avoid any harm to human life and were committed to practicing nonviolence.[2] Montoya and Recznicek were apprehended by officials after they issued a detailed public statement on July 24, 2017 laying out the moral and political grounds for their acts.[3]

Applying tough US domestic terrorism measures designed in part to thwart environmental saboteurs, US prosecutors indicted them on nine federal charges. In June 2021, Recznicek was sentenced to eight years in prison; in September 2022, Montoya received a six-year sentence.[4] They were also required to pay $3.2 million in restitution. During their trials, US District Judge Rebecca Goodgame Ebinger asserted that their protest had put the lives of firefighters and construction workers at risk. Describing their endeavors as "laudable but misguided," Ebinger agreed with prosecutors who viewed the women's action as "incredibly dangerous conduct."[5] Montoya and Recznicek have become a cause célèbre of sorts among environmental militants who view sabotage as a legitimate political tactic.[6]

2. During the 2014 "Umbrella Movement" Hong Kong pro-democracy protests, student activists remained principally committed to political non-violence interpreted as prohibiting harms to both persons and property. A second round of 2019–20 mass protests, however, took on a different coloration, with protestors engaging in violent battles with police and committing extensive property damage. The movement's radicalization seems to have represented a response to police repression and the refusal of PRC allies to compromise over Hong Kong's political fate. Official claims to the contrary, little random property destruction or looting seems to have occurred. Protestors targeted public and private property they viewed as implicated in the PRC's sought-for authoritarian makeover. Symbols of PRC influence and the offices of pro-PRC legislators were damaged, as were banks and businesses owned by those viewed as supporting the PRC. Some property damage was retaliatory: after the company operating Hong Kong's subways caved in to government pressure and closed down stops near planned protest sites, activists vandalized train stations. Boundaries between property destruction and physical violence, however, occasionally became blurry. Violence against police, usually justified as a form of self-defense, transpired alongside property damage.[7]

The pro-democracy movement's radicalization may have simply accelerated the PRC's authoritarian clampdown. Hong Kong activists, at any rate, have faced draconian legal penalties and lengthy prison sentences, and the PRC has quashed their efforts to achieve self-rule and preserve basic civil liberties.

3. The May 25, 2020 police murder of George Floyd in Minneapolis set off an astonishing wave of antiracist Black Lives Matter protests around the world, including about 30,000 public demonstrations in the United States involving an estimated 15 to 26 million participants.[8] Independent researchers as well as US police chiefs confirm what most participants and sympathizers have claimed: 93 percent of demonstrations connected to the movement involved neither violence against persons nor property destruction.[9] Nonetheless, opinion polls taken in the shadows of the protests suggested that as many as 42 percent of Americans viewed BLM as inciting violence and destructive of property.[10] In part fueled by incendiary comments by President Trump and

unsympathetic media coverage, this misperception nonetheless had some basis in reality. Hundreds of racist and colonialist public statues and monuments were defaced and toppled. Some were removed or damaged by activists, whereas others were taken down or relocated by public officials.[11] Street battles with police were a rare exception to the general (nonviolent) rule. Yet, looting and arson attacks, in Minneapolis, Portland, and other major cities, took place. Police stations and police vehicles were targeted. Luxury retail chains as well as small businesses suffered heavy damages, with the insurance industry reporting over $1 billion in losses.[12] As one Los Angeles looter told a *Los Angeles Times* writer, "We've got no other way of showing people how angry we are."[13] There and elsewhere, many minority-owned businesses tragically suffered damage at the hands of what appear to have been opportunistic acts of arson and looting. In Portland, Seattle and other cities, militants occupied public spaces and declared them "autonomous" no-go zones off limits to police and public officials, with fierce battles and fatalities ensuing. Many who fought with the police or engaged in property destruction soon faced criminal charges and penalties.

4. Since 2003 Anonymous, the decentralized, internationally based network of "hacktivists," has regularly targeted computer servers and websites to disrupt presumed wrongdoings. Some of its acts have resulted in property damage and economic losses. In 2021, for example, the group announced "Operation Jane" before hacking the website of the Texas Republican Party, flooding it with memes and inviting visitors to donate to Planned Parenthood and other groups opposed to the recently promulgated Texas Heartbeat Act, which banned abortions after six weeks of pregnancy.[14] Anonymous has a long history of illegally accessing and releasing data to shame persons and institutions. Some observers praise the group for generating public debate on matters of broad political concern, whereas critics accuse it of spreading misinformation, trolling innocent people, and sexual harassment.[15]

5. On January 8, 2023 supporters of outgoing Brazilian President Jair Bolsonaro engaged in substantial destruction of public property at capital buildings in Brasilia. Furniture and equipment were damaged, with the offices of the Workers' Party, Social Democratic Party, and other anti-Bolsonaro figures suffering extensive damage. Fires were set and hydrants damaged to prevent firefighters from responding. Protestors vandalized iconic art works by famous Brazilian artists and other symbols of national pride. Valuable patriotic items, including a ball signed by the soccer legend Neymar da Silva Santos, were stolen. Since Brazil's legislature was not in session, no lawmakers

were harmed.[16] Yet, as critics quickly pointed out, Bolsonaro sympathizers among police and security forces appear to have turned a blind eye during the attacks. Hundreds of participants were arrested and charged. Bolsonaro has been banned from seeking reelection for eight years and has faced a variety of legal charges. Inspired by the January 6, 2021 attack on the US Capitol, the Brasília protestors similarly aimed to subvert election results. The earlier Washington, DC protest also involved damage to targeted congressional offices (belonging, for example, to then–Speaker Nancy Pelosi) and statues of Thomas Jefferson and other national icons. Since the US Congress, in contrast, was in session and tasked with finalizing the presidential election results, property harms merged palpably with violence against and intimidation of capitol police and elected officials, including Pelosi and then–Vice President Mike Pence.

Countless examples could easily be added to this list. Like property itself—which can either be public or private, tangible or intangible—political acts that entail damage or harm to property can take myriad forms. We see politically oriented illegal property violations committed both by those professing and those rejecting nonviolent commitments. Some happen more or less spontaneously during protests. Others constitute discreet, carefully planned acts. Property disobedience can aim to serve democracy or undermine it; it can take on left- or right-wing contours. Participants might be locally based, part of a national or global movement, or loosely affiliated with cross-national networks whose affiliates have never met in person.

Property disobedients often face stiff penalties; protest-related property harms rarely enjoy legal protection.[17] However, public sympathy, as well as the legal penalties meted out, can vary. While US federal prosecutors and Judge Ebinger threw the book at Montoya and Recznicek, officials elsewhere have occasionally demonstrated leniency. Juries can respond either harshly or appreciatively. UK BLM activists who toppled a Bristol statue of the philanthropist and slave trader Edward Colston on June 7, 2020, for example, were found "not guilty" by a jury after their two-week trial in January 2022.[18]

No system of property can flourish if acts that damage, destroy, or seize property were made legal. But the fact that some of these acts are *politically* motivated, and that perpetrators aim to address broader publics and treat their political peers with *respect*, should matter, both in terms of our normative evaluation and the legal system's response. Property disobedients break the law, but they often do so in ways that distinguish them from ordinary criminals.

Viewed through a wider historical lens, recent incidents of property dis-obedience simply represent the latest installments in an unfinished narrative. In early modern Europe, Catholics and Protestants defaced and destroyed their rivals' sites of worship and residences as a way of ridding the world of so-called "moral pollution."[19] Christians vandalized synagogues and Jewish religious symbols during shockingly frequently pogroms. In many places, peasants and laborers damaged and seized property to express outrage or oppose injustice. They stole wood or smashed new time-saving devices or technology they considered culpable for their misfortunes.[20] Sometimes they participated in a "culture of retribution" directing their anger at officials and the economically privileged.[21] During economic crises, or when the prices of basic foodstuffs abruptly took off, hungry people seized bread from bakers or grain dealers, blocked shipments and retained them for their own use, and commandeered food supplies.[22]

African slaves who fled to Canada or free states in antebellum America—refusing to accept their status as someone else's property—engaged in prop-erty disobedience, as did abolitionists who aided their efforts.

During the twentieth century, anarchists, labor militants, partisan fighters trying to bring down fascism, South African anti-apartheid militants, suf-fragettes, and others embraced property damage as a political tactic. Figures as diverse as the Wobbly (International Workers of the World) Elizabeth Gurley Flynn, the British suffragette Emmeline Pankhurst, and the African National Congress' Nelson Mandela endorsed sabotage and political vandal-ism. More recently, environmentalists have spiked trees to obstruct logging companies, while others have damaged SUVs to protest their contributions to global warming. Animal rights defenders have broken into and damaged laboratories and company buildings to release animals. For their part, far-right extremists and racists have set fire to buses transporting migrants and refugees along with hotels and public buildings housing them.

Though historically commonplace, politically based property damage may now be on the rise when compared to the late twentieth century, when many democracies experienced general declines in political violence.[23] The global private insurance industry reports that recent protests have generated massive and probably unprecedented losses to businesses, going so far as to argue that they have "changed insurance forever" because of the incurred losses' enormity.[24] We still lack reliable empirical data, in part because politi-cally motivated property damage gets clumped by those quantifying protest types alongside other violent political acts. Since the early 2000s, there is some evidence of increases in protest-related violence, which typically include acts of property damage.[25]

Protest-related property damage's apparent increase likely has multiple sources. It remains striking, however, that it correlates with enhanced legal protections for private and especially corporate property, a direct consequence of a period in which both national governments and international organizations (e.g., the International Monetary Fund [IMF] and World Trade Organization [WTO]) embraced aggressively neoliberal economic policies.[26] A prominent legal historian of private property in the US characterizes the period since the 1980s as "property resurgent," as courts have made it more difficult for government to seize property for public purposes and have blurred the boundaries between ordinary regulatory endeavors and "takings" of private property requiring fair compensation.[27] Conservative legal thinkers have long called for stronger property protections; their efforts seem to have paid off.[28] At the global level, thousands of bilateral investment treaties, sometimes begrudgingly consented to by developing countries only at the behest of international organizations and powerful nation-states, have strengthened foreign investors' property rights.[29]

Neoliberalism has also helped pave the way for a far-reaching *proprietization* of creative activity, data, information, and knowledge, as corporations, universities and other major institutions have secured copyrights, patents, and trademarks giving them control over a wide array of intangible objects and services resulting from recent technological innovations. Key sources of wealth today do not necessarily depend on owning material or physical objects, but instead depend on property in concepts, ideas, images, and information. An economy in which companies increasingly "lease, rent, or charge an admission fees subscription, or membership dues" for access to immaterial goods has not, despite some initial expectations, undermined strict private property rights.[30] On the contrary, what Jeremy Rifkin aptly calls the "increasing commodification of all human experience" accompanying this shift relies both on creating novel types of private property and extending its scope.[31]

Some recent cases of property disobedience—for example, damage to businesses during the 1999 Seattle WTO or post–2008 financial crisis anti-austerity protests—expressly target neoliberalism. Yet most do not. Nonetheless, as social existence has become increasingly proprietized, with governments frustrating opportunities to transform property relations by ordinary political and legal means, it is hardly surprising that many people are opting to pursue extra-legal protests involving property harms.[32] With property increasingly beyond the effective reach of ordinary democratic electorates, it is not always clear what other options people have.

Journalists, political observers, and major scholars, at any rate, think something significant is afoot.[33] Since Mahatma Gandhi and Martin Luther King Jr., defenders of nonviolent civil disobedience have generally looked askance at violence not just against persons but also property. The liberal philosopher John Rawls famously defined civil disobedience as a "public, nonviolent, conscientious yet political act" of lawbreaking.[34] It was *political* in the sense that it sought political change or reform, and *civil* in part because strictly nonviolent. Civil disobedients were expected to provide evidence of respect for or fidelity to law, which in a basically democratic context was interpreted as generally in sync with the political community's shared sense of justice, as ensconced in the constitution and its core principles. Showing respect for the law or constitution typically required accepting legal penalties—for example, appearing in court and facing the prospect of sanctions.[35]

The story is a complicated one, but civil disobedience as practiced by Gandhi and King and theorized by Rawls and others soon morphed into what the contemporary philosopher Candice Delmas calls the "civil disobedience playbook," a selective and occasionally idealized interpretation of canonical ideas about it. In that playbook, property damage is off-limits.[36] According to this well-nigh universal view, property harm represents *uncivil* lawbreaking that, especially under liberal and democratic political conditions, cannot be justified. As the liberal philosopher Hugo Bedau pointedly declared, civil disobedience should never be "intentionally or negligently destructive of property or harmful to persons."[37]

In chapters to come, we explore the relationship between politically motivated property damage and nonviolent civil disobedience; it proves more complicated than first seems apparent. Why does it matter? Nonviolent civil disobedience possesses a moral and political cachet from which political agents sometimes benefit. By placing their acts under its rubric activists can conveniently associate their efforts with iconic figures such as Gandhi and King. There are no guarantees, but when participants successfully convince a judge or jury that they belong among the ranks of Gandhi's or King's political offspring they may face reduced penalties. Sorting the relationship between property and nonviolent civil disobedience is not simply a matter of conceptual calisthenics; it is politically consequential.

For the present, I simply note the existence of numerous recent—and perhaps increasing—cases of protests that abandon the standard civil disobedience playbook: militants seem more willing than their historical predecessors to condone so-called "violent" property damage. We may be undergoing a shift in what the political sociologist Charles Tilly dubbed protest *repertoires*. Tilly showed that during specific historical junctures people tend to cling to a relatively limited set of forms of collective protest; they modify them incrementally and slowly. When protesting they draw on "limits set by the repertoire already established" for a specific time and place.[38] Many of us have learned, for example, how to demonstrate peacefully, attend a mass rally, or participate in ritualized civil disobedience that requires nonviolence vis-à-vis both persons and property. We gained the requisite practical know-how by watching and sometimes joining with others pursuing such activities. At other historical junctures, political actors drew on different sets of similarly adaptable, widely shared protest repertoires. Early modern peasants, for example, were unfamiliar with picket lines and nonviolent sit-ins, but they knew how to loot food granaries and steal grain from merchants they deemed dishonest. By the outset of the twenty-first century, a range of nonviolent tactics constituted a widely shared, arguably globalized protest repertoire.[39] A growing willingness among our contemporaries to embrace property damage suggests that things may now be changing.

Yet, even if we reject broad empirical generalizations about property disobedience's apparent trajectory, there is no disputing its past and present significance. That fact alone calls for a systematic examination of its types and their political and normative challenges.

*   *   *

Unfortunately, we still lack a systematic scholarly discussion of political property damage.[40] To be sure, intellectuals and activists have long debated the pros and cons of some of its variants (for example, sabotage), while scholars have analyzed them as part of the messy mix of popular collective violence. However, property disobedience tends to get addressed incompletely or only in passing, with one result being a tendency to marginalize key normative and political questions—for example, under what conditions might it make sense to describe it as potentially *legitimate*? Which of its various types may be prospectively acceptable and which unacceptable? This neglect surely stems in part from political property damage's controversial contours: it is regularly characterized by influential political figures, voices in the media, and many others as "violent." Who wants their reputation tarred by defending those who "violently" damage private or public property?

It also partly stems from its association with a variety of morally and politically loaded terms. The word "vandalism," for example suggests brutish and "uncivilized" action, a linguistic oddity that probably reflects a misplaced soft spot for the civilized Roman Empire over those naughty Germanic Vandals who dared to sack Rome. The terms "vandalism" and "vandal" are "always stigmatizing, and imply blindness, ignorance, stupidity, baseness or lack of taste."[41] "Looting" probably has its roots in British colonial rule in India where it was used to "denigrate and racialize riotous subalterns" unfairly depicted as having a congenital weak spot for plunder.[42] (British colonials, it seems, were innocent of plunder or robbery.) "Riot," another term frequently used to cover incidents of property disobedience, has a similarly distasteful genealogy.[43] Sabotage derives from the French *sabot*, a wooden shoe, suggesting slow or clumsy work. Nor does "squatting," with the connotation of being "low to the ground," conjure up positive images, though it is at least less biased than "invasion," the term favored by those eager to discredit building or land occupations.

It seems unlikely that we will ever agree on neutral language to capture something as politically explosive as property disobedience. Nor will it help to jettison our existing, one-sidedly negative terms for positive, more upbeat linguistic alternatives.[44] Yet we can still try to develop an analytic framework that better addresses property disobedience's undeniable political challenges.

Political scientists, sociologists, and others have contributed to an impressive array of empirical studies comparing nonviolent and violent movements. Under a variety of terminological guises, property disobedience surfaces in that literature. Unfortunately, by day's end its specific contours tend to get pushed aside.

For instance, Erica Chenoweth and Maria J. Stephan's award-winning *Why Civil Resistance Works: The Strategic Logic of Nonviolent Conflict* (2011) makes a persuasive case for nonviolent protest's superiority as a source of lasting change. To support their thesis, the authors rely on coding hundreds of cases from the history of resistance movements as *either* principally violent *or* nonviolent. Focusing on nonviolent opposition to authoritarian regimes, military occupiers, and—least frequently—secessionist movements, they argue that nonviolent prove superior to violent movements because the former lowers "moral, physical, informational, and commitment barriers to participation" and thus opens the door to mass mobilization.[45] Such mobilization, in turn, plays a role in movements' resiliency, tactical creativity, and increased chances for civic disruption, all of which work to augment political pressures on governments. Nonviolent movements prove better than their rowdier violent cousins at generating "loyalty shifts involving . . . erstwhile supporters" of the regime, "including members of the security force."[46]

Where does politically motivated property damage fit into the story? On the one hand, *Why Civil Resistance Works* offers a strict definition of nonviolence that excludes "bombings, shootings, kidnappings, physical sabotage such as destruction of infrastructure, and other types of physical harm of people *and property.*"[47] On the other hand, the volume operationalizes violence more strictly as *armed insurgency,* in part because the datasets Chenoweth and Stephan tap demarcate insurgency from incidents of "unarmed" collective violence (e.g., riots, property damage and physical harms committed by unarmed civilians). What this incongruity means is that the authors' robust claims on behalf of nonviolence's effectiveness rely on examples "coded as nonviolent [but] includ[ing] significant elements of unarmed violence," for example, the supposedly nonviolent Iranian Revolution, in which protestors committed widespread property destruction.[48]

Consequently, we ultimately gain no clear sense of where precisely property harms fit in. Read sympathetically, Chenoweth and Stephan have perhaps demonstrated that *predominantly* nonviolent movements that allow for some so-called "violent" property damage may be more effective than their violent rivals.[49] We cannot be certain, however, since property damage simultaneously gets clumped together with violence targeting persons and other types of militant protest.

Too little empirical research zeroes in on politically motivated property damage and its specific features. Tilly, for example, defined collective violence broadly as referring to physical damage "on persons and/or objects."[50] Another researcher defines it as "intentionally caused or carelessly accepted damage to/destruction of property or injuring/killing people."[51] The prestigious *Oxford Handbook of Social Movements* follows suit: protest violence includes a heterogeneous range of activities that inflict "physical, psychological, and symbolic damage to individuals and/or property."[52]

Parallel ambiguities plague canonical normative theories of civil disobedience. Although the standard playbook rendition tends to occlude the realities of a messier, more interesting historical and philosophical story, both famous practitioners and influential theorists generally demoted property damage's role by declaring it violent and thus beyond the pale.[53] For Rawls, for example, violent lawbreaking—and, most likely, property damage—fell under the rubric of "militant resistance" but not civil disobedience, with the former justifiable chiefly in authoritarian settings. Since Rawls was primarily interested in formulating a theory of justice for liberal democracy, he and many who subsequently followed him ignored complicated questions concerning property disobedience.[54]

More recently, theorists have broadened the idea of civil disobedience by allowing for some violent forms.[55] But since they tend to place property damage under an analogously open-ended definition of violence, they similarly tend to ignore its specific contours and their challenges. The traditional and—as I argue in Chapter 2—flawed premise that severe violations of persons and property damage represent different subsets of violence blocks the more differentiated analysis we require.

Contemporary writers are energetically defending "disruptive disobedience," "resistance," and "uncivil" disobedience.[56] In this vein, Delmas outlines a wide-ranging defense of uncivil lawbreaking, defined as "disobedient acts that are principled yet also deliberately offensive, covert, anonymous, more than minimally destructive, not respectful of their targets, or which do not aim to communicate to an audience the need to reform laws, policies, or institutions."[57] Although those engaging in uncivil disobedience should act responsibly and minimize harms, even some of its messy, sometimes violent forms are justifiable—and sometimes *obligatory*—in basically liberal or democratic societies. Its myriad virtues notwithstanding, this approach risks clumping property disobedience together with a wide range of other supposedly uncivil and "violent" protest. For Delmas, uncivil disobedience covers not just nonviolent but morally offensive protest, but also sabotage, armed resistance, vigilantism, and whistleblowing. This framing invites a failure to delineate between and among different political scenarios as well as illegal protests that might prove most appropriate to them.[58] When, for example, has so-called sabotage or looting proven not only acceptable but politically advantageous, and for whom? What have their costs been? Who has borne them? Which general or at least provisional lessons, if any, might we draw? Here again, property disobedience as a distinct mode of political action tends to vanish from view.

Related weaknesses appear in some similarly imposing normative-minded philosophical discussions of riots. Riots are complex, multifaceted political phenomena. One general feature seems to be their "unexpected, convulsive nature."[59] The philosopher Avia Pasternak defines "political rioting" as a form of "spontaneous, disorganized collective violence" typically entailing harms to public and private property as well as other persons (generally, police officers).[60] Political scientist Jonathan Havercroft characterizes them as involving "violence against persons, vandalism and looting."[61]

Beyond the reality that a term as emotionally loaded as "riot" seems unlikely to fulfill the requisite analytic and normative tasks, a great deal of property disobedience seems neither spontaneous nor disorganized. Reliance on the broad category of "riot" reproduces a familiar problem: property damage gets grouped alongside other militant (and sometimes violent) acts. Admittedly, there are plausible empirical reasons for doing so; they sometimes seem closely related. However, there is no reason to assume, as this conceptual framing implicitly suggests, an underlying commonality or necessary link. Smashing a Confederate statue, for example, damages public property, but when no one is harmed, no physical violence results. In many riots, looting constitutes a central and perhaps decisive trait. Why not then instead zero in on looting's specific dynamics and their normative challenges?

We are better off disaggregating messy terms such as "uncivil disobedience" or "riots" if we are to make sense of their components and gain a better understanding of possible relationships between and among them. Overly inclusive categories fail to capture key empirical distinctions or identify some key normative and political challenges. By using them, we risk sidelining variations between and among politically based property damage's forms: spraying graffiti on a colonialist statue, for example, seems intuitively different from looting or even destroying a small business during a riot and potentially posing an existential threat to its owners.

*   *   *

Chapter 2 looks more closely at the nexus between political violence and property disobedience. How and why is it sensible to distinguish them? When, if ever, might we characterize political property damage as akin to or possibly related to violence? Before proceeding we first need to clear some basic conceptual and methodological ground.

Property disobedience refers to a range of politically motivated acts that illegally damage or harm property, negatively impacting public or private owners by violating their rights.[62] The property harm may be "real"—for instance, hacktivists damage a computer, protestors smash a statue, or a crowd seizes consumer goods from a shop. Yet even when so-called squatters, for example, *improve* and constructively repurpose buildings or land they have occupied, they still infringe on someone's property rights. State officials, predictably, will charge them with some illegality. In many and perhaps most cases, property disobedients acknowledge having violated the law, even as they may justify their acts with more general appeals to the law. As with civil disobedience, as Rawls pointed out, there is frequently "some uncertainty as to whether the dissenters' action will be held illegal or not. But this is merely a complicating element."[63] Even those property disobedients who insist on the legality of their endeavors may refuse "to desist should the courts eventually disagree with them."[64] Such complications should not lead us to overlook the fact that authorities will have identified *some* legal violation.[65] And those—usually property owners—whose interests tend to be most effectively protected by government will vocally assert that their rights have been denied. They are also typically best positioned to generate sympathetic legal and political responses.

Property disobedience is *political* in the sense that it aims to change laws or binding regulations backed by state or state-backed institutions (for example, the IMF or WTO). Where disobedients do not expressly focus on specific laws or policies, they will still seek to modify some complex of power relations that requires changes to law and other binding rules. BLM protestors, for example, were not primarily protesting specific statutes but instead, more generally, racist policing as part of a broader system of white supremacy. Yet their acts remained indisputably political: dismantling racism necessitates ambitious overhauls to power relations within government, economy, culture, and education, a project that calls for extensive *state*—and always in part *legal*—action.

Here again, there are borderline cases. What about angry working-class teens who smash school windows or spray obscene graffiti on storefronts?[66] Or individual squatters who surreptitiously occupy private residences? There is no question that their—and many similar—acts have political contours. But here I am interested in scenarios where property is targeted because of some more or less self-declared political aims. Property damage limited to expressing inchoate frustration with the status quo will have to be sidelined, since it would simply take us too far afield. Despite the difficulties, most of the time it will not be difficult to distinguish property disobedience from nonpolitical property crimes. If I steal your laptop merely because I can get away with it and prefer yours to mine, that is a very different matter than Anonymous hacking and damaging Texas GOP computer servers to aid reproductive rights activists.

Similarly, my analysis brackets property damage by state or state-backed actors, some types of which—incidents of looting or sabotage, for example, when coordinated by officials—may resemble political acts by individuals and groups in civil society. I sideline such cases not because they are insignificant; on the contrary, they deserve careful attention. But here I focus on what we might roughly dub "bottom-up" protest-related property disobedience aimed at political change, not "top-down" efforts by state actors to advance the national interest or shape public opinion. Even if some empirical episodes blur this delineation, it should suffice for our purposes.

What about rebels or revolutionaries pursuing property disobedience as part of their efforts to construct a new political or social order? I bracket them as well, chiefly because I am interested in property disobedience within *functioning*, institutionalized, more or less democratic, basically orderly political contexts. Why *more or less* democratic? Because all existing democracies are flawed; democracy remains an incomplete project. Yet clear differences separate democratic from authoritarian polities.[67] Many of the examples explored come from my own country, the United States, primarily because the author is most familiar with them. On any reasonable measure, the United States represents an unfinished, terribly imperfect experiment in self-government, yet one still in possession—as I write—of some embattled democratic credentials.

Here as well, there are borderline cases. Until the recent PRC clampdown, for example, Hong Kongers enjoyed significant liberties, even if local sovereignty was subject to top-down decisions by Beijing. Admittedly, democratic backsliding and decay complicate this focus, with many present-day political regimes falling in the grey zone between democracy and authoritarianism. Even old democracies such as the United State remain vulnerable to such tendencies. Later in our analysis, we will explore their consequences for property disobedience.

The causes motivating protest-related property disobedience take myriad forms, some of which readers will understandably reject. It would be naive and historically myopic to assume that only the oppressed or disadvantaged pursue it, or that they always do so in morally acceptable or politically astute ways. In US history, a great deal of politically oriented property damage has transpired in the context of "white riots" in which racist whites destroyed Black-owned homes and property.[68] My aim is not to provide normative cover for heinous, destructive political acts by authoritarians, racists, or the like.

Yet, in a pluralistic political community we need to be mindful of the dangers of repressively shunting unpopular political positions aside. How then to evaluate property disobedience fairly? We need a measuring rod for property disobedience that tells us when it is unacceptable, even when undertaken by those with whom we sympathize. Defenders of democracy, the expansion of women's rights, antiracists, and many others have damaged property in morally and politically ambivalent ways. What general standards should they as well as less palatable property disobedients be expected to meet?

What follows is an effort to tackle that question. Although I write as a political theorist, I find it illuminating to focus on real-life historical and contemporary examples. I do not seek to posit some abstract, nominally universal theory of property disobedience and then mechanically deduce answers. Instead, my exposition relies on digging into the particulars of some of property disobedience's more revealing episodes. My discussion partly rests, to be sure, on conceptual and theoretical claims; Chapter 2 defends key ones pertaining to democracy and political violence. But the general argument's theoretical skeleton only takes on flesh and bones through a careful exploration of concrete cases. Unavoidably, I draw not just on political theory and philosophy but also history, political science, sociology, and the writings of journalists, political commentators, and movement participants.

The term *property disobedience* is borrowed from the legal scholars Eduardo Moises Peñalver and Sonia K. Katyal, who introduced it as a way of exploring how those committing property crimes may, in fact, counterintuitively update and improve property law. In their pathbreaking *Property Outlaws: How Squatters, Pirates, and Protestors Improve the Law of Ownership* (2010), property disobedience refers to violations of property law and the potentially constructive role they play within the design of a system of private ownership.[69] Here the category is used more broadly to capture identifiably political acts in which property rights are challenged or violated, even if the disobedient is only peripherally—or perhaps fundamentally—uninterested in property law per se. Hong Kong activists who trashed pro-PRC businesses, for example, were not aiming chiefly to reshape property relations but instead advance democracy and local autonomy. BLM sympathizers who tore down racist statues or looted chain stores were targeting racism and racist policing.

Some sympathized with efforts to change economic policies and the material injustices that undergird white supremacy. But they did so as part of a broader political project.

For other property disobedients, the desired changes pertain directly to property and its legal underpinnings. For example, squatters may seek major shifts in home or land ownership; hacktivists target the intellectual property rights status quo. Property disobedience in the sense used here covers such cases as well as those in which participants seek wider political changes and violate property rights as part of those efforts, without necessarily aiming *primarily* to modify property or its legal supports.

Nonetheless, the fact that politically lawbreaking impacts *property* and *ownership rights* remains consequential, even in the context of those protests having broader goals. The legal scholar Edwin Baker has persuasively argued that it makes sense to disaggregate the general notion of property by recognizing its separate, and by no means always congruent, social functions. Traditional thinking about property either conflates or simply ignores some of them while privileging others.[70] Property entails most basically the *use* or consumption, as well as *allocation*, of resources, both tangible and intangible. Property additionally serves a basic *welfare* function: it secures claims for people on resources the community deems essential to their well-being. People also define themselves in relation to and identify with their property, in part because they may see it as resulting from personal initiative and essential to their identity, a view Baker describes as property's *personhood* function. Property functions to *protect* individuals from exploitation or oppression from government and other people. Finally, property allows for some people to control and exercise power over others. This final *sovereignty* function grants both capitalists and managers of state-owned far-reaching decision-making privileges and authority vis-à-vis employees. According to Baker, the "significance of the sovereignty function tends to depend primarily on the distribution of resources in society."[71] When people lack property that would allow them to survive or flourish, property's sovereignty functions loom large: they will be effectively forced to seek employment and become subject to extensive workplace controls and regulations.

Property comes in different shapes and sizes, most of which can be grouped provisionally under the general categories of *private* and *public* property. As a legal entity, private property takes different forms—for example, sole proprietorships, partnerships, and corporations. We can also disaggregate public property into different subtypes—in other words, collective (or state) property and common property, in which "rules governing access to and control of material resources are organized on the basis that each resource is in principle available for the use of every member alike."[72] On the standard view, private property can be interpreted as consisting of a bundle of rights-based claims—for example, the owner's right to control and thus exclude others, use, manage, derive income from, alienate or transfer, and bequeath, all for a potentially unlimited duration.[73] It entails not just a relationship between the owner and some possessions but, more fundamentally, legally mediated *social* ties between persons. Proprietors have a duty not to use their resources to harm others; nonowners are expected to respect property rights. For contemporary libertarians, "property embraces the absolute right to exclude" others from using or taking advantage of them.[74] In the context of public property, by contrast, resources are governed by the general community and regulated by rules ensuring fair access and prohibiting individuals or groups from using them to preclude or disadvantage others.[75]

Legal systems typically treat and regulate public and private property differently. The extent to which civil and political liberties can be effectively exercised is partly determined by whether those doing so act in the context of private or public property.

With only slight exaggeration, a Harvard Business School professor once observed that "[o]nce a US citizen steps through the plant or office door at 9 a.m., she is nearly rightless until 5 p.m., Monday through Friday."[76] Fundamental civil and political rights such as free expression are only protected to a limited degree for employees and others within private businesses. The US Constitution, with some exceptions, "protects individuals against action by government, not by private agents."[77] Although basic rights remain in principle more secure in the context of public than private property, the differences sometimes blur. As the history of modern social movements quickly attests, protestors in public parks, on streets, or at other designated public sites can be charged with trespassing or failing to comply with a host of complex and sometimes arcane regulations. When King and other civil rights activists took to Birmingham's streets in 1963, they were charged with "parading without a permit" and encountered armed police aiming to enforce a court injunction. Inspired by the Spanish *Indignados* and Occupy Wall Street, in 2011 and 2012 protestors occupied parks and plazas worldwide to protest material inequality and neoliberal economic policies. Many soon faced forced removals by security officials who charged them with violating rules and regulations concerning the proper use of public space.

In democracies citizens possess rights to free speech and the right to assemble peaceably in identifiably public sites. But even those rights are hemmed in by specific—and by no means uncontroversial—norms and rules concerning their fair use. A messy collection of "judicial precedents, laws, regulations, common law actions, policing practices, and embedded norms" regulates public protests.[78] Many public properties are basically out of bounds even to peaceful protestors.[79] Even public universities have complicated and understandably controversial rules restricting protests.[80] According to one legal scholar, in the contemporary US "a citizen's right to come out to protest—or merely express solidarity with others—in response to a current event depends significantly on local officials' tolerance for inconvenience and disorder."[81] Consequently, even when protest "behavior has been nonviolent and would traditionally have been understood to be peaceable, participants . . . have frequently been charged with various misdemeanors, from disorderly conduct and breach of the peace to trespass and disobeying lawful police orders."[82] From the perspective of protestors, "what was legal can [seem to] become illegal from one minute to the next if a completely peaceful demonstration disturbs the peace or voluntarily or involuntarily trespasses."[83] A leading expert on the legal regulation of public protest, Timothy Zick, describes the existing US approach as a system of restrictively "managed dissent," in which officials are generally permitted to "over-regulate nonviolent assemblies, over-punish civil disobedience, impose burdensome costs and liabilities on protestors, respond to even the most peaceful protest with violence and aggression, and far too often escape liability for their actions."[84]

Protest participants only engage in *property* disobedience as interpreted here when their acts involve some appreciable harm to or violation of public or private ownership rights. Admittedly, this standard is contestable; some cases will not fall neatly under it. But most of the time it provides sufficient guidance. Antinuclear activists who briefly "sit in" at nuclear missile sites, for example, typically aim to protest nuclear policy but not the missiles' status as public property. When they secretly break into a missile site and damage or destroy expensive destructive weapons, however, they commit tangible, potentially costly harms to public property.

During the worldwide Occupy protests, large crowds gathered in parks, plazas, and public squares usually chosen because of their links, symbolic or otherwise, to major sites of political and economic power. Even as militants resisted efforts by state authorities to dismantle their encampments, it is doubtful that protestors chiefly aimed to harm or damage public spaces, though many of them assuredly favored a renegotiation of the rules regulating protest.[85] In some contrast perhaps, when Occupy Wall Street selected the privately owned Zuccotti Park as an occupation site, doing so in part to raise critical questions about the creeping privatization of public space, the group's efforts arguably constituted property disobedience. In effect, activists were repurposing what New York City zoning laws designate a "privately owned public space" (POPS) owned by the Brookfield Company and Goldman Sachs.[86] From the perspective of the park's corporate owners (and a series of court rulings that backed their claims), the protest generated sizable property harms.

This initial demarcation still leaves some unanswered questions. For example, how exactly should we evaluate tangible harms to property rights, and when should activists avoid incurring them? I hope to provide provisional answers in the analysis to follow.

Property disobedience, at any rate, comes in different shapes and sizes. To make progress, we need an analytically nuanced, empirically useful account of its various forms. In chapters to follow, I sketch a series of *idealized models* or *ideal types* to gain a better framework for making sense of the messy empirical cases we encounter in political life. Only with such a typology in hand can we tackle the difficult normative and political challenges posed by them. Ideal models or types, it is important to recall, are never found in a pristine form in social reality, even as they should enable a better understanding of its essential features.[87] They are always abstractions that heighten or accentuate, in an occasionally exaggerated manner, some of social reality's traits. Readers, of course, will have to decide whether my ideal types help make sense of property disobedience. The proof, as they say, is in the pudding. For now, I conclude by simply pointing out that the contemporary examples of property disobedience briefly noted at the start of this chapter already hint at the ideal-typical models I outline.

Hong Kong activists targeted symbols of PRC political and economic muscle as a way of symbolizing their opposition to Beijing's authoritarian agenda. Similarly, BLM protestors toppled Confederate and segregationist statues to publicly express hostility to racist policing and white supremacy. They and many other possible examples illustrate the centrality of *symbolic property disobedience*, in which legally unauthorized damage to or destruction of property is directed against a target that has been selected primarily because of its symbolic or expressive value. In neither case did militants probably expect that defacing or damaging prominent symbols of perceived injustices would, on its own, put an end to them.

Montoya and Recznicek sought to disable the Dakota Pipeline and in the process prevent possible toxic leaks into Iowa groundwater. Summer 2020 BLM protestors who damaged police stations and vehicles hoped to obstruct racialized policing. These are cases of what I call *disruptive* property disobedience. While usually having expressive or symbolic contours, these acts *additionally* aim to disrupt some practice viewed as unjust or illegitimate, with the targeted property interpreted as essential to the wrongdoing in question.

Some looters who ransacked businesses during the summer 2020 BLM protests were *seizing* private property. Hacktivists who have broken into and stolen confidential information have appropriated public as well as private property. Their political interventions contain not only symbolic and disruptive elements but also entail outright seizures of property, in which militants take and sometimes use what authorities standardly view as somebody else's property. They do so to challenge—and ideally correct for—some perceived injustice or inequity.

Politically oriented seizures probably represent property disobedience's most complicated variety. Because of their complexities, I identify three main subsets, namely: property *repossession*; *repurposing* and/or *reusage*; and *consumption* or *use* (typically, of consumer goods). Later I say more about why this categorization makes sense. For now, let me just briefly hint at the reasons behind it.

In the Dakota Access Pipeline protests, for example, Indigenous activists occupied land and joined Montoya and Recznicek in trying to protect water supplies, claiming that they were reclaiming and repossessing rights to territory that had been illegally taken from them. Poor farmers or unhoused urban residents may similarly assert that squatted lands or buildings are rightfully theirs. However, they generally do not posit that the properties *previously* belonged to them; they repurpose but do not reclaim property. Both property repossessions and repurposings often *prefigure* some new and ostensibly improved political or social universe. Their acts constitute efforts to create a reformed—and sometimes dramatically reorganized—set of property relations and concomitant political alternative. By doing so, they hope to communicate a political message to their peers while taking concrete steps toward creating the changed world they seek.[88] Rioters who loot businesses typically take, use up, or even destroy consumer goods. In contrast to those who repossess or repurpose land or buildings, however, their acts rarely point to the outlines of some alternative political or social vision. They often appear *retaliatory*: they punish those (for example, local businesses) they view as directly complicit in injustices against them.

Because there is no greater hurdle to a sound analysis of property disobedience than the well-nigh universal assumption that it is intrinsically *violent*, we now turn to explore the knotty debate about violence, and how best to define it.

CHAPTER 2

Violence and Property

When journalists and pundits discuss politically motivated property harms, they almost always characterize them as *violent*, as do most politicians and state officials. Even scholars seeking an objective assessment place property disobedience under the rubric of political violence, or at least presuppose some commonality between violence directed against persons and destructive activities against property. In this chapter I critically interrogate the sources of the widely held premise that property disobedience is basically violent. There are, in fact, sound reasons for viewing some types of property disobedience as *related* to violence. Nonetheless, the tendency to assume—without any real investigation—its violent contours is misleading. And it gets in the way of a systematic analysis of the challenges posed by property disobedience.

Since the word "violence" usually has negative connotations, its association with property disobedience makes an impartial assessment difficult if not impossible. Not only politically contestable but intrinsically polemical, the term "violence" functions "to change the way in which persons see their world."[1] Recourse to it loads the deck—ideologically, legally, and politically— against any endeavor to sketch a politically responsible justification for property disobedience. Not surprisingly, protestors who violate property rights frequently resist characterizing their efforts as violent, instead emphasizing their nonviolent bona fides. This chapter tries to take that claim seriously.

Admittedly, the standard view has an imposing pedigree and rests on rich genealogical sources. No less a source than the venerable *Oxford English Dictionary* (*OED*) defines violence as: "The exercise of physical force so as to inflict injury on or damage to persons *or property*; action or conduct characterized by this" (emphasis mine). Other reference guides to the English term *violence*—and similar guides to other languages—also join property damage and violence at the hip.[2] Doing so has long been part of linguistic usage, everyday political thinking, and high-brow intellectual analysis. Nonetheless, the basic idea motivating this convention is confused. We need to do better.

In this spirit, I start by briefly revisiting some now canonical statements, mostly from philosophers and political theorists, about how to conceive of and understand violence. I do so not because these scholars have somehow directly shaped everyday usage of the term or recent political debates; their real-life influence has been limited. Instead, they proffer what are accurately viewed as the most sophisticated attempts available to make sense of the idea of violence. If we can successfully demonstrate that even their auspicious efforts fail to justify the longstanding marriage of property damage to violence, our reasons for opposing it will have gained some footing. In the process, we can undermine the conventional wisdom, which often rests on less systematic versions of what the philosophers have to say about the concept of violence. So our exploration of scholarly debates about violence represents more than ivory-tower theorizing.

By examining where and how theorists have gone wrong, we can identify key ideational differences between violence and property damage. Doing so is crucial if we are to gain a more nuanced understanding of their relationship. Only by challenging the conventional wisdom can we then reconsider possible connections between property damage and violence. Scrutinizing possible causal relations is more productive than presupposing their basic equivalence.

The chapter then returns more directly to the political field. I revisit some insightful, mostly posthumously published remarks about property damage from Dr. Martin Luther King Jr., who presciently anticipated the necessity of delimiting the concept of political violence. Writing in the aftermath of massively destructive riots that shook Detroit, Newark, and about 160 other US cities in the summer of 1967, King pointedly insisted on distinguishing harm to property from violence. Significant for our purposes in this chapter is that he suggested a version of political nonviolence that would rest on a principled "core of nonviolence towards persons."[3] I use King's reflections as a launching pad for salvaging a view of nonviolence that can serve as a basis for a theory of property disobedience. To successfully do so we will need to consider some of King's implicit assumptions about property.

*   *   *

The philosopher Vittorio Bufacchi has helpfully distinguished between *minimalist* and *maximalist* or comprehensive conceptions of violence. Proponents of the former typically define violence as "an intentional act of destructive force," whereas the latter defend broader views in which it encompasses a wide "range of rights violations" and, in extreme cases, myriad social injustices (e.g., the denial of educational opportunities, poverty, gender inequality, racism, etc.).[4] Some scholars associate the former with a liberal and the latter a radical political standpoint, though this delineation hardly seems necessary let alone self-evident.[5] Some minimalists are located on the political left; one can easily imagine a comprehensive view having mainstream or conservative credentials.

Among those committed to a comprehensive view, the peace researcher Johan Galtung argued in an influential 1969 essay that violence was present "whenever human beings are being influenced so that their actual somatic and mental realizations are below their potential realizations," either because of some intentional activity or as a consequence of potentially indirect or "structural" sources.[6] While defenders of the minimalist reading usually focus on violence's intentionality and physicality, Galtung envisioned it as having additional psychological as well as social and institutional contours. A wide variety of avoidable restrictions on personal and collective self-development and human flourishing could be viewed as violent. Even if no one intentionally injures another person, violence can be built into social structures and manifest "as unequal power and consequently as uneven life chances."[7] In capitalism, for example, authority to determine the distribution of resources is unequally shared, resulting in systemic or structural gaps between actual and potential somatic or mental realizations—in other words, unnecessary restrictions on possibilities for self-realization especially among lower income groups.[8] From this perspective, capitalism is a system of *structural* or, alternately, *institutional* violence.[9]

On his maximalist or comprehensive view, Galtung conceded, there is little that distinguishes violence from myriad social injustices.[10] Precisely this element of Galtung's view has irked minimalists such as the philosopher C. A. J. Coady, who—with some undeniable justification—have retorted that maximalists stretch the term's uses to sacrifice its primary association with destructive, typically harmful or injurious acts. Comprehensive views inadvertently sideline violence's most basic—and typically onerous—facets. As violence becomes ever more conceptually inclusive, it becomes unproductively amorphous: "as the range of things denoted by the term expands, its descriptive force contracts."[11] When reconfigured as the keystone of a wide range of injustices, what, if anything, remains special about violence?

For Coady and other minimalists, broad definitions along the lines of Galtung's encourage "the cosey but stultifying belief that there is one problem, the problem of (wide) violence, and hence it must be solved as a whole with one set of techniques."[12] Overly inclusive definitions transform the concept of violence into a stand-in for a range of social injustices, which are then reductively interpreted as different facets of violence and, in principle, all capable of being resolved by the same devices. Yet "it may well be that quite different techniques, strategies, and remedies are required to deal with . . . violence than are needed to deal with such issues as wage injustice, educational inequalities and entrenched privileged."[13] Achieving nonviolence or peace is not the same thing as reducing material inequality or entrenched gender or racial inequities. Comprehensive accounts of violence get in the way of both nuanced social analysis and effective political action.

Between these two extremes, we find a range of theoretical positions that, while transcending narrow views of violence as harmful, destructive activity, aim to avoid the excesses of Galtung's and similarly comprehensive accounts. Much of the debate occupies this intermediate space. Interlocutors have addressed a range of complicated issues—for instance, whether violence requires intentionality and some sort of action, or instead can transpire absent intentionality and even in the context of what philosophers call act omissions, or failures to act.

Some of the debate centers around how violence should be interpreted in relation to cognate terms such as *force* and *coercion*. Despite some linguistic and conceptual overlap, most writers prefer to differentiate them.[14] They are probably right to do so. We might plausibly define force, for example, as the general "ability to work some change in the world by the expenditure of physical effort," without any physical or psychological injuries necessarily ensuing.[15] Chopping and splitting wood harvested from a dead tree requires force; ordinary English speakers will probably deem it unusual to call those doing so "violent." Coercion can include forms of compulsion (e.g., moral blackmail) unrelated to violence. Even some canonical practitioners of nonviolent civil disobedience such as Gandhi and King viewed their efforts as potentially coercive. Joan V. Bondurant, one of Gandhi's early American enthusiasts, noted that his movement relied on methods involving "an element of compulsion which may effect a change on the part of an opponent which initially was contrary" to his or her will and may prove costly to them. She pointed out that "[n]on-cooperation, boycott, strike" all involved "an element of compulsion."[16] King, Gandhi's greatest American disciple, concurred. In his famous "Letter from Birmingham City Jail" he conceded that civil rights activists sought "to create a crisis and establish such creative tension that a community that has constantly refused to negotiate is *forced* to confront the issue."[17] More recent theorists of nonviolent civil disobedience have made a persuasive case for its congruence with a wide range of identifiably coercive behaviors.[18]

Crucial for our purposes here is that defenders of both minimalist and more comprehensive views, as well as politically mainstream and more radical writers, too often presuppose the orthodox view that damage to property is intrinsically violent. Despite their otherwise imposing philosophical efforts, they rarely try to justify that position. In those rare cases where they *do* address it, their reflections are, more often than not, brief and unsatisfactory.

Coady, for example, endorses a modified version of the *OED* view of violence as physical force that inflicts injury or damage to persons or property. His admirable quest to cleanse the idea of violence of undesirable accretions and ambiguities notwithstanding, he preserves—without any explanation— the traditional view of property damage as violence. After rigorously criticizing Galtung's expansive view of violence, he defends modest revisions to the *OED* definition. As he accurately notes, there are cases where extreme psychological harm can prove just as debilitating to persons as physical force; damage to persons can also happen absent physical coercion or violence—for example, when poison is dropped into somebody's drink.[19] But his updates leave property untouched. One reason why Coady is eager to categorize his minimalist version as liberal perhaps stems from the implicit suggestion that violence to persons and property destruction are somehow equivalent, and that both persons and property are morally valuable. That view coheres with traditional liberal ideas about the sanctity of private property. Since Coady says nothing about property in his amendment to the OED view, however, we cannot know for sure whether that is his aim. At any rate, his purportedly minimalist concept turns out to be less minimal than first appears: it presupposes the commonplace view of property damage as basically violent.

More surprisingly, radical philosophers and theorists do so as well. Ted Honderich, for example, defines violence as "a considerable or destroying use of force against persons or things," with even less attention than the *OED* or Coady to the question of whether the object or "thing" in question represents somebody's property.[20] Smashing my neighbor's living room window, for example, seems different from destroying the windshield of an abandoned and ostensibly unowned car on a vacant lot. In a related vein, Robert Paul Wolff insists that nonviolent protests that negatively impact property rights can prove more violent than physical force: a peaceful sit-in bankrupting the lunch counter owner, for example, might imply "greater injury than would be accomplished by a mere beating in a dark alley."[21]

One can, to be sure, debate whether nonviolent protest unavoidably relies on—or perhaps inadvertently generates—violence. There is a longstanding debate about fringe or "flank" violence in otherwise basically nonviolent social movements.[22] But the more immediate problem is that writers embrace an expansive view of violence as including physical harm or injury to *both* persons *and* property, with inadequate attention to the resulting oddities. The social philosopher Robin Celikates, for example, asserts that illegal protest can include violence, which potentially encompasses property damage and blockades of streets, railroads, or buildings.[23] Because nonviolent protests can be harmful, it no longer makes sense to insist on civil disobedience taking strictly nonviolent forms.[24] He and others endorsing revised, relatively broad notions of civil disobedience tend to endorse correspondingly wide views of violence.[25]

Vital distinctions risk getting lost. When a torturer viciously brutalizes a young anti-government protestor with a billy club, the activist will likely suffer deeply injurious "shock, bruises, scratches, swelling or headaches to broken bones," whereas if the torturer uses the same club to smash the activist's cell phone or the chair to which he or she had been tied, something very different transpires.[26] The activist will have been violated in deeply injurious and psychologically traumatic ways. In contrast, a chair or cell phone will not experience excruciating pain, injuries, or lasting psychological trauma. The militant will probably require medical and psychological care; the chair or laptop gets disposed of and forgotten, with their owners perhaps inconvenienced but maybe not much more. The acts may initially appear similar, but their *effects* are quite different.

This is likely why some writers who defend the idea of violence as covering property damage say a bit more, typically by suggesting that property represents *extensions* of the person. On this view, damage to property is factually inseparable from violence against persons. For Bufacchi, for example, violence is best characterized as a "violation of integrity" that "may occur at the physical or psychological level."[27] His account, he tells us, presupposes a "metaphysical conception of the self as something violable."[28] Since damage to property or possessions represents one way in which violations of selfhood transpire, he argues, it constitutes violence.

Here we can discern the makings of what Baker calls property's personhood function, namely that people's control over "unique objects and . . . specific spaces" is "fundamentally intertwined with their present and developing individual personality or group identity."[29] In this vein, the legal theorist Margaret Jane Radin defends a "personality theory" of property, according to which control over resources is essential to autonomy and self-development.[30] Unfortunately, this intuition is rarely if ever carefully developed among theorists of violence. It too often gets quickly supplanted by references to John Locke and some version of a labor theory of property. In a widely read essay, for example, Newton Garver has noted that since the "right to the product of one's labor, which has played an important role in the theory of both capitalism and communism," is fundamental to personhood and autonomy, destruction of property represents violence.[31] Damage to property eo ipso is destructive of persons. The same underlying intuition regularly surfaces among commentators skeptical of protest-related property destruction. Conservative *National Review* editor Rich Lowry, for example, criticized BLM-related property damage during the 2020 protests by arguing that "people pour themselves into their property, using their earnings to pay for it, improving it, becoming identified with it." Property is not a lifeless "abstraction." Because people put themselves into their property, it represents an unmediated extension of their persons and is no less deplorable than violent acts directed at persons.[32] Although BLM sympathizers sometimes sought to distinguish property damage from violence, Lowry countered, doing so misunderstands the social significance of property along with its moral bases.

Admittedly, there is something to be said in favor of this position. For now, I make two brief critical observations.

First, Locke's account and related labor theories of property remain controversial; they require more attention than they receive among those debating violence.[33] One problem is that it seems unlikely that Locke can help us make sense of property disobedience in the context of public property (e.g., damage to public monuments or statues). More generally, Lockean theory fails to capture the complex realities of a modern economy in which massive, bureaucratically organized private corporations loom so large.[34] Despite some attempts to proffer a loosely Lockean defense of modern capitalism, doing so generates difficulties. Some business owners have undeniably "mixed" their labor and "poured themselves" into their enterprises. But is not that also true for the workers, for example, at an automobile plant owned by wealthy stockholders?[35] Like many US academics, I have "property" in retirement funds invested in a range of firms I could not even name. It seems odd to assert that I have somehow mixed my labor with the commodities they produce and sell. Property does not, at present, take one standard type; that fact raises questions for Locke and overly simple accounts based on a labor theory of property. Contemporary capitalism relies for ideological support on labor theories while in fact frequently disconnected from and sometimes openly violating them.[36]

In this spirit, the philosopher Tony Milligan correctly notes that "because of the mixed nature of property, because of the fact that that so many things can be claimed as possessions, the idea that property must be respected does not generalize."[37] Limited protest-related damage to a multimillion-dollar corporate hotel is one thing. Setting fire to a small family-owned business or the local mayor's personal home seems like another.

Second, the personality theory does not purport to identify essential links between *all* or even most existing property, but only with objects connected to or bound up with persons and their opportunities to develop and flourish. A home or apartment, for example, arguably provides a necessary space for privacy and self-development in a way that other forms of private or public property may not. Revealingly, Radin calls for material redistribution in order "for all citizens to have whatever property is necessary for personhood."[38] The implicitly Hegelian inspiration for these views, Jeremy Waldron has pointed out, is "more applicable to a petit-bourgeois economy of small owner-occupiers than to an advanced capitalist economy."[39] The personality theory posits that property is an extension of persons in some but by no means all contexts. It cannot ground indiscriminately conflating violence against persons with property destruction, especially under existing economic conditions, though it admittedly suggests that in *some* instances the two may turn out to be linked.

In fairness, some writers occasionally intuit something approaching this necessary refinement. Even as they try to hold on to the traditional, overly broad view of violence, what ultimately bothers them about property damage is that it tends to "get at" persons, in other words, that it directly contributes to tangible harms or injuries. Property's relation to persons is what counts.[40] These writers implicitly admit that violence to persons and property differ, with the former representing its primary and normatively most troublesome type.[41] The philosopher Kai Nielsen has commented that it is "extremely important to distinguish between violence against property and violence against persons. The sacking of the ROTC office is one thing; the shooting of an ROTC officer is another."[42] Versions of this intuition appear regularly in writings by and directed at political activists.[43] Among recent theorists of civil disobedience, it takes the form of outlining more demanding standards for violence against persons than property destruction. Though still wedded to broad definitions of violence, these writers recommend that activists do whatever they possibly can to avoid the former but not always the latter.[44] While the OED definition and writers such as Coady make no distinction between violence against persons or property, these writers start to do so. They introduce a conceptual modification that poses a bigger challenge than they acknowledge: when push comes to shove, it is "the *effect* of violence upon persons that invests it with moral significance."[45] Or, as Mark Vorobej comments, "property matters, from a moral perspective, only insofar as that damage somehow *affects* the well-being of sentient creatures," including—of course—human beings.[46] Property damage is violent in the secondary sense that it potentially contributes to physical or severe psychological injuries to persons, impacting or *affecting* them in deeply injurious ways.

The long tradition of thinking about property damage as intrinsically violent impedes scholars from following up on this crucial lead. Robert Audi, another philosopher and author of a classical essay on violence, not only illustrates this general tendency but allows us to see more clearly why it should worry us. Like others, Audi concedes that violence to persons (and, he adds, other sentient beings) can be distinguished from violence to property. So why not see them as ideationally different? Why continue to group them under one overly inclusive idea of violence? For Audi, violence to persons takes the form of "the vigorous physical abuse of, or vigorous physical struggle against a person"; violence to property can be characterized as a "highly vigorous, or incendiary, or malicious and vigorous, destruction or damaging of property or potential property."[47] What links violence's two faces is ultimately "the notion of vigorous abuse," which for Audi comes "very close to forming a kind of core; for virtually all instances of violence involve vigorous abuse."[48]

To its credit, this view nicely captures some ordinary linguistic usages of "violence." We might, for instance, describe a raging neighbor who vigorously punches a hole in a living room wall as "violent." On one level, this account makes sense: it is hard to deny that what we characteristically call violence involves "vigorous abuse." On another level, something seems amiss. What concerns us about the vigorous abuse of persons, as Audi concedes, is that it potentially results in terrible injuries and, frequently, pain and suffering.

Its effects on persons are different from those on property or objects: they experience no such injuries or related symptoms, though damage to them *may* sometimes *lead to* or *cause* such injuries to persons. But many incidents of property disobedience will not. If student activists kick a hole in a college administrator's office wall, for example, the administrator will be understandably angry, and the cleanup costs will need to be covered by somebody. Yet it seems odd and somehow misleading to describe their acts as "vigorous abuse" generative of meaningful injuries or harms to persons.

This is more than mere semantics. The problem is that fidelity to the conventional idea of violence as encompassing severe injuries to both persons and property not only invites us to overlook meaningful differences; it also obfuscates what remains so alarming about violence. The political theorist John Keane rightly distinguishes violence from property damage, with only the former entailing "unwanted physical interference by groups and/or individuals with the bodies of others, which are consequently made to suffer a series of effects ranging from shock, bruises, scratches, swelling or headaches to broken bones, heart attacks, loss of limbs or even death."[49] Unwanted "vigorous abuse" that forcefully violates persons—and, yes, possibly other sentient beings as well—usually produces pain, suffering, and a host of related traumas. Treating such experiences as somehow parallel or equivalent to property damage recalls G. W. F. Hegel's sarcastic quip about the night where all cows look black: it gets in the way of making necessary distinctions. Expansive views that conflate persons and property obscure violence's most chilling real-life traits and effects. They sloppily confuse property crimes with what Elaine Scarry describes as the traumatic experiences of "the body in pain."[50] Violent attacks, physical abuse, rape, and torture are not directly analogous to violations of property rights. By attributing to property something akin to the status of "independent beings endowed with life, and entering into relations both with one another and the human race," this view mystifies both what is at stake in property damage and violence's potentially alarming threats to human subjectivity.[51]

Admittedly, severe violations to persons potentially transpire absent pain or suffering. It is hard for us even to begin to fathom what those horrifically but rapidly killed at Hiroshima and Nagasaki, for example, experienced during their final moments. Some poisons kill without victims apparently ever really knowing what happened. Nonetheless, it still makes sense to delineate severe violations to persons from property damage. In most cases of the former, those fortunate enough to survive will experience physical and psychological traumas. Among the less fortunate, there can be no question that both their bodies and psyches will have been violated, in fatally destructive ways.[52]

Modern criminal law standardly treats violent crimes against persons differently from property violations, with more severe sanctions meted out for crimes that entail injurious violations to persons than objects.[53] The law generally captures what philosophers, political theorists, and many others downplay: violence is a "relational act in which the object of violence is treated, not as a subject whose 'otherness' is recognized and respected, but rather as a mere object potentially worthy of bodily harm, or even annihilation."[54] Property damage may, in some cases, be directly implicated in or crucial to violence, but oftentimes will not. In those cases where a clear link can be identified, property rights violations, accordingly, are treated differently from those where there is no negative impact on anyone's core bodily and psychic integrity.

Only persons can be robbed of their personhood or subjectivity. That is precisely what makes violence morally suspect and, in its extreme forms, horrible: its perpetrators reduce other human beings to objects of abuse to be stepped on or kicked aside at will.

Violence is perilously impactful because we are physically and psychologically vulnerable creatures, and thus our bodies and psyches are subject to violent "injury, pain, and ultimately death."[55] Such vulnerability is arguably central to our humanity.[56] To be sure, it is shaped by social and political conditions that exacerbate it for some and limit its impact on others. Such differences matter. Yet our shared vulnerability remains pivotal if we are to avoiding losing sight of violence's core—and normatively most decisive—features. Human beings, not inanimate objects or property, are physical and psychological creatures potentially subject to violence "in its most terrifying way, a way in which we are given over, without control, to the will of another, a way of life in which life itself can be expunged by the willful action of another. To the extent that we commit violence, we are acting on another, putting the other at risk, causing the other damage, threatening to expunge the other."[57] We "live in the world as embodied and physically vulnerable creatures," with our physical vulnerabilities typically linked to psychological ones; there is no clear boundary between mind and body.[58] Violence against the body tends to result in psychological harm and emotional trauma. Analogously, psychological damage can play a decisive role in bodily violations: teens subject to psychological abuse are more likely to attempt self-harm, starve themselves, or manifest a variety of physically self-destructive ailments.

Even if property damage can sometimes contribute to or facilitate human pain or suffering, or function to intimidate and threaten other persons in worrisome ways, it is not conceptually useful to clump them together. When there *is* preliminary evidence of some relationship between them, it becomes incumbent on us to make sense of the possible causal processes at hand. Labeling everything we tend to find politically reprehensible "violent" is not a productive way to proceed, intellectually or politically.

Does this mean that we should favor relatively minimalist views of violence? Conceiving violence to highlight applications of destructive force that are injurious to persons, both physically and psychologically, makes a great deal of sense. The minimalist position allows us to delineate violence from property damage; it also meshes better with a what many of us ordinarily view as violence's most disturbing attributes.[59] Doing so still permits us to see that social injustice can be related to violence. But it calls for appropriately nuanced accounts of the nexus between them. There is no question, for example, that severe poverty is both physically and psychologically injurious in ways that understandably might lead us to link it to violence.[60] Yet poverty is a multisided phenomenon. Describing all or even most of its traits as violent loses sight of its distinctive features and complex social causes. Going hungry certainly seems "violent" in ways that directly recall the term's core association with severe physical and psychological injuries. In contrast, a school kid in a wealthy country whose parents cannot afford new school clothes every year, or take their kids on a summer vacation, suffers from social disadvantages but arguably nothing akin to severe physical or psychological abuse. To call the kid's lack of new shoes at the start of the new school year violent does not seem helpful or illuminating. Nor is poverty's undesirable status thereby reduced, especially if doing so impedes the requisite analysis of its social dynamics and sources. We cannot reduce the complexities of capitalism, racism, or sexism to violence without distorting their relatively autonomous contours and thereby trivializing violence's worst components.

Property disobedience is a no less complicated phenomenon that comes in different shapes and sizes. Rather than a priori declaring them violent, we need to do the difficult—but potentially illuminating—work of examining its various types and considering possible ties or connections to violence. We should not try to solve by conceptual or definitional fiat what only careful political and social analysis can disclose.

Even those who might still reject my view and instead hold on to more expansive notions of violence should be able to endorse this basic point. Bufacchi, as already noted, relies on a morally ambitious idea of integrity to make sense of violence. A contemporary theorist of civil disobedience, Piero Moraro, tracks Bufacchi in endorsing a broad notion of violence as a "violation of integrity" and similarly interprets property as an extension of the person. For him as well, property destruction directly threatens the person's integrity.[61] Both writers may be right that property damage represents a "typical consequence" of integrity's violation.[62] But it remains crucial that we identify *what* types of property damage under *which* conditions violate integrity; we cannot assume that they always go hand in hand. In part simply because property comes in different shapes and sizes, some cases of property disobedience are likely to prove more troublesome than others.

Relatedly, if we opt to associate violence with violations of human dignity, defined as the idea that everyone deserves to be treated with respect, and that each of us has a life to lead of our own choosing, we cannot presuppose that property damage is necessarily violent. In this vein, Todd May suggests that deciding whether property disobedience constitutes or contributes to violence depends "on the particular property being destroyed" as well as the particulars of the political act.[63] Some acts involving property damage pose more of a threat to human dignity than others. If, for example, private residences of regime supporters are marked with spray paint in orders to identify who should be subjected to physical violence, that is decidedly more alarming than if a statue is toppled by protestors hoping to show that they no longer fear the regime.[64]

The bottom line: even if we interpret violence more expansively, we still face complicated questions about property damage. We cannot simply assume its violent credentials. It is time to abandon the old but deeply flawed idea of violence as an exercise of physical force that inflicts injury on or damage to *both* persons *and* property.

*   *   *

Speaking on Canadian public radio in the wake of destructive riots that shook US cities during the summer of 1967, King highlighted some of the same key conceptual and political distinctions whose advantages I been trying to highlight. "I am aware," he noted, "there are many who wince at a distinction between property and persons—who hold both sacrosanct. My views are not so rigid. A life is sacred. Property is intended to serve life, and no matter how much we surround it with rights and respect, it has no personal being. It is part of the earth man walks on; it is not man."[65]

Distinguishing *violence against persons* from *damage to property*, King told his audience that riots in Detroit, Newark, and elsewhere had chiefly targeted "property rather than people."[66] Hostile politicians and pundits neglected this crucial distinction. With occasionally fatal consequences for rioters, police and military forces had treated "acts of petty larceny as equal to murder."[67] King conceded that "a handful of Negroes used gunfire substantially to intimidate," but "not to kill."[68] Alarmed nonetheless by reports of snipers firing weapons, King emphasized that violence against persons had been committed overwhelmingly by overzealous—and sometimes openly racist—police and National Guardsmen: "It is clear that the riots were exacerbated by police action that was designed to injure or even kill people."[69] King emphasized that

far more rioters took chances with their own lives, in their attacks on property, than threatened the life of anyone else. Why were they so violent with property then? Because violence represents the white power structure, which they were attacking and trying to destroy. A curious proof of the symbolic aspect of the looting for some who took part in it is the fact that, after the riots, police received hundreds of calls from Negroes trying to return merchandise they had taken. Those people wanted the experience of taking, of redressing the power imbalance that property represents. Possession, afterward, was secondary.[70]

Theirs were acts in which protesters symbolically enacted an alternative society in which blacks and whites shared more equitably in America's enormous wealth, with shocking imbalances in property ownership reduced. In previous remarks on the 1965 Watts riots, King analogously noted that the upheavals should have surprised no one: Los Angeles had become "the luminous symbol of luxurious living for whites," a site for conspicuous consumption whose temptations television regularly beamed into the "wretched homes" of poor blacks, located "only steps away." He continued, "The looting in Watts was a form of social protest very common through the ages as a dramatic and destructive gesture of the poor toward symbols of their needs."[71] Even if we continue to abide by the familiar linguistic convention—as King frequently did—and call politically motivated property damage violent, it was a very different creature from violence against persons.

In 1967 King conceded that the rioters' arson, "which was far more dangerous than the looting," expressed an even "deeper level of hostility." Yet even arson attacks were usually "directed against symbols of exploitation and . . . designed to express the depth of anger in the community."[72] Rioters had committed crimes. Nevertheless, they had done so in response to lawless white police officers, corrupt city officials, local businesses charging bloated prices, and overall social conditions that left blacks with few opportunities for economic advance: "In our society it is murder, psychologically, to deprive a man of a job or an income. You are in substance saying to that man that he has no right to exist."[73] While delineating violence against persons from property damage, King still described racialized poverty as complicit in violence. In an editorial for the *New York Amsterdam News*, he noted that poverty "destroys the souls and bodies of people" and thus partakes of violence.[74]

Concerned that the riots buttressed those considering nonviolent strategies obsolescent, King insisted that even when "emotions were exploding" one found support for "a core of nonviolence towards persons," and thus that "nonviolence should not be written off."[75] Of course, King celebrated neither the riots nor the resulting economic losses. He condemned those who armed themselves and sought to engage in intimidation. Riots were destructive and terribly unsettling events, often exploited by criminal elements. They included a range of activities, some manifestly incongruent with the disciplined nonviolent practices King favored, and too often politically counterproductive. Widespread looting, as we will see in Chapter Five, worried him, and he rejected it as a political tool. He also emphasized rioting's tragic futility: "It is understandable that the white community should fear the outbreak of riots. They are indefensible as weapons of struggle, and Negroes must sympathize with whites who feel menaced by them. Indeed, Negroes are themselves no less menaced, and those living in the ghetto always suffer most directly from the destructive turbulence of a riot."[76] Too often, protest-related violence and property damage emboldened reactionary whites and generated draconian political backlashes. Disproportionately poor and working-class African Americans would simply be left to clean up the debris of devastated neighborhoods likely to suffer further decay as remaining businesses fled elsewhere.

I have referenced King's remarks at length because his desire to reframe the association of property damage with physical violence remains useful.

Property should serve to preserve and protect human beings. It is a means toward an end, but only that end—the human person—is sacrosanct or inviolable. It might be going too far to claim that, by 1967, King believed that political nonviolence principally prohibited *only* violence "toward persons." Yet it remains the case that his grounds for opposing property damage or destruction—which, to be sure, he condemned—appear to rely chiefly on tactical considerations.[77] Property damage constituted a "derivative crime" that paled in comparison to the violence against protestors committed by the police and National Guard.[78] In King's thinking, "those who fret much about property are in error for they really value property more than persons."[79] Politically based property damage called for hardheaded political analysis and criticism. Yet, King's criticism rested on different and less categorical grounds than his condemnations of violence against persons. King never recommended or whitewashed the dangers of politically motivated property damage. Yet he refused to place it on the same normative plane as violence against persons.

From King's Christian perspective, this distinction made sense. As creatures made in divinity's image, human beings are ends-in-themselves deserving of equal respect, whereas property is merely an institution that serves them. Even the most hateful person is worthy of equal regard since the "dignity and worth of all human personality" rests on sturdy metaphysical—and spiritual—foundations.[80] Not surprisingly, King worried less about property destruction than damage to persons brought about by the existing economic order and its conservative, usually white defenders.[81] By implication, property that *directly buttresses or supports human beings* possesses a privileged position vis-à-vis property that does so only indirectly, or perhaps not at all. It would not have surprised King that many of us still instinctively wince at property disobedience when connected to tangible injuries to persons (for example, the destruction of a small shopkeeper's business and, as a result, loss of livelihood), while we tend to be less vexed by acts unrelated to any damage to human persons or their well-being. Nor would he be jolted to discover that those who treat violence to persons and property damage as equivalent still seem more vested in preserving the economic status quo than realizing a political order premised on equal respect.

In the chapters to follow, I intend to tap King's distinction between property damage and violence against persons, as well as the inference that we should evaluate the former by carefully considering possible relations to violence against persons—in other words, the extent to which property damage "gets at" people in harmful and destructive ways. To be sure, property damage *can be* "linked with larger uses of violence," in part "because of the way that men in particular are taught both to repress and vent their anger," with violence resulting "as an exaggerated representation of masculinity."[82] When property disobedience undermines our core physical and psychological identity, or aims to intimidate or frighten as part of a violent attack on others, it becomes objectionable. Can we salvage this intuition without endorsing King's Christian philosophy? Can we circumvent its sectarian contours?

I think so: King's own Christianity notwithstanding, nonviolence vis-à-vis persons can be grounded on decidedly less controversial theoretical grounds.[83]

A principled—though unavoidably imperfect—commitment to nonviolence follows from the aspiration to live together with others in a shared political community in which everyone deserves basic respect. The problem with violence is that it prospectively means treating others as mere objects "potentially worthy of bodily harm, or even annihilation," not as equal participants in a political project.[84] Stated in the simplest terms: violence invites mistreating both actual and prospective partners in a common political endeavor, something that makes no sense. It implicitly presupposes the "rule of the strongest," with political outcomes determined by violence's vagaries rather than justificatory practices among and between political equals.[85] All defensible ideas about democracy "place political equality somewhere at the center."[86] Keane rightly notes that "democracy, considered as a set of institutions and as a way of life, is a nonviolent means of equally apportioning and publicly monitoring power within and among overlapping communities of people who live according to a wide variety of morals."[87] Violence against persons becomes principally suspect as soon as we take seriously the commitment to communicate with and try to persuade political opponents, often amid deep disagreements, recognizing that perfect consensus may never materialize. It is inconsonant with maintaining some basic sense of a common project—and shared willingness to move forward, despite conditions of injustice—necessary to shared cooperation and its possible success. Violence and communal political existence where we work and hope to thrive together are like oil and water: they do not mix. There are sound reasons, in sum, why nonviolence constitutes the "best form of democratic claims-making."[88]

Admittedly this principled but identifiably *political* defense of nonviolence raises tough questions. Outside democracies, as well as in relations between states, political nonviolence rests on less secure footing than *within* democracies. While moral and prudential reasons may then advise against violence's deployment, it sometimes becomes tragically necessary. Furthermore, political boundaries are subject to contestation; democracies are regularly reconstructed in novel and sometimes far-reaching ways. As seemingly straightforward a matter as who belongs to "our" community, and to whom political respect is owed, becomes complicated. Even so, it is hard to see why nonviolence within political communities should be limited only to relations between citizens and not, for example, migrants, refugees, and other partners in the community's common affairs. If recent political history has taught us anything, it is that yesterday's political "outsiders" can rapidly become political consociates and full citizens.

Since democracy also remains everywhere a not yet fully realized—or perhaps never fully realizable—project, additional complications result. How can we know if we are in fact participating, actually or prospectively, in a common political project deserving of fidelity? When can we be sure that other participants will abide the necessary conditions of basic respect? Nonviolence follows out of our commitments to mutual respect and political equality. What should we do when those commitments are ignored or violated? How do we know, in other words, whether more militant, potentially violent resistance is called for? With authoritarian populists making sizable inroads even in longstanding liberal democracies, these questions are by no means purely academic.

Many thinkers, of course, have tried to address these issues. But Rawls' brief—and appropriately modest—response still seems illuminating. In deciding whether or not to discard nonviolence and pursue more militant political responses, Rawls emphasized that "we have to balance imponderables: How great must the likelihood be [of regime change without excessive loss of life]? How unjust the regime?–and much else? These questions have no precise answer and depend, as one says, on judgment. Political philosophy cannot formulate a precise procedure of judgment . . . There is no avoiding, then, having to reach a complex judgment weighing many different imponderables, about which reasonable persons are bound to differ."[89] Such considerations always involve tangled empirical questions and complex matters of political judgment. Rawls rightly thought that those living in basically democratic societies should avoid political violence, "especially against persons," as a way of evincing respect for them as political equals.[90] Yet he recognized that in many real-life polities we would likely disagree about the relevant imponderables. Existing democracies include messy mixes of just and unjust elements that are likely to produce heated political disputes. For this reason, Rawls left some circumscribed space in real-existing liberal democratic states for more militant protest: "I do not at all mean to say that only this form of dissent [i.e., nonviolent civil disobedience] is ever justified in a democratic state."[91] When nonviolent protest fails "in its purpose, forceful resistance may later be entertained."[92]

Anyone who entertains violence risks violating ideals of equal respect without which democracy makes no sense: the justificatory hurdles they face are extraordinarily high. Political action that potentially involves bodily or severe psychological violations to others will have to meet the strictest tests. It can only be justified under circumstances of extreme injustice.[93] In robust, well-functioning democracies, such instances are likely to be rare and ideally nonexistent.

Damage to or destruction of property, however, remains in principle a different matter. Because property is "not a potential member of the political project of living together, destroying property does not set anyone outside the political project and so does not contradict a commitment to that project."[94] Property is not per se deserving of our equal respect; we have no categorical reason to favor nonviolence in relation to it. To be sure, some forms of property damage may invidiously harm or injure persons, disabling or removing them from the shared political enterprise. Then it potentially undermines political equality's necessary presuppositions. Using property damage to frighten and intimidate, perhaps as a precursor to violence against persons, risks doing so as well. Yet a great deal of property damage will have little if any negative impact on persons' physical and psychological integrity or their chances to remain partners in a common political project. Whether or not property disobedience destructively impacts persons always requires careful examination and cannot simply be taken for granted.

So we can endorse what King dubbed a "core of nonviolence towards persons." Although I cannot sketch a full-fledged nonviolent political theory, I conclude this section by recalling this modestly updated rendition's strengths.

First, it circumvents the standard but unproductive contrast of *absolute ethical or moral* to *pragmatic political* nonviolence.[95] Nonviolence vis-à-vis persons, I have suggested, can be grounded on principled political grounds that are weightier than matters of mere strategy or tactics. Participants in a shared political project premised on some idea of basic respect should be expected to practice nonviolence. Yet, the messy continencies and imponderables of political life, as well as the fact that democracy typically remains imperfect and incomplete, infer that under extreme circumstances nonviolence may prove unrealistic or undesirable, even as a heavy burden of proof rests on anyone who abandons nonviolence. Interpreted this way, political nonviolence has significant moral and ethical content. But it does not necessarily depend on controversial religious or sectarian metaphysical views, though it clearly is consistent with some of them.

Second, this rendition can still build on valuable insights that that have long been part of the nonviolent political tradition. When King commented that "All men are caught in an inescapable network of mutuality, tied in a single garment of destiny. Whatever affects one directly, affects all indirectly," he was describing a key *socio-theoretical* basis for nonviolence.[96] Nonviolence rejects an implausible, hyper-individualistic account of society and persons, instead envisioning the "self" and "other" as deeply and unavoidably inter-meshed and mutually dependent. Violence directed against other persons is, potentially, violence against oneself. According to Judith Butler, "Violence against the other is . . . violence against oneself, something that becomes clear when we recognize that violence assaults the living interdependency that is . . . our social world."[97] Stated more prosaically: the perpetrator's violence tends to ricochet back with harmful and sometimes devastating consequences. For both Gandhi and King, violence aimed at the agents of oppression inevitably damaged and impaired those fighting oppression, oftentimes in deeply disturbing ways. Because of the web of mutuality between oppressed and oppressors, such violence was always potentially self-destructive.

Third, this update continues to benefit from some of nonviolence's widely discussed *strategic* and *tactical* advantages. Nonviolent politics, Gene Sharp has famously argued, builds on a supple understanding of the operations of political power. It recognizes that political power depends on the more or less implicit consent of its subjects; a wide range of nonviolent tactics can work to delegitimize and eventually destabilize power holders.[98] It also helps break the all-too-familiar *cycle of violence* in which political violence generates unnecessary distrust, hatred, and additional violence. Nonviolent movements tend to disable opponents—and even state officials, for instance, the police or military—by directly challenging an escalatory logic of violence that opponents previously had confidently followed.[99] Whereas violence tends to generate polarization, its nonviolent cousin places a premium on reaching out even to hardened opponents: it enlarges possible areas of agreement and integrates even those who may initially seem irrevocably hostile.

Fourth, nonviolence vis-à-vis persons actively anticipates a prospective order in which unnecessary violence has been fruitfully reduced. Stellan

Vinthagen notes that nonviolence represents a future-oriented "utopian enactment" where political agents *already* are "acting in a way that looks toward the future" as a place where human beings live together in respect and mutuality.[100] Practicing nonviolence means that activists are in fact presently embodying and actively building the political future they aim more fully to realize. Nonviolence potentially engenders political self-education and self-transformation, with those acting in concert acquiring essential skills (e.g., a refusal to demonize political opponents as existential "enemies") necessary to a future order where persons are no longer treated as "things" but as equals deserving of respect.

Fifth, while many who celebrate political violence recklessly downplay its unpredictable, risky contours, misleadingly treating political action as controllable by decisive, violent action, a nonviolent approach takes the complexities of political life seriously. According to the feminist and peace advocate Barbara Deming, nonviolent protest provides for enhanced control over and better possibilities for navigating political conflict and its unpredictable exigencies.[101] It breaks with the masculinist idea that violence best counters political contingencies. Nonviolent theorists have long viewed political *means* and *ends* as inextricably interwoven, with one key result being the insight that nonviolence is not only morally preferable but also better equipped to mitigate the unavoidable dangers of political action whose consequences are always hard to calculate in advance.[102]

*   *   *

King, as we have seen, delineated property destruction from violence, in part because he refused to grant property the same moral standing as human persons. Property, on his view, represents a means toward an end, possessing only secondary but not primary value. Property is a tool or instrument, whose value can only be determined by examining the extent to which it effectively serves human beings.

My general sympathy with this view undergirds my analysis of property disobedience. Yet there is no question that it rests on some controversial claims.

Some political thinkers have usefully categorized property theories as falling under two general types, namely: *instrumental* theories that conceive of property as a means toward some higher end, in contrast to *self-developmental* views, which attribute to property a superior normative status and sometimes depict it as an end in itself.[103] Instrumental views depict property ownership as lacking intrinsic value or significance. Whether property rights yield social benefits or not remains, fundamentally, an open question, with property expected to serve some higher purpose. In contradistinction, a noninstrumental or self-developmental account envisions the relationship between persons and what they own as "intrinsically significant; there is a substantial bond between a man and his property," with property envisioned as indispensable to the individual's personhood and moral development.[104] This second view meshes with property's personhood functions and related theories that highlight how access to and control over resources is necessary to individuality and autonomy.

In the former view, property ownership, along with the specific institutional form property takes, is simply a matter of convenience. What counts is some higher moral good, whereas in the latter view, as embraced by Immanuel Kant, Hegel, and their disciples, a particular system of (usually private) property ownership is required if human beings are to successfully cultivate their capacities and gain freedom. On this second view, personhood and property are inextricably linked: human beings require property to be autonomous and morally "complete." As we have observed, it, some theorists of violence who interpret property as extended personhood occasionally hint at this idea.

Of course, King was no theorist of property; it would be silly to expect him to have resolved complicated disputes between these two rival theoretical approaches. Nevertheless, he was deeply influenced by German Idealism and perhaps sympathized with elements of the self-developmental account.[105] At the same time, many of his comments seem to presuppose an instrumental view: they envisage property as serving a higher goal, or what King sometimes called human "life," which as a devout Christian he held in the highest regard. We know from speeches and writings that he was a critic of capitalism and probably a democratic socialist.[106] Like many on the political left then and now, he worried that contemporary capitalism disfigured the proper relationship between persons and material objects: in capitalism, we worship things while degrading human beings. In contrast, a more just economy would prioritize human life by treating material objects as means toward a higher end: "We must rapidly begin the shift from a 'thing'-oriented society to a 'person'-oriented society. When machines and computers, profit motives and property rights are considered more important than people, the giant triplets of racism, materialism, and militarism are incapable of being conquered."[107] Because capitalism subordinates human values to "blind

economic forces, human beings can become human scrap."[108] Required was
a drastic overhaul to the economy so that it might better guarantee universal economic security and allow all persons to flourish. While rejecting Karl
Marx's atheism and criticizing Soviet-style communism, King credited Marx
for seeing that "capitalism is always in danger of inspiring men to be more
concerned about making a living than making a life. We are prone to judge
success by the index of our salaries or the size of our automobiles, rather
than by the quality of our service and relationship to humanity—thus capitalism can lead to a practical materialism that is as pernicious as the materialism taught by communism."[109] King's views overlap illuminatingly with
those of a prominent Canadian theorist of property, C. B. Macpherson, who
embraced an instrumental theory according to which property should entail
at its core nothing more than access "to the means of life."[110] What counted
first and foremost, for both King and Macpherson, was property's "welfare
function," namely its role in securing "individuals' claims on those resources
that a community considers essential for meaningful life."[111] The traditional
notion of private property as implying exclusive or sovereign control over
some object or thing, Macpherson argued accordingly, should be jettisoned
for the idea of a basic universal right to the material goods necessary to gain
full "enjoyment of one's human capacities."[112] Some liberal ideas of property
that allowed some to exercise sovereignty over others, and to exclude them
from productive resources, no longer made sense. The democratic welfare
state, Macpherson claimed, had already taken steps toward discarding them.
It was high time, at any rate, to reconfigure property rights as *social rights* to
a modicum of economic well-being.[113]

What if we instead favor a self-developmental account and view property
as having a higher normative status? In principle, then even relatively limited
types of politically motivated property damage would likely face high normative hurdles. Even when property damage is unrelated to tangible injuries
or harms to concrete persons sound reasons for acknowledging property's
sanctity would remain. On a self-developmental view, for example, damaging
or stealing from a privately owned business could be interpreted as an attack
on the individual owner's autonomy or dignity. Accordingly, we would "do
violence to a person, then, not only by doing him bodily harm or by dimin-
ishing his autonomy through coercion, but also by not respecting his right to
own and control property."[114] The conceptual distinctions I have tried to draw
between violence against persons and property damage might blur. If private property is something persons need to develop their capacities and gain

autonomy, even minimal property damage potentially entails a direct assault on persons, even absent evident bodily or psychological damage.

One observation allows us provisionally to defang this critical retort. Self-developmental theories provide no clear reasons for assuming that *existing* property relations build or rest on them. Radin's personality-centered account, for example, justifies ownership over resources indispensable to personhood. However, many types of existing public and private property seem distant from or even disconnected from personhood; personhood accounts provide no justification for the massive inequalities that characterize existing ownership patterns. In fact, Radin bluntly declares that her view demands "that government should rearrange property rights" so that everyone can fully enjoy some benefits.[115]

Similarly, Waldron has noted that the intuition that "property-owning is necessary for ethical development" implies universal property ownership, and therefore that present-day disinterest in "the moral and material plight of those who own nothing" is morally unjustifiable.[116] Property as a fundamental moral good, and perhaps even an end in itself, allows for a great deal of institutional and policy leeway in terms of how best to realize it. Nonetheless, it provides no "justification for a society in which some people have lots of property and many have next to none." A self-developmental account of property can "only disingenuously . . . legitimize the massive inequality that we find in modern capitalist countries."[117] Such a theory demands a significantly more egalitarian distribution of property and economic resources than exists today in the United States or probably *any* existing society. We might favor a self-developmental theory, yet it still possesses only limited relevance vis-à-vis existing property relations.

By implication, even when we bring self-developmental theories into the mix, good reasons remain for preserving space for potentially justifiable politically motivated property damage. Under the ideal material conditions outlined in some theories, property might indeed deserve a more privileged normative status. But such conditions have not been realized: we cannot justify today's massive property inequalities on the basis of self-developmental views. Given this gap, it makes sense to continue to prioritize human persons— and their need to survive and, hopefully, flourish—and allow for property disobedience, so long as doing so circumvents violence against persons and meets other conditions we need to say more about.

The exposition in the chapters to follow, in short, need not be interpreted as necessarily relying on overly controversial ideas about property. As we will see, some property disobedients in fact *build* on influential views of it. When squatters occupy land or buildings, for example, they make normative claims that will be recognizable to defenders of both instrumental and self-developmental views. They frequently contest existing property relations by tapping widely held intuitions, claiming that existing property relations fail to correspond to them. It is frequently difficult to discern how their illegalities are either necessarily violent or represent attacks on property qua property.

As King would likely remind us, damage or destruction to property can engender a terribly counterproductive backlash. It is not to be undertaken carelessly or recklessly. Strategic and tactical reasons often militate against it. Nonetheless, there may be circumstances under which politically based property damage is appropriate and perhaps necessary. We now need to turn and consider what they might be.

CHAPTER 3

Symbolic Property Disobedience

Protestors who damage or destroy property frequently do so because of its symbolic traits. In 1773, Massachusetts colonists dressed as Native Americans boarded vessels in Boston Harbor and despoiled tea shipments to express their anger over the Tea Act, a burdensome tax approved by parliament. As every US school kid learns, Boston's Sons of Liberty viewed the tax as an assault on the principle of "no taxation without representation." The rich symbolic messaging of what Americans came to call the Boston Tea Party helped crystallize support for independence. During the late 1960s, college students opposing US military intervention in Vietnam and a controversial conscription system that determined who would fight burned draft cards and trashed draft-related records. While invigorating public debate about the military draft and the war, their acts never gained a similarly iconic historical status.[1]

We could easily identify other examples of property disobedience where targets have been selected because they embody or express some perceived injustice. Symbols are commonplace in political life. They display something not immediately present, ideally providing a roadmap that aids people negotiating a complex political and social universe.[2] When the represented entity or state of affairs becomes intensely controversial, its meanings prove especially contestable. The "stars and stripes" stands for the United States, for example, but whether it functions as an object of reverence or enmity depends on both audience and context. What the legal scholar Sanford Levinson describes as political symbols' "necessary plurality of meaning" accurately indicates their essential contestability.[3] Political symbols aim to evoke cognitive and normative messages, but much of their appeal stems from emotional associations. Those that matter in the context of political protest serve as launching pads for "collective action through the normative structuring, interpretative resonance, and projection" of messages having both cognitive and affective traits.[4] They tell a story about some more abstract set of political and social relationships so as to render them immediately tangible and motivate people to act.

It is probably impossible to conceive of property disobedience absent some symbolic contours, however imperfectly conceived or executed. When poor farmers occupy land owned by wealthy landowners, or political militants damage the businesses of those hostile to their cause, the resulting property rights violations say something crucial about the target's (alleged) role in some injustice. Disruptive property disobedience, as well as political acts that involve directly seizing or repurposing property, also include symbolic features. *Symbolic property disobedience* constitutes a core building block on which its other ideal-typical variants are constructed.

Because property disobedience's intended symbolic contours are ubiquitous, we need to get a better handle on their core features. Here I do so by focusing on cases of property disobedience where symbolism plays a central and perhaps overriding role, that is, protestors target an object that directly symbolizes an unjust condition. These examples of predominantly *symbolic* property disobedience will, admittedly, sometimes blur into other types. But one distinctive feature is that participants direct their ire against some artifact or object that in their eyes represents a concrete instantiation of injustice. They focus on symbolic targets that become pivotal to their efforts "as structuring elements of movement culture."[5] Even when protestors view the impacted property as complicit in the perceived inequity, they usually appear to grasp that by targeting it their act becomes deeply—and perhaps chiefly—symbolic in character.

Recent BLM protesters who defaced and toppled Confederate memorials, for example, surely did not believe that doing so would immediately disable racism, even as they hoped to gain political support and communicate a message about white supremacy. By directly confronting white supremacy's publicly visible representations, they wanted to take a step toward purging it. Although occasionally claiming that Confederate memorials directly harmed African Americans, activists grasped that what made them potent targets were the ways in which they stood in for the inadequacy of previous efforts to dismantle racism: if hundreds of monuments honoring the Confederacy were still prominently displayed at public sites, white supremacy clearly remained a powerful force that had to be taken down, in part by literally taking down statues memorializing Confederate dignitaries and veterans.[6]

Partly due to its political importance, and partly because of general theoretical lessons it usefully highlights, recent politically disobedient action in
the US directed against Confederate and other racist monuments serves as
this chapter's focal point.[7] As an exemplary case of symbolic property damage, it allows us to see why it is mistaken to conflate politically motivated
property damage a priori with violence. When monuments are placed on
public property and protestors meet certain conditions, symbolic property
disobedience potentially approximates features of what we have traditionally
called *nonviolent civil disobedience*. Symbolic property damage in this vein
can be principally justifiable, even when specific incidents prove pruden-
tially or strategically unsound. I side with those in the ongoing debate who
have pointed out that US antiracist activists have had few options *except* to
act in violation of the law, given the ways in which political oversight of the
monuments has been unfairly rigged to impede legal change. Unfortunately,
confused ideas about the protests' allegedly violent nature get in the way of
thinking productively about the real challenges they pose.

Before examining the particulars of the debate over Confederate statues,
we need to explore more deeply what makes symbolic property disobedience *symbolic* in the first place. Only then can we grasp what is at stake in
the debate about racist statues. To underline the difficult challenges posed by
symbolic property disobedience, I briefly explore recent climate activists' art
museum protests.

*   *   *

We can tap the impressive scholarly literature on social movements to capture symbolic property disobedience's general traits. That literature suggests
that the targeted property's symbolic attributes help perform different but
potentially incongruent functions for protest movements. They can "make
declarations, represent constituencies, attract attention, inspire responses,
stigmatize or legitimize actions, and afford authority, vulnerability, or other
reputational attributes. Accordingly, the potency of a given symbolic object
can differ quite considerably depending on the item in question."[8] A symbolically powerful target potentially helps cement existing support and gain
additional followers—or at least the begrudging sympathy of the erstwhile
skeptical. Effective protests will usually rely on some more or less easily com-
municable link between property violations and the movement cause. Just as

1960s civil rights militants chose the most viciously segregationist US locales for acts of civil disobedience, so too do symbolic property disobedients aim at objects that vividly exemplify injustices they hope to overcome.

To prove effective, such acts ideally perform some combination of diagnostic, prognostic, and motivational functions. This is rarely easy: since politically pertinent symbols are subject to rival interpretations, acts of property disobedience that speak effectively to movement insiders and sympathizers may irritate or even put off many others. Toppling a statue of General Robert E. Lee likely makes sense to BLM activists, for example, but risks alienating conservative white Southerners. For a protest to succeed, the selected property will probably have to possess a symbolic significance comprehensible both to some broader public—or, at least, some carefully targeted audience—as well as the movement's sympathizers. Rival symbolic interpretations will inevitably surface. When gaps between and among them prove large or unbridgeable, symbolic property disobedients will frequently struggle to gain new supporters.[9]

When smartly selected, the targeted property prospectively changes existing political narratives and helps generate new ones. Efficacious symbolic property disobedience ideally aims at objects that "underscore and embellish the seriousness and injustice of a social condition or redefine as unjust and immoral what was previously seen as unfortunate but perhaps tolerable."[10] Then the earmarked property can constructively illuminate an unfair state of affairs that cries out for political intervention. When protestors successfully do so they may be able to produce a cognitively as well as emotionally effective "frame" that justifies their efforts and allows for their message to reach a wider audience.[11] This is essential if they are to garner attention and generate a desirable political response. In an informational environment plagued by inequalities in access and control, creative symbolic protests can pierce an otherwise indifferent news and media landscape, momentarily leveling the playing field and gaining attention for perspectives that are otherwise likely to be marginalized. Symbolic property disobedients, in short, can play a decisive role in thematizing injustices and rejuvenating public debate.

Political movements are always forced to "compete with other movements, media agents, and the state" in shaping public discussion.[12] Given the intense time pressures of a complex political environment subject to intensified social acceleration, a symbolically fertile target can speak volumes—and directly egg on others to speak as well—in a way that other protests may fail to accomplish. When a successful political performance, symbolic property disobedience potentially aids in transforming an individual's inchoate sense of dissatisfaction and unease about some social condition into expressly political terms. In the process, it can reshape individual as well as collective political identities: those cognitively and emotionally affected by a symbolically laden protest may join the cause or even rethink their own place in the political and social world.

When intended as an identifiably political act aimed at persuading peers, property disobedience will typically operate as just one prong of a broader strategy. Yet an astutely selected symbolic object lends credibility to even relatively complex viewpoints. As the sociologist James M. Jasper has argued, rich "condensing symbols" that resonate cognitively and emotionally, in part by attracting "charged meanings and connotations," are frequently used by social movements to recruit new members.[13] They are pivotal to the "moral shocks" that accompany an "unexpected event or piece of information" and generate a sense of outrage.[14] Such moral shocks, Jasper suggests, are crucial to political mobilization. They are usually "embodied in, translatable into, and summed up by powerful condensing symbols" that persuade because of their implicit emotional as well as moral appeals.[15]

In the 1970s, for example, Cesar Chavez's United Farm Workers Movement turned a nationwide grapes boycott into a potent political symbol that generated wide-ranging public debate and helped gain new sympathizers. During the 1980s, antiabortion activists did the same with alarming images of aborted fetuses. A condensing political symbol produces "symbolic power," which Jasper defines as referring to "how many people are familiar with an event, the strength of emotional responses to it, and its ability to symbolize moral and cognitive meanings" and persuade others to join the cause.[16]

Some of the toughest challenges posed by symbolic property disobedience are illustrated by recent climate change protests targeting art museums. To bring attention to the climate emergency, activists have blocked roads and highways, impaired SUVs, and spray-painted and sometimes smashed window fronts of financial institutions that bankroll fossil fuel firms. Whatever the controversies raised by them, their symbolic messages, for the most part, have been relatively clear: the targeted property can be plausibly viewed as more or less directly linked to global warming and its sources. Even those politically unsympathetic to the protests can grasp what they are about.

At the same time, some activists have targeted paintings and sculptures by famous artists.[17] These so-called "soup-throwers" have glued their hands to picture frames and splashed mashed potatoes, tomato soup, maple syrup, and other materials onto the glass cases protecting paintings and sculptures. Generally, they have made a conscientious effort to avoid incurring damage; some have consulted art conservators in advance to ensure that glues and other materials used cause no lasting damage. Hoping to avoid injuring either persons or property, they interpret their acts as basically nonviolent. It seems absurd to associate their acts, as some prominent German government officials recently did, with attacks on artworks like those pursued by the Taliban.[18]

Yet, museum directors have been forced to reallocate scarce resources and staff time to clean up the artworks and, as a preventive measure, hire additional security guards and encase possible protest targets. From their perspective, these efforts are unnecessarily costly given the budget restraints facing nonprofit and public cultural institutions. Museums have not always sought to enforce possible legal sanctions against the protestors, though some have done so. Two activists who smeared paint on the glass enclosures of an Edgar Degas sculpture at the National Art Gallery in Washington, DC, for example, were charged with crimes potentially resulting in five-year prison sentences and fines of up to $250,000 each, despite the undamaged state of the sculpture and cleanup costs amounting to an estimated $2,400.[19]

The soup-throwers have inspired copycats worldwide. Here I focus exclusively on their efforts to make a symbolically meaningful and politically resonant statement.

Why target iconic works of art to raise awareness about climate change? Large protest movements typically bring together diverse constituencies and speak in different voices. Still, the museum climate activists proffer an extreme multiplicity of explanations for their acts. Some participants say they hope to focus attention on the hypocrisy that leads people to decry damage to art while turning a blind eye to the vastly greater harms resulting from climate change. In the words of one UK-based Stop Oil activist, "By targeting something that is precious and valuable, the people feel a sense of shock and discomfort . . . That is really the emotion that we need to be feeling when we are seeing the decisions our governments are making and the devastation being wreaked by the climate catastrophe."[20] Others assert that they aim to show that on a planet decimated by climate change, future generations will be denied the pleasures of enjoying art or the natural beauty it can capture. In this vein, activists tossed liquids on paintings depicting natural landscapes (e.g., Vincent Van Gogh's *Sunflowers*) as a way of symbolizing impending environmental catastrophe.[21] Norwegian protestors attached themselves to a wall adjacent to Edvard Munch's *The Scream* to express their intense anger and fears about climate change. Yet others have gone after museum collections because of their financial dependence on sponsorship from large fossil fuel companies and the banks that fund them.[22] Stop Oil members who threw soup on Van Gogh's *Peace Trees in Blossom* did so partly to protest rising living costs, which they attribute to fossil fuel companies reaping record profits. In the words of one participant, "Is art worth more than life? More than food? More than justice?"[23] Others say they are acting to protect nature's own rights, an idea that has gained traction among climate activists and other environmentalists.[24] Many appear to have jumped on the bandwagon because soup-throwing protests have proven attention-grabbling, in contrast to some protest acts directly targeting the fossils fuel infrastructure but frequently failing to gain media traction.

It would be ungenerous to deny that climate activists have engaged in creative protests and sought to draw the requisite symbolic links. The decidedly mixed reaction even from sympathetic media and cultural representatives, however, suggests that their symbolic messaging has not always resonated well.[25] The protests have energized climate activists and generated debate. At the same time, observers have been surprised and even angered by what they view as the protests' inappropriate symbolic targeting. As the art historian David Freedberg argued in response to the Stop Oil protests, "We should stop oil. But what's the connection with allowing people to go on enjoying works of art that they love, which means something to them? There's no conceivable connection. . . . It's a kind of logical absurdity . . . to do away with one great salvation of civilization for the sake of saving civilization from climate change. Seems to me a confusion of aims."[26] The protests have certainly shocked some. Whether they have made use of plausible condensing symbols that encapsulate a cognitively and emotionally persuasive view of climate change and the necessity for resolute political action, however, remains unclear. The ensuing sense of moral shock has frequently focused on harms—real or otherwise—to artworks and the resulting inconveniences to museums, not climate change per se.

Controversial protests always generate a variety of divergent responses. One can surely empathize with the protestors and their growing sense of desperation about climate change. Given its perils, does it not make sense to seek attention whenever and wherever possible, even if doing so involves odd symbolic acts? Maybe some future generation will look back and view the soup-throwers as far-sighted prophets. Who among us can say for sure?

Nonetheless, confused symbolic efforts come at a high political cost. Successful movements need to speak effectively to people busy with their jobs, taking care of loved ones, and worried about getting on with their lives.[27] Many of us just do not have the time or energy to try to decipher overly complex symbolic codes that risk confusing rather than illuminating contentious political aims. Perhaps in some more ideal future, democratic political community citizens will have the requisite time and energy. But we do not live in that political world. At present, symbolical misfires are easily exploited by political opponents and risk diverting public attention from the issues at hand. A movement that engages in lousy symbolic messaging is likely to fail to offer cognitively and emotionally effective frames.

Will soup throwers successfully shift mainstream views of climate change and generate a new narrative that invites political action? There are at least some grounds for skepticism, in part for a simple reason identified by the radical Swedish environmentalist Andreas Malm: "Vincent Van Gogh is not responsible for our climate breakdown."[28]

*   *   *

More than two thousand publicly sponsored memorials to the Confederacy dot the American landscape, including over seven hundred statues, primarily located in the US South, at courthouses, town squares, state capitols, and other public sites.[29] Most monuments were erected between 1900 and 1920, as white supremacists regained political power and aggressively promoted the historically revisionist myth of the Lost Cause. A smaller number of memorials appeared in the 1960s, as a direct response to the civil rights movement. They take a variety of forms, with most commemorating Confederate war dead and leaders such as Robert E. Lee.[30] Generally, they were donated to public authorities or privately financed by the Daughters of the Confederacy and the Sons of Confederate Veterans, two groups that have long promoted revisionist views of the Confederacy and slavery. Even when subsequent maintenance has remained in the hands of ostensibly private groups, they and related groups have continued to benefit from public subsidies.[31]

Since the 2015 white supremacist murder of nine African Americans at a Charleston, South Carolina church, more than two hundred memorials have been removed, relocated, or renamed, mostly by municipalities responding to organized efforts spearheaded by local African Americans. The vast majority of changes transpired in the aftermath of the 2020 Black Lives Matters protests, during which activists defaced and damaged Confederate and other statues they viewed as glorifying racism.[32] Inspired by those protests, activists opposed to colonialism, police violence, and racism in many other countries followed suit and damaged and sometimes toppled monuments as well.[33]

In some rare instances, BLM-related protests engaged in weird and probably counterproductive symbolic politics—for example, knocking over a San Francisco statue of Ulysses Grant and another in Madison, Wisconsin of a nineteenth-century Norwegian American abolitionist, Hans Christian Heg. Even sympathetic commentators, quite rightly, have raised concerns about these and similar acts.[34] In some extreme instances, the defacement or toppling of statues has also been directly linked to the intimidation of and violence against political opponents.[35] Yet such incidents seem to have been rare. Overwhelmingly, unarmed activists directed their ire at identifiably Confederate monuments, including many generic mass-produced statues of a solitary standing Confederate soldier displayed throughout the South. Unfortunately, the heated media coverage and subsequent political debate has obscured crucial features of the protests.

First, twenty-first-century activists are by no means the first to recognize the possible advantages of targeting symbolically suitable public monuments. Nor have they been first to face the accusation of having vandalized valuable artistic and cultural artifacts. At least since the French Revolution, ideological or politically motivated *iconoclasm* has occurred during moments of dramatic political and social change, ideal-typically taking both "top-down" (i.e., regime-driven) and "bottom-up" (public or movement-driven) varieties.[36] From revolutionary France to the 1989 uprisings in Eastern Europe and beyond, popular protest-related iconoclasm has played a significant role. Public artworks and monuments have served as "privileged targets because of their ideological function and public accessibility, as well as because statues may be deformed and thus transformed."[37] For example, statues can be easily "beheaded," or painted over with messages that counter their original meanings. Since monuments as publicly endorsed symbols "are used to express, impose, and legitimize a power," they have frequently been fixed on by those seeking political change. Art historian Dario Gamboni has observed that every public memorial tends to "share the fluctuating fate of what it symbolizes."[38] The complex relationship between the object and that which it represents, along with the sometimes rapidly changing views of both, invites the politically engaged to damage or seek creative modifications of public symbols of the status quo.

Second, only a limited number of Confederate monuments have been impacted by recent protests; the vast majority still stand.[39] Even many removed monuments have been relocated to less visible locations (for example, private cemeteries, historical sites) or placed in temporary storage pending a final decision about their fate. Some have been returned to the organizations that originally donated them, with the very real prospect that they will be put back on display at some nonpublic yet possibly prominent location.[40] By day's end, recent BLM protests may unwittingly end up contributing to the privatization, but not elimination, of Confederate and racist statues.[41]

Third, local authorities acting in accordance with existing regulations are responsible for almost all removals.[42] Even when motivated by a desire to placate protestors, it is simply wrong to see the removals as *directly* resulting from spontaneous "mob" action. Significantly, the officially sanctioned removals represented, in many localities, the culmination of longstanding efforts to remove or at least contextualize the monuments—for example, by adding an explanatory historical marker or some sort of corrective statement. Since the 1960s (and in some cases even earlier), activists have lobbied for local authorities to review the public status of Confederate memorials.[43] Crucially, their endeavors were regularly stymied, a fact whose consequential implications we will presently explore.

Many controversies surrounding them notwithstanding, recent protests targeting Confederate statues offer an illuminating example of symbolic property disobedience. Protestors have been charged with a variety of legal violations, ranging from minor property damage misdemeanors to more serious crimes. Most of the protests have earmarked *public* property. Even so, they raise messy property law–related issues we will need to consider. The protests uncovered deep political divides and sharply competing interpretations of the monuments and what they represent; nor have they succeeded in removing most of them. Yet most sides in the ensuing debate have implicitly acknowledged what is at stake: how should contemporary Americans grapple with our troubled racial past? It has been relatively clear, in other words, what the protests have been *about*, even as they have revealed disagreements about the targeted objects and their precise symbolic contours. If only briefly, the protests successfully focused public attention on America's terrible racial legacy. For many activists, at any rate, damaged and/or toppled monuments have functioned as efficacious, quickly recognizable "condensing symbols" that express a vital political meaning.

BLM activists and sympathizers tend to see the monuments as direct expressions of a system of white supremacy that continues to shape American life. On this view, the statues legitimize and thereby buttress contemporary racism. Racists and white supremacists also identify a direct symbolic link between the monuments and white supremacy. But they worry about the latter's (alleged) decline and seek to preserve the monuments to maintain what remains of a racist hierarchical order they celebrate. Many white Southerners and their mostly conservative allies elsewhere say they reject racism and white supremacy.[44] They interpret the monuments chiefly as commemorating the heroism and valor of ancestors whose memory should not be "erased." On a sympathetic reading of this position, one need not be a racist or Confederate apologist to desire preserving monuments celebrating Southern war dead any more than those who praise Maya Lin's Washington, DC Vietnam Veterans Memorial necessarily endorse the Vietnam War or US military intervention in Southeast Asia.[45]

Scholars have disagreed as well, with some defending protestors' efforts to remove or even destroy the monuments, and others favoring their defacement as the best way to counter their original racist intentions.[46] Advocates of preservation, including many historians, hope to contextualize them by adding historical markers, or by carefully considered relocations that counter any suggestion that their racist messages have a public imprimatur.[47]

The protests have also effectively highlighted why public symbols, and thus by implication protests targeting them, *matter* to people in the first place. One critic of the protests, the British architectural critic Robert Bevan, asks: "Do we really need to see ourselves in monuments to feel like we belong?"[48] Why care so much about monuments and statues? Wouldn't it be smarter for activists to focus their energies on more tangible, down-to-earth injustices? Many of us simply ignore politically unpalatable or poorly understood public memorials. Knocking down a statue doesn't feed a hungry kid or guarantee political rights to those denied them.

The fact that battles over Confederate statues have generated political heat suggests that we cannot ignore symbolic property disobedience's potency. Fights over symbols can function as a first step toward overhauling a social universe in need of far-reaching change. The philosopher Michele Moody-Adams correctly notes that recent "challenges to the symbolic celebration of colonialism and racism" help remind us of the fact that we cannot remake the world "unless we first reimagine it."[49] More often than not, symbolic property disobedience is part of organized efforts to do so.

When situated on public space and maintained by government, memorials constitute *state-sponsored* symbolic expressions—that is, crucial instruments by means of which government speaks to its citizens. Public memorials allow the state to communicate its favored interpretation of the polity's "values, beliefs, ideals, and relations with other communities."[50] Monuments typically aspire to "reflect and shape how we see ourselves," calling "attention to history in order to shape the future."[51] Constitutional restrictions on state decisions about how best to do so in the United States remain relatively lax; courts typically defer to governments' preferences about historical commemoration, even at the cost of condoning historically tendentious, frequently racist public memorials.[52]

Nonetheless, most of us would prefer to live in a world where public memorials do not degrade or stigmatize us or posit that some groups are inherently superior. Ideally, in an inclusive democratic society, monuments would provide what the philosopher Johannes Schulz aptly describes as *assurance*, that is, they express "the idea that all persons have equal standing" and are equally worthy.[53] We can and should reasonably expect that they uphold core ideals of political equality and equal respect and not endorse dehumanizing views of participants in our shared political life. We indeed "live by symbols," as US Supreme Court Justice Oliver Wendell Holmes quipped, and thus it matters in a democracy that monuments and other state-sanctioned symbolic expressions reflect fundamental egalitarian commitments.[54] Political monuments that communicate contempt for entire categories or citizens or endorse their unequal or subordinate status are always suspect and should be subject to critical scrutiny. Even if the courts have not yet acknowledged stricter preconditions for legitimate state speech, good normative reasons remain for insisting on them.

Matters are made more complicated by the fact that the question of *who* deserves equal respect was answered differently in the past than the present, and that *every* existing democracy builds on a history riddled with injustices, many of which continue to shape the present. In pluralistic communities, people inevitably disagree about how to interpret history and advance shared political ideals. Recent battles over Confederate memorials highlight a question that can be answered with rival, more or less plausible, responses: how can democracy's symbolic public landscape express our highest ideals and provide *assurance*, while also acknowledging the community's tainted past, if

only to avoid repeating previous wrongdoing? Those calling for removal usually focus on some version of the former condition, whereas preservationists
emphasize the latter. Yet both concerns seem, in principle, legitimate.[55]

Every political community has public monuments that reflect anachronistic and now tendentious historical views. Some of them will unavoidably irritate, offend, or cause psychological discomfort: I cringe every time
I encounter an interstate highway named after Ronald Reagan, a political
figure whose positions I still find deplorable. If we were to prohibit governments from creating any but the most anodyne memorials we would likely be
left with a politically bland and historically uninspiring symbolic landscape.
Memorials would fail to perform basic functions many of us deem essential to effective citizenship. They might not, for example, successfully "spotlight people whose lives and deeds viewers are supposed to emulate," in part
because even the most admirable of historical figures are morally imperfect
and products of a specific time and place.[56]

Nonetheless, public markers that systematically degrade or stigmatize
some groups or members of the community fall into a special category. They
challenge the basic ideal of equal respect without which democracy becomes
impossible. They cross the line by marshalling the prestige and power of the
state to communicate to entire categories of people that they are undeserving
or unequal. They not only endorse troublesome views about history or policy
but function to preclude entire groups of people from cooperating as equals
in a shared political project.

How then do we decide which public monuments are to be removed,
relocated, or reframed? Symbolic property disobedients who have targeted
Confederate monuments have already implicitly proffered one response.
Their answer reproduces key traits of what conventionally has been described
as nonviolent civil disobedience. To see why, however, we first need to provide grounds for *not* characterizing damage to or toppling of statues a priori
as political violence.

*   *   *

Some defenders of recent BLM-inspired protests have described Confederate
statues as *harmful* to African Americans while not characterizing them as
inherently *violent*.[57] In contrast, others have done just that, at the risk, predictably, of confusingly conflating violence with a wide array of social ills.
According to Chelsey Carter, for example, racist monuments are part of a

system of white supremacy that exposes Blacks "to educational and residential segregation, economic injustice, state-sanctioned violence, political exclusion, stereotypes in media and popular culture, racial slurs, and negative imaging in the form of monuments," which she calls "psychosocial stressors that lead to deleterious health incomes."[58] Carter is right to highlight empirical evidence of racism's myriad harms to African Americans. Nonetheless, the precise role played by public memorials in causally producing concrete bodily and traumatic psychological injuries is never really explained.[59]

This position finds some unsettling resonance among those on the political right who have characterized iconoclasm *against* Confederate statues as "violent." In a fiery Executive Order issued on June 26, 2020, President Trump promised to mobilize the full force of federal power to prosecute "violent extremists" (that is, so-called anarchists, Marxists, and other left-wingers on the "radical fringe") who participated in so-called mob attacks against "revered American monuments." While Trump and his allies lambasted BLM for seeking to "defund the police," the decree in fact did so: it required federal agencies to defund "state and local law enforcement agencies that have failed to protect public monuments, memorials, and statues from destruction or vandalism."[60] It clumped together a broad array of acts, ranging from relatively minor acts of graffiti and vandalism to removals and topplings. Trump may have meant to claim that we (allegedly) *know* in advance that anarchists, Marxists, and other supposedly dangerous radicals seek to overthrow the US system and thus, by definition, *any* of their destructive acts, however minor or inconsequential, are prospectively or imminently violent. Revealingly, no real evidence for that over-the-top claim was provided. Once again, an overly general view of violence distorts rather than illuminates the complex issues at hand.

Another right-leaning critic of recent statue defacing and toppling, Alexander Adams, similarly describes them as violent. Why? Iconoclasm's sordid history proves that attacks on public monuments are always "an immediate precursor to suppression, persecution, expulsion and massacres of people," a strong general claim that does not, however, withstand careful scrutiny.[61] To be sure, some incidents of statue topplings have been linked to violence against persons. Social scientific research also shows that politically motivated property damage tends to raise protest-related tensions among police officers, contributing to a climate in which physical violence is more likely to transpire. Yet that research also suggests that the relevant tensions are partly driven by unthinking fidelity to the idea that property damage is equivalent to violence against persons, or that it necessarily leads to it.[62]

In recent BLM-related incidents of symbolic property disobedience, at any rate, the connections to violence were tenuous: some rare assaults on Confederate statues were assuredly part of identifiably violent protests that targeted police officers and others, but the vast majority were not. The political philosopher Ten-Herng Lai characterizes the protests targeting Confederate statues as examples of *uncivil* disobedience because they involve vandalism that "is a form of violence."[63] Unfortunately, Lai reproduces the commonplace but flawed view of violence covering severe damage to persons and/or property. A more satisfactory defense of iconoclasm's violent credentials might instead be reconstructed on the base of a claim we encountered in Chapter 2, namely that property represents a direct *extension* of persons, and thus that attacks on it eo ipso constitute an assault on persons. One variant of this intuition appears in the writings of the classicist Alexander Demandt, who considers destructive iconoclasm violence directed not only against cultural artifacts but also, more fundamentally, those who created them, as well as those who enjoy and later benefit.[64] Artists and other creative minds embody their skills and ideas in their artworks; by doing so, they speak to future generations. By implication, when iconoclasm damages or destroys their achievements, it eliminates links to the past and assaults the creative minds behind them. Demandt believes such attacks simultaneously entail violence against those who presently appreciate and value their artworks: those engaged in its reception, it seems, somehow commune with its creators, and thus iconoclasm also involves violence against contemporary audiences.

On this logic, those defacing or damaging Confederate memorials violently assault both their creators and those appreciative of their beauty. Crucial here is the idea of a direct link between the personhood of the creative artist and the products of his or her work. When Trump railed against BLM protestors tampering with "beautiful statues and monuments," some echoes of this intuition occasionally surfaced.[65] Some right-wing critics worried about "erasing" the past might also perhaps be interpreted in this light.

The immediate problem with this position is that it suggests that political statues and monuments are structurally analogous to the works of Michelangelo or Picasso. Trump's comments on the beauty of racist monuments notwithstanding, the issue of aesthetics, revealingly, has been sidelined in recent political battles about their fate.[66] Relatively few proponents of preserving Confederate memorials emphasize their aesthetic merits, in part because large numbers were inexpensively mass produced by a Connecticut-based firm during the early twentieth century.[67] Even those praising their aesthetic

merits, like Trump, remain preoccupied with their historical and political significance. This is probably why no one seems to have spoken on behalf of the
Confederate monument's original creators' so-called "moral rights" to their
works, which ordinarily prohibit owners from dismembering or disfiguring
them in ways their creators might find unacceptable.[68]

Yet, even if we *were* to agree with Trump and others about Confederate statues' aesthetic merits, it remains the case that their creators are long
gone, and that no tangible harm or injury to them results when an activist
defaces or beheads a statue of General Lee or another Confederate bigwig. It
is even less clear what violence is done when they are removed or relocated
to a museum or cemetery. Like other overly inclusive views of violence, this
one downplays its distinctive traits and their very real perils. If violence is
redefined to cover severe violations not only to *living* persons and property,
but also those already deceased, and even those who value and admire their
cultural achievements, the concept becomes uselessly amorphous.

Those favoring preservation of the monuments might legitimately point
out that their destruction or removal potentially results in tangible cultural
and historical losses. Future generations, for example, might no longer find
themselves forced to confront real-life symbolic reminders of white supremacy, reminders that potentially, when effectively contextualized, perform educational and political functions. But to describe such losses as "violence"
simply confuses matters.

*   *   *

Philosophers and political theorists sometimes infer that if we could agree on
one interpretation of public memorials, the myriad puzzles they raise could be
quickly solved. In principle, memorials that violate inclusive ideals of political equality have no place in democracy's symbolic landscape. In irrepressibly
conflict-laden, diverse polities, however, we will likely disagree about *which*
memorials fail to pass the test, how best to weigh core democratic commitments vis-à-vis concerns about preserving historical artifacts, and the role
such artifacts should play in educating citizens about past and present injustices. As Schulz has noted, when it comes to real-life decisions about their
fate, "there is no one-size-fits-all solution . . . Removal, narrow contextualization, relocation to a museum, all of these can be legitimate options depending
on the specific context of the practice and the struggle surrounding it."[69] The
only answer in a democratic community in which citizens deserve an equal

say in determining their fate are sufficiently deliberative, fair and inclusive, well-functioning mechanisms to decide. In other words, we require "clear, transparent processes around our public art," with citizens empowered "to lodge complaints and check" that their "responses to monuments are really being considered by people with the power to take action."[70] Both defenders of removal as well as preservationists should in principle agree that any action impacting public monuments "should proceed deliberately, legally, and through the most legitimate procedures available."[71] Unfortunately, those who instinctively flinched at the recent BLM protests seem to assume that suitable procedures *already* exist, whereas sympathizers rightly underscore their myriad irregularities.

I cannot review the mindboggling array of byzantine mechanisms that have been established to oversee US public monuments.[72] Unfortunately, they tend to be burdensome and opaque—or worse, systematically rigged against those desiring contextualization, modification, or removal. Alabama, Arkansas, Georgia, Kentucky, North Carolina, Mississippi, and Tennessee all have laws that effectively prevent localities from modifying or removing them.[73] Many GOP-controlled state legislatures have introduced similar measures.[74] The particulars vary, but some involve sizable hurdles for localities forced to seek exceptions from a general prohibition by petitioning unelected statewide review boards designed in part to thwart their efforts. Some states (for example, South Carolina) only allow changes to memorials by means of a (two-thirds) legislative supermajority, rendering them effectively unfeasible. Placing oversight power in the hands of state legislatures and review boards means neutralizing the preferences of mostly Black-majority cities and localities that have sought change, while benefiting gerrymandered legislatures dominated by predominantly conservative, oftentimes rural whites. The real aim behind much of this legislation is revealingly captured by a 2002 Georgia statute mandating that "the memorial to the heroes of the Confederate States of America graven upon the face of Stone Mountain shall never be altered, removed or concealed, or obscured in any fashion and shall be preserved and protected *for all time* as a tribute to the bravery and heroism of the citizens of this state who suffered and died in their cause."[75] The Confederate memorials at Stone Mountain, in short, should stand unchanged for perpetuity, a status denied even the Georgia Constitution, which can be amended by two-thirds of the members of each chamber followed by a popular vote.[76] Confederate monuments, it seems, deserve a privileged and indeed sacred legal status, while Georgia's fundamental political rules of the game do not.

Many Confederate monuments were donated by powerful groups that lobbied successfully for their installation, frequently with little political deliberation and limited attention to the usual procedural formalities of self-government.[77] Their establishment, in other words, rests on less-than-ideal democratic grounds. We also know that state legislatures have created onerous mechanisms effectively removing them from the scope of ordinary decision-making. The dilemma is not simply, as Carl Fox has correctly pointed out, that the statues were intended to stand indefinitely, in the process blocking future generations' rights to review public art.[78] Just as alarming, recent political efforts have sought to codify Confederate memorials' unchangeable, permanent status in violation of basic democratic ideals.

No wonder that in many places "the pace of legal processes has been too slow or the corresponding government entities," designed to block possible changes, systematically favoring those "not on board with removal."[79] In principle, public property in a democracy is deserving of basic respect. But public symbols that degrade and aim to exclude some members of the community from political life forfeit that respect. The management of public memorials should, of course, be in *public* hands, and thus accountable in recognizably democratic ways. When oversight mechanisms have instead been designed to obstruct change, or to impede effective participation by those most likely to be most impacted, their legitimacy becomes questionable.

Additional impediments are thrown up by some messy property law–related issues. Many protest targets, as noted, were donated by private individuals and groups sympathetic to the Confederacy, though they have long been situated on public property and maintained with public funds. On June 8, 2020, William C. Gregory, the great-grandson of the original donor of a Richmond, Virginia Robert E. Lee monument faced with the prospect of removal, filed a complaint in state court by appealing to deed restrictions his great-grandfather had included as part of the original bequest: the monument and surrounding area were to remain "perpetually sacred" and the state "faithfully guard . . . and affectionately protect it."[80] Although the court eventually ruled against Gregory, determining that the monument now "belongs to the people," this was hardly the only episode where those speaking on behalf of the original donors asserted property claims as a way to thwart removal efforts.[81] Existing public records pertaining to original donations are often incomplete. Yet the confusing interplay of public and private property offers a convenient launching pad for those opposing democratic oversight.[82]

In other cases, for example, those opposing removal have tried to return them to their original owners, with sympathetic courts occasionally seeing "heritage groups as appropriate owners because of their interest in caring for (and paying for) the monuments without displaying them on public lands."[83] For those hoping to strip Confederate monuments of any public imprimatur this might seem like a reasonable compromise. Yet it might just mean more private—yet still prominent—monuments that gain enhanced legal protections: when situated on private property the monuments' owners enjoy robust First Amendment free expression rights to display them.[84]

Unsurprisingly, many African Americans and their political allies have long fought, with depressingly meager results, to contextualize or remove Confederate and other racist monuments.[85] Nor is it surprising that those who have repeatedly encountered rigged political games, unsympathetic courts, and Kafkaesque review mechanisms have reluctantly decided to take matters into their own hands. Given the substantial roadblocks to legal change, what alternatives do they realistically have?

What then might we reasonably expect from those pursuing symbolic property disobedience? Some activists have already suggested a plausible answer: many recent statue and monument defacements and topplings can be plausibly characterized as analogous to nonviolent civil disobedience.

Civil disobedience has been conceived and practiced in different ways. Yet most writers have argued that its legitimacy depends on evidence of civility, publicity or openness, nonviolence, and fundamental respect for or fidelity to law.[86] In King's eloquent words, "I submit that an individual who breaks the law that conscience tells him is unjust . . . is in reality expressing the very highest respect for the law."[87] On the standard view, civil disobedience is most legitimate only when normal political and legal channels for redress have already been exhausted. A commonplace defense interprets it as principally justifiable when aiming to correct for democratic deficits, when civil disobedience compensates for sclerotic political mechanisms that fail to allow for meaningful political participation.

Although protestors targeting Confederate statues have not, admittedly, typically grounded their acts with recourse to ambitious ideas about democracy, they frequently acted with an appreciable sense that previous, long-standing legal efforts to remove them were regularly stymied. Their protests can be interpreted as a last resort taken only after ordinary political devices failed.

To the extent that defacements and topplings involve no tangible harms to persons, they also remain fundamentally nonviolent. Prominent liberal theorists defending otherwise stringent views of civil disobedience long ago suggested that damage to public property can be justifiable, so long as injuries to persons are minimized and the targeted property is symbolically significant.[88] Many recent protests meet those conditions. By the same logic, when attacks on memorials and statues aim to threaten and intimidate political opponents and, in extreme circumstances, foreshadow real political violence to come, they should be rejected. Then political equality and the fundaments of common political life are likely to suffer.

But such episodes have been exceedingly rare in the BLM protests that defaced, damaged, and sometimes knocked over monuments. Protest participants acted for the most part civilly: jolting the body politic into confronting racism's perseverance, they demonstrated a commitment to the public good. By taking aim at prominent public Confederate monuments, they made clear, public statements about racial injustice. To be sure, some activists might have thought harder about how to communicate their messages: writing "racist" on a statue of a Confederate soldier, for example, is more expressive than simply "tagging" it by spray-painting some personalized reference or mentioning some group.[89] Issuing additional public declarations justifying their acts, as a way of recognizing that even well-selected symbolic protests benefit from interpretative augmentation, is always useful.

BLM, of course, was chiefly targeting racialized, oftentimes violent policing, a practice that rests on the "use of boundless police discretion" and thus represents the very antithesis of the rule of law, when viewed as requiring generality, predictability, and stability within law.[90] In that vein, some protest participants appeared in court as a way of making their case to a broader public. They targeted symbols representing fundamental injustices but did not waste energy on politically unappealing symbols of lesser gravity—hence their preoccupation with racist and Confederate monuments. Legal infractions were committed with the hope of generating political, social, and, yes, also *legal* reform: a core BLM goal, of course, is the abolition of racialized policing. Although some illegal BLM-related protests surely might have surprised King and other canonical civil disobedients, many demonstrated something akin to "respect for law," when not viewed in overly cramped ways. The vast preponderance of protestors, Trump's shrill executive order notwithstanding, were assuredly *not* anarchists or others bent on violent resistance and the destruction of American democracy.

Why should we care? Even if nonviolent civil disobedience often proves controversial, it possesses a moral and political cachet that other modes of protest-based political illegality frequently lack. Its key elements conform to fundamental democratic notions of accountable, public, law-based government.[91] It effectively communicates to political peers a clear sense of moral and political seriousness. Significantly, nonviolence gives expression to basic ideals of mutual respect and political equality without which democracy is impossible. By remaining nonviolent, protestors avoid contributing to an unnecessarily more violent—and dangerously polarized—political climate. Finally, civil disobedience is premised on the key insight that even in more or less functioning real-life democracies, systemic injustices and institutional deficits are often only undermined by movements that pursue extralegal paths.

With this moral and political cachet also come some political and legal benefits. Protestors who successfully take on the mantle of Gandhi or King are more likely to garner valuable public recognition. If they can convince a jury or judge that they are not ordinary criminals or rioters, but participants in a venerable political tradition, they may get off with a reduced sentence or some realistic expectation of clemency in the future. It would be a mistake for intelligent political actors to ignore such advantages.

In this vein, Minnesota Indigenous activists decided to bring down a statue of Christopher Columbus at the state capitol in Saint Paul on June 10, 2020, a day after BLM protestors had toppled a Columbus statue in Richmond, Virginia. They followed much of the standard template for civil disobedience. They spent decades peacefully protesting, petitioning, and calling on officials to bring down the statue because of its colonialist and racist connotations. They worked hard to elect Peggy Flanagan, a member of the White Earth Band of Ojibwe, to the Minnesota House of Representatives and then, in 2018, Lieutenant Governor, in part because of her promise to remove it. Revealingly, even her efforts to do so lawfully appear to have been waylaid by the state's opaque mechanisms for reviewing public art.[92]

Activists announced the statue's removal in advance and invited officials, including Minnesota Governor Tim Walz, to participate. Though Walz turned down the invitation, they proceeded to pull it down in daylight, taking "full, public responsibility for" their acts, with the protest's key organizer, Mike Forcia, turning himself in and facing felony charges for criminal damage to property. Those charges were dropped after Forcia agreed to perform community service: a hundred hours educating people about the traumatic history that had led him to topple the statue.[93]

Most symbolic property disobedients are unlikely to face government officials as sympathetic to their cause as Minnesota's Attorney General. Even protests that hew close to the civil disobedience playbook often prove controversial and set off political firestorms. Nonetheless, they pose only a comparatively limited range of normative challenges. When intended as communicative acts aimed at changing public opinion, resulting in no bodily or psychological violation of persons and with protestors accepting possible legal consequences, they prospectively gain both a moral status and possible legal and political benefits frequently denied participants in other types of militant protest.

Things are more ambivalent when symbolic property damage occurs secretly, or activists circumvent legal consequences. Moody-Adams notes correctly that we should look askance at a "remove-and-destroy-first" approach to racist memorials that ignores the importance of careful moral, political, and strategic reflection.[94] It was precisely those acting absent serious planning and with little deliberation who, by targeting monuments to Grant and Heg, misfired badly in 2020 in their selection and helped fuel a political backlash. Some protestors have also "hid their face or struck at night," in part because they worried about racist violence and sought to avoid "potentially heavy criminal and financial penalties," tangible possibilities given repressive laws aimed at impeding their efforts.[95]

Nonetheless, to the extent that recent BLM protestors made concerted efforts to communicate reasons for their acts, they approximated core features of civil disobedience. Even if they sometimes failed the strictest tests within the standard civil disobedience playbook, the fact that activists strove to meet many of them should count for something. In politics, things are rarely perfect or even close to it. Even if we take demanding ideas of civil disobedience as our yardstick, contextualized political judgment remains indispensable.

There may be reasons for criticizing symbolic property disobedients who act surreptitiously or refuse responsibility for their acts. Those who pursue them to intimidate and threaten others should be condemned. By the same token, the normative commitment to publicity within civil disobedience should not be interpreted in unduly narrow ways. Activists may think it unwise to reveal their personal identities, for example, yet still issue some sort of public statement outlining their acts. Activists can "own" their acts in a multiplicity of ways. As the philosopher Peter Singer noted decades ago, in extreme scenarios where state authorities "prevent dissenters from publicizing their views," the evasion of legal sanctions seems justifiable.[96] In some contexts, there may be politically more effective and normatively justifiably ways to evince respect for or fidelity to law than accepting draconian penalties. Civil disobedience is an irrepressibly contested concept that takes different shapes and sizes. We should avoid interpreting it in a way that risks blinding us to the messy complexities of real-life politics and movement struggles.

Of course, symbolic disobedients can select inappropriate targets, in the process failing to impart the desired message. Their cause may be manifestly unjust: those seeking to uphold racism and white supremacy have defaced and tried to bring down monuments to Martin Luther King and other praiseworthy figures.[97] On grounds of political ideology and judgment we can legitimately condemn their acts: those rejecting fundamental ideas of political equality and equal respect on which democracy—indeed, *any* decent political community—depends can and should be condemned. Moreover, anyone engaging in symbolic property disobedience with the aim of reshaping public life will always need to pay attention to possibly negative political repercussions. As Rawls correctly noted, even if legitimate political lawbreaking's preconditions have been satisfied, considerations of prudence may lead to rejecting it when likely "to provoke the harsh retaliation of the majority" and a political backlash.[98] Such considerations are always pertinent in the context of controversial efforts at symbolic property disobedience.

*   *   *

This chapter has explored the challenges of symbolic property disobedience by discussing recent climate and antiracist political protests. Both examples involved targets that were frequently public property—or at least, in the case of climate museum protestors, artworks owned by nonprofit institutions that enjoy some privileges (e.g., tax-free status) that private owners usually lack. Especially in the case of BLM-inspired symbolic disobedience, protestors were only marginally interested in questions raised by their acts as *property* harms as such. The source of this neglect probably derives from an implicit sense that public monuments and statues are legitimate objects for public contestation and protest since they are, of course, *public* property. They belong to "the people," and with mechanisms for oversight badly rigged extralegal protest becomes appropriate.

What about cases where symbolic property disobedients target private property? Would that alter the story I have tried to sketch? Would it still make sense to describe symbolic disobedience as potentially congruent with nonviolent civil disobedience?

There are complicated legal questions I cannot explore here: protests impacting private enjoy decidedly fewer protections than those impacting public property.[99] We can, however, offer some provisional observations.

Symbolic property disobedience targeting private property can potentially contribute or be related to tangible, potentially serious injuries to persons. Recent Hong Kong pro-democracy protestors, for example, damaged property owned by those identified as supportive of PRC policies. During the 1960s US urban riots, participants initially did the same to some white-owned small businesses. We could surely debate the symbolic merits of such acts. To the extent that they aimed to intimidate and threaten store owners, the lines between property damage and violence fade. In some cases, it seems possible to trace an identifiable causal link to manifest physical and psychological harms. A targeted shopkeeper, for example, loses her business, can no longer take care of loved ones, and faces the prospect of bankruptcy. As "embodied and physically vulnerable persons" she and others impacted might face existential consequences.[100] It seems implausible to describe such political acts as nonviolent or consistent with treating political equals with basic respect.

Whether this or other similar cases of symbolic disobedience involving private property should be so characterized will depend on a variety of contingencies and contextual conditions. It cannot be decided in advance. One measuring rod will be the general political context: even prior to the PRC clampdown, Hong Kong could hardly be described as a basically democratic regime, though its residents enjoyed crucial liberties. In authoritarian contexts, the main political grounds for privileging nonviolence vis-à-vis persons become uncertain, though there still may be pressing moral and strategic reasons for favoring it.

At the same time, we can easily conceive of scenarios involving *public* property where a similar dynamic plays out. Imagine militants opposed to some recent shift in health care policy who target a public clinic by committing severe damages to it, resulting in its temporary or permanent closure and patients in dire medical straits consequently denied necessary health care. Here again, the conceptual borders between property damage and violence blur. In such scenarios, symbolic property disobedience's relationship to nonviolent civil disobedience becomes tenuous.

Even in our own very imperfect democracies, principled nonviolence vis-à-vis fellow citizens and other political peers is indispensable. Violence against them means undermining their rightful status as partners in a common political project. When symbolic disobedients choose targets that potentially result in severe injuries, they risk attacking democracy's core presuppositions. It becomes hard to see how their acts could be justified, even when possibly motivated by an understandable or legitimate sense of injustice. Whatever symbolic message they otherwise intended is likely to be badly obstructed by a failure to treat others as equal persons deserving of respect. By communicating fundamental disrespect, theirs become symbolic acts that seem perilously self-destructive: only a more or less thriving democracy provides sufficiently possibilities for free-wheeling political contestation. Without those possibilities symbolic property disobedience seems unlikely to succeed. Violence threatens to destroy the very possibility of a community in which we can engage effectively in protest in the first place.

CHAPTER 4

Disruptive Property Disobedience

isruptive property disobedience aims to obstruct practices viewed as unjust or unfair, with the targeted property seen as essential to some identified wrongdoing. While typically having symbolic and communicative contours, illegal disruptive disobedience blocks presumed injustices from continuing or ever taking place.[1] The desired change, in other words, is brought about straight away—though in most instances, only temporarily—by incurring damage or destruction to public or private property. Even when engaging in direct action, practitioners usually hope that their efforts will inspire others and ignite wider political and social change.

Disruptive property disobedience is often more contentious than its symbolic but predominantly nondisruptive cousin. Defacing a Confederate statue is one thing; vandalizing a police vehicle or station to impede racialized law enforcement is generally considered something else altogether. Disruptive property disobedience's most controversial types are frequently called *sabotage*, a term deriving from the French *sabot*, referring to wooden shoes or clogs, with sabotage suggesting clumsy work, that is, to work as though one were wearing wooden clogs. Many work-related practices associated with sabotage predate its reinvention as a self-consciously radical political tactic favored by nineteenth- and early twentieth-century anarcho-syndicalists and leftist labor militants. Ordinary people throughout history have practiced its constantly evolving, multiform varieties, often without express political goals and in relatively isolated, highly individualized ways.[2] Most famously perhaps, England's so-called "Luddites" engaged in "machine-breaking" to resist early industrializing capitalism.[3]

By the start of the twentieth century, "sabotage" referenced a diversity of politically motivated acts chiefly targeting business owners, ranging from worker "slowdowns" to orchestrated efforts to damage the means of production.[4] It was embraced by the Industrial Workers of the World (IWW), or Wobblies, "the first and only labor group in American history to officially advocate sabotage," before the group disavowed it in the face of massive state repression in the context of the so-called Red Scare.[5] The IWW's ill-fated espousal of sabotage, I argue in this chapter, contains lessons for sabotage's present-day proponents.

The discourse of sabotage, along with techniques associated with it, subsequently migrated into military strategy.[6] It was recommended to those living under Nazi-occupied Europe, for example, by US intelligence services.[7] Most importantly for our purposes, today the term is typically used to describe a major subset of politically motivated acts involving property damage or destruction, with saboteurs frequently acting secretly and hoping to avoid legal repercussions. Theorists and political commentators are again formulating principled defenses of sabotage, in part because of its growing prominence among radical environmentalists—and, most recently, climate activists—advocating *ecotage*, or ecological sabotage.[8]

Because present-day ecotage both usefully illustrates core traits of disruptive property disobedience as well as possible perils, this chapter devotes special attention to it. To their credit, eco-saboteurs have usually acted nonviolently in relation to persons. Still, they have too often muddied the waters so as unnecessarily to invite a political backlash. Unwittingly, they have reproduced vexing ambiguities that plagued radical labor's recourse to sabotage during the early decades of the twentieth century. By comparing the Wobblies and recent environmental militants, we can get a better sense of some general dangers.

In what King astutely called a "a 'thing'-oriented society" in which "machines and computers, profit motives and property rights" are considered at least as—and sometimes more—valuable than people, attacks especially on private property always pose sizable political risks.[9] Officials tasked with enforcing the law will usually aim to exploit widely shared but flawed, overly broad ideas about violence to justify harsh responses. Given private property's sacrosanct status, property disobedients will have a hard time avoiding severe penalties. They should avoid, at a minimum, inviting any association of their protests with paramilitary activities, something saboteurs have not always successfully accomplished because of their ambivalence about political violence. Unfortunately, sabotage's widespread association with small numbers of militants operating secretly risks opening the door to an inappropriately martial outlook.

Since it takes a wide variety of forms, we begin by analyzing disruptive property disobedience's general traits and relationship to its symbolic cousin. Some of its variants are now relatively commonplace and pose few novel political or theoretical questions, whereas others are more controversial and appear more difficult to justify.

*   *   *

Disruptive property disobedience contains symbolic features, even as it seeks to block some wrongdoing. This simple but pivotal point sometimes gets lost in the scholarly literature, which often relies on excessively stylized juxtapositions of deliberative civil disobedience to militant direct action. Theorists start with idealized, sometimes counterfactual ideas about civil disobedience as a communicative practice, before pointing out that direct action—potentially including property damage—follows a different political logic.[10] In fact, disruptive property disobedience relies heavily on *cost-levying*, that is, dramatically raising the political (and often material) costs for those pursuing some disputed practice. Militant climate activists, for example, sabotage the fossil fuels infrastructure hoping that by doing so, industry profits can be slashed and investors will shift resources to less environmentally destructive opportunities. Some consider this a politically smarter, more realistic way to generate change than conventional democratic politics—for example, lobbying political leaders, or joining the ranks of a peaceful demonstration.

There is also no question that disruptive property disobedience sometimes takes on *coercive* features, especially when contrasted to civil disobedience conceived along strictly deliberative lines. A blockade of a public highway, for example, keeps motorists from using it. An occupation or sit-in at a private company potentially brings operations to a standstill, preventing business transactions and reducing profits. Recent US and Canadian Indigenous activists who occupied construction sites for the Dakota Access Pipeline, for example, were not simply making a public or deliberative case, but also actively impeding those who believed they had legal authority to proceed. Activists insisted that the proposed pipeline directly threatened Native lands, and that large utility companies were illegally violating environmental protections those lands rightfully enjoyed.[11] Unsurprisingly perhaps, some prominent liberal theorists of civil disobedience have criticized blockades and similarly disruptive protests, many of which potentially impact property rights, describing them as morally troublesome blackmail.[12]

Yet, it would be wrong to ignore disruptive property disobedience's identifiably symbolic and frequently communicative credentials. A blockade or occupation affecting property rights is likely to be experienced as intrusively coercive by those negatively impacted. However, it still aims to make a public statement. Militants block *gas* but not *water* pipelines, for example, to disrupt a wrongdoing *and* communicate a message. The tendency to overstate contrasts vis-à-vis civil disobedience downplays the familiar historical fact that even some of its iconic exemplars included coercive traits. Gandhi counseled "a positive element of coercion . . . [and] element of compulsion which may affect a change on the part of an opponent."[13] Disruptive property damage arguably exemplifies a *different* mode of persuasion than what academic theorists have associated with civil disobedience, but it remains in crucial respects communicative. It seems unfair, at any rate, to see it as nothing more than coercive blackmail, even if some of its more controversial forms pose tough questions.

Property targeted by activists, for example, is typically supposed to have symbolic significance, even if activists may still fail to make the necessary connections. The reason is obvious: protestors want to broadcast a political message. Those who damage or destroy property for political reasons hope to encourage others to rethink their views and join the cause. Eco-saboteurs, for example, have damaged SUVs but not hybrid or electric vehicles, and then issued declarations outlining the grounds behind their choice.[14] Opponents of Elon Musk's Department of Government Efficiency (DOGE) cost-cutting measures have targeted Tesla vehicles and dealerships. Even when disruptive property damage is done secretly and anonymously, real-life examples contain "elements of political theater that seem explicitly designed to appeal to a wider audience."[15] Admittedly, those engaging in disruptive property disobedience may express disdain for "mere talk" and conventional protest politics, but they still spend time and energy thinking about how their acts should spur others to join them. Disruptive property disobedience may look different from the sorts of protests found in stringently deliberative editions of the civil disobedience playbook, yet it also generally seeks to persuade and mobilize.

* * *

Since disruptive property disobedience takes myriad possible forms, it may be helpful to conceive it as prospectively located at different points on a series of spectra or scales. The first would capture the *intensity* or *extent* of

protest-related damage to property and the resulting infringements on ownership rights. On one end of this first spectrum, for example, we might situate
1980s antinuclear protests that blockaded rail tracks and roads to stall shipments of uranium or atomic waste, causing an inconvenience to affected proprietors by cutting into profits, but with relatively limited lasting economic
losses.[16] Toward the other end we could place an Earth Liberation Front 1998
attack on a Vail, Colorado ski resort that generated an estimated $12 million
in damage.[17] In cases involving public property, BLM blockades of roads or
highways, resulting in minor inconveniences to motorists and others, would
fall on one end, whereas arson attacks destructive of significant public property (e.g., police vehicles or stations) might fall on the other.

    This first spectrum overlaps but potentially diverges from a second one
that captures disruptive property disobedience's *temporal* contours, that is,
the extent to which property damage is brief and temporary, rather than long
lasting and durable. Many severe cases of property damage will fall under
the latter and the less extreme cases under the former part of the scale. But
temporality and intensity constitute different measures: an expensive piece of
construction equipment, for example, can be destroyed at a high price to its
owner but quickly replaced. At some point, ongoing and seemingly permanent violations of property rights become more than merely or exclusively
disruptive: property is then being *taken* from its legal owners, and violations of their rights are correspondingly significant. In such scenarios—for
example, when squatters occupy a building or land and refuse to vacate it—
disruptive property disobedience merges into property *seizures*, a phenomenon we explore in Chapter 5.

    Finally, we might classify incidents of disruptive property disobedience
in relation to familiar ideas about *nonviolent civil disobedience*. In Chapter 3,
I suggested that some predominantly symbolic protests targeting property
approximate civil disobedience when conceived as politically motivated violations of law that exemplify *civility, conscientiousness, publicity, fidelity to
law,* and *nonviolence*. Provisionally, this also seems like a helpful basis for
analyzing disruptive property disobedience, even if its political logic and
emphasis on cost-levying conflict with stringent models of civil disobedience.
Do disruptive property disobedients make a public case for their acts? Can
their acts be viewed as attempts to change and improve law? Have activists
taken responsibility for them?

    Crucially, have disruptive property disobedients practiced nonviolence
vis-à-vis persons? When entailing no bodily or severe psychological harm,

their acts remain in principle nonviolent. In contrast, when property damage is tangibly linked—or more or less directly complicit in—violence against persons, it conflicts with political nonviolence; then there frequently will be legitimate reasons, in a more or less well-functioning democracy, to reject it. Only property damage that remains nonviolent vis-à-vis persons can provide evidence that participants take ideas of basic respect and political equality essential to democracy seriously.

In sum, disruptive protest's relationship to nonviolent civil disobedience provides us with initial evaluative criteria, even if we might justifiably worry about mechanically applying them. Nonetheless, there is a relatively broad, well-founded consensus among intellectuals and some political and legal officials that lawbreaking in accord with its features deserves *some measure* of respect, in contrast to ordinary criminality. When illegal protests exhibit a substantial mix of civility, conscientiousness, publicity, fidelity to law, and nonviolence, their compatibility with core democratic ideals can be reasonably inferred. Disruptive disobedients who act openly or make public declarations defending their acts, for example, implicitly suggest their preference for a political order where binding decisions are made via open *public* exchange. By making legal or constitutional appeals they express fidelity to or respect for the rule of law and constitutional government. Disruptive disobedience that embodies familiar traits of nonviolent civil disobedience provides preliminary grounds for inferring that activists presuppose valuable political intuitions. To the extent that they fail to do so, their acts may be more difficult to justify.

On one end of this third scale, we could locate numerous real-life examples of open, peaceful blockades or occupations of public or private property. At the other end, secret and violent protests, in which participants make little or no attempt to sway peers or show anything akin to respect for or fidelity to law, would fall.

These three scales illuminate key features of disruptive property disobedience's variegated types, along with some key normative and political questions they pose. Take, for example, the canonical case of the 1960s student sit-ins, a crucial conjuncture in the US civil rights movement. Ignited by four college students who politely requested service at a segregated Greensboro, NC, Woolworth lunch counter on February 1, 1960, copycat sit-ins—involving approximately 70,000 predominantly working-class African American students in over 100 localities—soon rippled across the south.[18] What we have come to dub "the sit-in movement" is now commonly viewed as crucial to the revitalization of the civil rights struggle. Although theirs was not the first lunch counter sit-in targeting racism, the Greensboro Four grabbed the national media spotlight, launching a wave of similar protests. At the time, the sit-inners many Americans now lionize "were maligned as threatening sacred rights of private property and the rule of law."[19] Segregationists and leading public figures such as former president Harry Truman described their protests as recklessly disruptive, violent, and implicitly socialistic because of their challenge to the business owner's traditional right to engage in racial discrimination.[20]

Nonetheless, the sit-inners were able to gain a measure of public sympathy—and eventually ward off a repressive legal response—in part because their protests were public, self-consciously nonviolent, and strove to demonstrate civility, conscientiousness, and respect for law. In a series of major rulings, the US Supreme Court sided with the protestors, in part because the Court majority sidelined critics' accusations that the protests recklessly infringed property rights. Indeed, the sit-ins had only briefly obstructed "business as usual" for diners and restaurants; the Court sensibly pushed back against overheated interpretations of their protests as violent threats to private property and American capitalism, though many people at the time rejected that assessment.[21]

The sit-ins helped trigger landmark federal legislation, the Civil Rights Act of 1964, prohibiting racial discrimination in public accommodations. They also served, not surprisingly, as an immediate inspiration for prominent liberal intellectuals, including Rawls, who were soon preoccupied with outlining strict models of nonviolent civil disobedience.[22] Here we have a canonical case of disruptive property disobedience in which key decision-makers and significant swaths of public opinion determined that damage to property and infringement of ownership rights were both temporary and negligible, with activists abiding by core elements of the nonviolent civil disobedience playbook.

We could easily identify other incidents of disruptive property disobedience analogous to the civil rights sit-ins and, in principle, potentially justifiable. Similar disruptive protests have sometimes briefly impeded using public property or cut into business profits. Nonetheless, when remaining conscientious, public, nonviolent, and expressive of fidelity to law, it probably makes sense to place them under the rubric of nonviolent civil disobedience. Philosophers and political thinkers have already done so.[23] When inconveniences to property owners are limited, the acts in question pose few if any novel normative challenges; in most cases, it will be difficult to see them as complicit in or contributing to tangible violence vis-à-vis persons. Of course, we might disagree with the causes advanced or worry about their timing and appropriateness. But, in many contexts, they make constructive contributions to public life and remain in principle justifiable.

Admittedly, even when disruptive property disobedients produce only limited damage or infringe only briefly on property rights and follow the standard civil disobedience playbook, there is no guarantee that judges and juries will respond favorably. Beginning in December 2016, a group of self-described nonviolent "valve turners" associated with the group Climate Direct Action successfully turned emergency shut-off values to close oil pipelines in Canada and the United States. The group's affiliates warned utilities in advance so that they could take necessary safety measures; they waited to be arrested and hoped to use the courtroom to raise awareness about climate change. Although they briefly reduced the flow of oil, no permanent damage to property resulted, and overall economic losses seem to have been modest. Nevertheless, the activists have been treated harshly by officials and unsympathetic courts, with the US Department of Homeland Security classifying them as a dangerous "extremist" organization akin to violent white supremacists.[24]

More complicated are those situations where disruptive disobedients reproduce some but not all elements of nonviolent civil disobedience. The cases of Catholic Workers and environmental activists Montoya and Recznick perhaps fall under this rubric. Their ecotage targeting the Dakota Access Pipeline was initially secret; only later did they publicly admit to their illegalities, claiming that they had vandalized property as a last resort, after "exploring and exhausting all avenues of process."[25] Both were imprisoned and required to pay massive fines. One reason why we focus on the case of ecotage later in this chapter is precisely because it represents a complex— and thus particularly illuminating—mode of present-day disruptive property disobedience.

By no means, however, is ecotage the only messy, controversial variety. For example, politically minded hacktivists have surreptitiously disabled and occasionally damaged computer servers of large firms and state agencies, without always owning up to their acts or accepting legal consequences. Even when lawyers creatively repackaged their protests as updated versions of civil disobedience, and no tangible injuries to persons could be identified, judges and juries have usually refused to take the bait. Hacktivists have faced severe legal repercussions, with judges often categorically dismissing comparisons to civil disobedience.[26] Similarly, recent animal rights defenders who damaged expensive laboratories and other property, and sometimes freed animals from confinement, have faced harsh official responses. In 2006, the United States passed the Animal Enterprise Terrorism Act, an open-ended statute that treats interferences with laboratories as acts of terrorism and promulgates stiff penalties. While terrorism has standardly been defined as random violence directed against innocent civilians with the aim of fomenting fear, the legislation covers targeted, discriminate property damage, with criminal penalties resulting even "if the offense does not instill in another the reasonable fear of serious bodily injury or death."[27] In July 2014, a Los Angeles-based activist, Kevin Johnson, participated in the release of two thousand fox and mink from fur farms. Prosecuted under the statute, he subsequently spent three years in prison.[28] As we will see, many US states have promulgated similarly open-ended laws targeting so-called "eco-terrorists."

Yet, nothing stands in the way of disruptive property damage remaining fundamentally nonviolent by conscientiously avoiding any prospect of severe harm or injury to persons. At the same time, there is no question that it sometimes involves risk-taking that may generate complicity in or pave the way for acts of violence against persons.

For example, tree-spiking—a controversial tactic embraced by a small number of militant eco-saboteurs—poses real threats to loggers, though not perhaps the owners or shareholders of the companies employing them. Arson attacks are always dangerous, for the obvious reason that fires can spread rapidly and become uncontrolled, threatening persons as well as property unrelated to any targeted injustice.

We can identify recent examples that undermine the basic norm of nonviolence vis-à-vis persons on which political equality and democracy rest. It is hard to see how they could ever be interpreted as justifiable disruptive property disobedience within a more or less democratic political setting.

For example, the January 6, 2021 attack on the US Capitol—and copycat January 8, 2023 attack on Brazilian government buildings in Brasilia—involved substantial property destruction intended to obstruct the peaceful democratic transfer of power. Both protests should be condemned not only because of their overtly antidemocratic aims, but also because they recklessly blurred boundaries between property damage and violence against persons.[29] Much of the property destruction at the Capitol targeted offices (for example, House Speaker Nancy Pelosi's) and monuments to Thomas Jefferson, Ulysses Grant, and others. Its symbolism, for the most part, was sufficiently clear, even if most contemporary observers deemed it unpalatable. Crucially, the damage was perpetrated by protestors—many of whom were heavily armed and had prior military training—who sought to intimidate and potentially commit violence against elected officials. A hangman's noose was exhibited on gallows constructed outside the Capitol, and participants hunted down Vice President Mike Pence while chanting "hang Mike Pence." Participants attacked and severely injured police officers. Some of their acts were disturbingly evocative of the sort of political violence that occurs during civil wars: it constituted a retaliatory attack on political "enemies," not an attempt to engage political peers in a common project.[30]

Despite President Trump's subsequent pardons, participants in the January 6 upheavals rightly faced assault or related charges, or were charged and sometimes found guilty of using a dangerous weapon or causing serious bodily harm to officers.[31] In this case, drawing a strict line between property damage and violence to persons seems implausible: the former was intended to serve the form.[32] Protestors damaged Speaker Pelosi's office, for example, to scare and recklessly endanger her. It is one thing when *unarmed* protestors engage in limited, carefully targeted symbolic or disruptive protest. But it is something else altogether when they are *armed* and pursue wide-ranging property damage to instill fear.[33] Then the divide between property damage and violence breaks down, with the former becoming little more than an accessory to the latter.

Here, as in other real-life examples we might recall, the differences between armed militants engaging in property damage as an accessory to violence, and unarmed activists pursuing limited, carefully selected property disobedience, are generally clear enough. Fortunately, examples of the former remain relatively rare within existing democracies. Most of us, I hope, will condemn them.

∗   ∗   ∗

I now turn to the case of the IWW, the radical labor union that espoused sabotage between 1910 and (roughly) 1917. I do so partly because the Wobblies remain the most significant US political organization to have openly endorsed sabotage, but also—and more importantly—because internal tensions plaguing their dalliance with it resurface in contemporary defenses of ecotage. The Wobblies' brief endorsement of disruptive property disobedience is of more than antiquarian interest.

Founded in 1905, the Wobblies endorsed revolutionary industrial unionism, promoting "one big union" that tried to organize so-called "native-born," immigrant, skilled, and unskilled workers, including many in industries neglected by mainline craft-based labor unions.[34] Resting on a mix of anarcho-syndicalist and Marxist ideas, and favoring militant forms of direct action, the IWW positioned itself as a radical alternative both to the mainstream American Federation of Labor (AFL) and a Socialist Party (SP) committed to political reform by electoral means. Its greatest organizing successes were in the American West, with peak membership reaching an estimated 150,000 in 1917, and the group's rapid decline occurring in the years immediately thereafter. Unfortunately, the Wobblies' links to sabotage appear to have been crucial to its demise: government officials used it to justify a repressive clampdown that decimated the IWW. The fact that the IWW occasionally highlighted workplace sabotage's basically nonviolent credentials, and that it remains unclear how widely it was ever in fact practiced, failed to thwart state repression.

According to labor historians, sabotage became crucial to IWW political thinking in 1910, after the group's leaders became acquainted with the ideas of the French labor militant and anarcho-syndicalist Emile Pouget, a pivotal figure in the early years of the French Confederation Generale du Travail (General Confederation of Labor).[35] Pouget's work was translated and introduced by the Italian-American Wobbly Arturo Giovannitti, and then circulated by the IWW, as were related pamphlets defending sabotage by prominent members, including Elizabeth Gurley Flynn, Walker C. Smith, and William E. Trautmann.[36] Until 1917, when key Wobblies disavowed sabotage, it constituted one prong of a broader tactical agenda focused on worker direct action. That single prong, however, was soon given an oversize status by critics.

The story is a complicated one, but a few elements stand out. First, the Wobblies followed Pouget in characterizing sabotage as encompassing a wide range of tactics to reduce profits—worker slowdowns, "quickie" strikes, and shoddy work resulting in subpar goods or services. It consisted of disruptive—oftentimes rapidly evolving, contextually specific—acts targeting capitalists and their decision-making prerogatives. Crucially, the IWW counseled against indiscriminate property damage and advised militants to select targets carefully, recommending that sabotage be undertaken only during strikes. Sabotage might disable capitalist-owned machines, for example, to render them temporarily unusable, with workers urged to avoid incurring lasting or permanent destruction.[37] (The workers, of course, hoped to take control of productive instruments in some postcapitalist, cooperative economy.) They were also told to avoid damaging goods in ways harmful to consumers.

Nonetheless, the borders between property damage and destruction occasionally blurred: temporary harm to the means of production or consumer goods sometimes blurred into calls for more lasting property destruction.[38] That slippage was effectively seized on by powerful critics, with the IWW soon linked in the public mind with wanton violence.

The IWW also repeatedly drew a line separating sabotage from violence against persons. As Smith put it (in language regularly echoed by other Wobblies), sabotage "does not seek nor desire to take human life," since it targeted what Pouget dubbed "machines and tools, that is . . . inert, painless and lifeless" objects.[39] The Wobblies delineated property damage, at least when directed against *capitalist* property in the means of production, from violence, whose deployment they generally condemned for any but extreme political circumstances. Indeed, to the extent that sabotage empowered the proletariat in its struggle against capitalist exploitation, it placed "human life—and especially the life of the only useful class—higher than all else in the universe."[40] By preventing capitalists from immiserating workers and their families, sabotage was central to the "struggle for life" itself.[41] Since capitalist property was culpable for many tangible harms, it was not sacrosanct. Might not sabotage endanger capitalists? It disrupted the capitalist's sovereign power to control production, but that was a very different matter from incurring violence to them or those dependent on them.

With some justification, recent commentators have described IWW sabotage as consistent with nonviolence vis-à-vis persons.[42] Wobbly writers pictured sabotage as life-preserving *self-defense*, directed against the capitalist's pursuit of profits and the real damages and injuries to workers—and also consumers, some Wobblies added—systematically generated by an economic system in which the means of production were privately owned.[43] This was no mere hyperbole: during the first decades of the twentieth century, about 25,000 died annually in the United States as a direct result of work-related injuries, with another 1.5 million suffering major injuries.[44] The IWW also pointed out that irresponsible, dangerously life-threatening sabotage was regularly practiced by capitalists and sanctified by law. When workers sought to unionize and improve working conditions, owners responded with lockouts, employment blacklists for labor organizers, and hirings of poorly trained scabs. Such practices posed potentially life-or-death threats to workers, while undermining efficiency and the optimal employment of the means of production, all for the sake of preserving ownership prerogatives. For all intents and purposes, capitalists engaged in top-down sabotage, even as their anti-unionism was protected by law and widely celebrated by the business community. In contrast, when workers pursued bottom-up disruptive practices, their acts, in contrast, were labelled and prosecuted as lawless, violent acts of sabotage.[45]

Two additional features of the Wobbly dalliance with sabotage deserve attention. First, Wobblies tapped labor theories of property. Since it was the working class whose labor had made capitalist machinery and consumer goods possible in the first place, workers had a right to damage the capitalist's property: property did not rightfully belong to capitalists.[46] In Chapter 2, I noted that ideas about property as an extension of personhood have some-times functioned to justify viewing property damage as violent. The Wob-blies embraced analogous ideas about personhood and property instead to posit that capitalist property legitimately and rightfully belonged to workers, who therefore could do with it as they pleased. For some Wobblies, sabotage anticipated or prefigured a new postcapitalist social order in which workers managed and controlled production.[47]

Second, the IWW's endorsement of sabotage rested on deep skepticism about existing political mechanisms. Since the liberal state systematically favored capitalists, it was naive to expect much if any meaningful reform. Direct action targeting capitalists, in contrast, represented a viable alternative. Trautmann went so far as to argue that the capitalist workplace was as repres-sive and undemocratic as the most autocratic of contemporary states.[48] Denied basic liberties at work, laborers had little choice but to engage in sabotage, to be pursued anonymously and secretly, with direct parallels to tactics employed by anyone seeking political and social change within autocratic states.

Massive state repression during the Red Scare of 1917–20 soon neutralized the IWW. One crucial legal tool was a collection of vaguely drafted state-level "criminal syndicalism" statutes, for which the business community and its allies had aggressively lobbied, aimed at debilitating the IWW by zooming in on its embrace of supposedly violent sabotage. The statutes willfully ignored the IWW's delineation of property damage from violence against persons, relying instead on open-ended definitions of both sabotage and violence to provide a convenient basis for a crackdown. A legal expert on the Wobblies claims the "unrelenting agitation of capitalists and their champions in the media" as the driving force behind the legislation and resulting crackdown.[49] Vague legal language meant that officials could interpret them selectively and sometimes arbitrarily, often with little attention to identifiable criminal offense; mere association with the IWW and its allegedly subversive activities sufficed.[50] Revealingly, "no prosecutor ever convicted any IWW member of actually committing industrial sabotage," yet countless Wobblies still ended up in jail or deported.[51] The federal government played a pivotal role in the clampdown. The US Post Office, for example, prohibited any mail containing the word "sabotage," while Attorney General Michael Palmer relied on the open-ended clauses of the Espionage Act (1917) to imprison or deport Wobblies. Indictments often rested exclusively on statements Wobblies had allegedly made, not concrete offenses relating to theft or sabotage.[52]

State repression followed myriad legal and administrative routes; we cannot explore them all here. By the early 1920s, at any rate, the IWW was a shadow of its former self, with its remaining members struggling to disassociate themselves from sabotage.

Present-day practitioners of militant disruptive property disobedience would do well to attend to the IWW experience. One lesson they might draw is that even conscientious defenses of sabotage, in which property damage is carefully delineated from physical violence, will not necessarily ward off a public backlash and tough legal penalties. Symbolic property disobedience targeting public property (for example, statues) is controversial enough; disruptive protest targeting privileged forms of private property is typically viewed as beyond the pale. Unfortunately, in contemporary society "machines and computers, profit motives and property rights" are still valued at least as highly as human beings.[53] Attacks on them are easily discredited, especially when impacting privileged, well-organized economic groups. Business executives are not only well regarded but frequently idolized in our and other societies. The mere specter of damage to capitalist property will energize politically influential, well-funded economic interests to demonize political militants, even if doing so means exaggerating the threats at hand.

The tragic irony is that the IWW seems only rarely to have engaged in sabotage, and then only the least destructive types.[54] Nonetheless, their frequently fiery rhetoric was seized on by defenders of the economic status quo: "Most students of the IWW agree that the organization's reputation for practicing sabotage was a creation of public hysteria," whipped up by the business community and its political allies to discredit the group.[55] Still, the overheated public reaction may have unwittingly been "encouraged by big-talking Wobblies who spoke so casually about" sabotage as to open the door to a crackdown.[56]

The perils of such "big talk" should not be ignored. Even as the Wobblies distinguished sabotage from violence against persons, they frequently depicted it with martial and paramilitary hues. Sabotage was described as a crucial tool in the "guerrilla war" waged by workers against capitalists, a necessary "war measure" required by the violent conditions of capitalist society, with labor saboteurs akin to "sharpshooters" turning their guns on the class enemy, the bourgeoisie.[57] According to Puget, labor and capital are "nothing but two belligerent armies in a state of permanent warfare."[58] At a minimum, such remarks invited misunderstandings and manipulation by well-positioned foes. One source was the Marxist idea of class struggle as *warfare*, a metaphor that risked conflating class conflict with openly violent battle. Another was the undeniably violent nature of capital-labor relations in the United States during the late nineteenth and early twentieth centuries, when capitalists, government officials, and local vigilantes joined forces to violently suppress labor and leftist movements. The Wobblies' anarcho-syndicalism was a third source. It meant that their nonviolent commitments were generally strategic but not principled, with most Wobblies believing that capitalists would never give up their privileges peacefully, and that organized collective violence might prove necessary. Alongside pamphlets advocating sabotage, for example, the IWW distributed Georges Sorel's *Reflections on Violence* (1915), a work that not only defended but romanticized workers' counterviolence against capitalists.[59]

Given the awful repression Wobblies suffered, it seems unfair to hector them for ambiguous rhetoric and confused strategizing. Less loose "big talk" probably would not have spared them. Still, sympathetic commentators are right to note how tensions within IWW rhetoric and thinking about violence sometimes made things too easy for opponents.

Why should we care? Recent political thinking among ecotage's advocates reproduces parallel ambiguities. Like the Wobblies, ecotage's proponents describe property damage as nonviolent while unnecessarily muddying the waters. Not surprisingly, some eco-saboteurs have been subjected to inordinately repressive state responses. In the United States and elsewhere, they are now frequently categorized as "eco-terrorists."

Of course, from the heights of some versions of normative political theory or philosophy, such mundane matters will seem marginal to the question of sabotage's possible justifiability. We should, in fact, delineate questions concerning normative justifiability from those relating to effectiveness. For real-world political actors, however, the latter are always crucial. It would be irresponsible for this or any other writer to ignore them. Property disobedience's justifiability should not depend exclusively or even primarily on the likelihood of a positive outcome. By the same token, activists who take on the heavy burden of pursuing it should still try to learn from previous experiences. As far as the possible legitimacy of Wobbly property damage goes, this at least should be said: it is very difficult to see how the astonishingly harsh criminal penalties meted out to the IWW were warranted. Too many Wobblies were given inordinately long prison terms for little more than participating in protests or circulating literature, frequently on trumped up charges disconnected from any clearly defined criminal act. By any measure, state and federal repression of the Wobblies represents one of US democracy's darker moments.[60] The Wobblies' main crime, it seems, was challenging capitalism and well-nigh universal assumptions about its virtues. Such matters should never be out of bounds in any self-respecting democratic political community.

*   *   *

Modern North American ecotage's Ur-text is Edward Abbey's *The Monkey Wrench Gang* (1975), an irreverent novel chronicling a motley gang of misfit activists in the US Southwest who come together to disrupt development projects threatening wilderness.[61] Historians of US environmentalism tell us that Abbey's book directly inspired activists—most prominently, David Foreman—frustrated with mainstream environmentalism and looking for radical alternatives.[62] Foreman helped found the militant group EarthFirst! in 1980, with his *Ecodefense: A Field Guide to Monkeywrenching* (1985), serving as the group's unofficial ecotage handbook.[63] EarthFirst! members damaged bulldozers, severed power lines and utility towers, and initially endorsed tree-spiking as a way to put a stop to logging, before disavowing the practice in 1990. Another organization formed in the 1980s, the Sea Shepherds, employed sabotage to thwart activities harmful to sea life and marine conservation with members, for example, ramming and damaging whaling vessels. Yet another group, Earth Liberation Front (ELF), emerged in the early 1990s, in part because of worries that EarthFirst! had become insufficiently militant. Operating secretly and by means of loosely connected local cells, ELF's most spectacular act of ecotage was probably the 1998 arson attack on a Vail ski resort.

Beginning in the 1980s, ecotage took many different forms and was pursued by a variety of political actors, including some who envisioned their acts as complementing nonviolent civil disobedience, and yet others who modeled themselves on guerrilla fighters. It mostly involved limited, temporary property damage, with activists expressly committed to nonviolence vis-à-vis persons. But some acts involved extensive property destruction by clandestine groups that pointedly rejected civil disobedience and viewed themselves as "warriors" defending nature. Ecotage's recent incidents, in sum, can be positioned at various locations on the scales described previously in this chapter.

Looking back at North American ecotage extending roughly from the 1980s until the start of the twenty-first century, we can identify some revealing parallels to the IWW experience. Like the Wobblies, green saboteurs have embraced skeptical and sometimes dismissive assessments of existing political institutions, even as their thinking sometimes draws on libertarianism rather than radical leftism. In the words of *Monkey Wrench Gang's* Doc Sarvis, the self-described "anarcho-syndicalist libertarian" who serves as Abbey's ideological mouthpiece: "I don't believe in majority rule . . . I am against all forms of government, including good government."[64] Thus, direct action targeting environmentally destructive practices, not appeals to incorrigible political elites or badly corrupted institutions, is the best way to end them. Ecotage's defenders have also frequently depicted it as basically *defensive*, with saboteurs serving as frontline eco-*defenders* resisting the ongoing destruction of wilderness areas and related violence against living creatures. Neither private nor public property rights should be strictly upheld when destructive of human beings, other living creatures, or nature more generally.

Like the Wobblies, ecotage's recent proponents have consistently underscored their commitment to nonviolence vis-à-vis persons but not things or property. For Doc Sarvis, there is a "cardinal rule: no violence to human beings."[65] Similarly, Foreman's influential *Ecodefense* affirmed ecotage's nonviolent credentials: "It is not directed towards harming human beings or other forms of life. It is aimed at inanimate machines and tools. Care is always taken to minimize any possible threat to other people."[66] Most US-based eco-saboteurs beginning in the '80s followed suit, with militants frequently endorsing some version of the idea of nonviolence vis-à-vis persons.[67]

Yet, revealingly, even as ecotage's defenders embraced nonviolence, martial and paramilitary ideas and images resurfaced. One member of Abbey's fictional monkey wrench gang, Hayduke, is a heavily armed Vietnam veteran; the book ends with Hayduke exchanging gunfire with government officials sent to capture him. The narrative "is filled with paramilitary operations," as the environmental ethicist Eugene Hargrove correctly noted in an early critical discussion, with the saboteurs trying "to keep their identities a secret and avoid capture."[68] That tension is even more apparent in Foreman's *Ecodefense*, which espoused nonviolence yet expressly imitated the sort of practical field guide tailored to military or counterinsurgency activities. Foreman's volume sought to provide practical advice to individuals and small groups of self-selected saboteurs, working secretly and hoping to circumvent legal repercussions. Their recommended activities recall elements of underground guerrilla warfare, though focused on "killing machines, rather than humans."[69]

This initial wave of ecotage, at any case, effectively came to an end during the first decade of the present century, when eco-saboteurs faced a repressive backlash with unseemly similarities to the ugliest moments of the Red Scare. Beginning in the 1980s, right-wing pro-business intellectuals and organizations fought aggressively to brand even relatively limited acts of environmentally motivated property damage as *ecoterrorism* subject to harsh penalties.[70] Such efforts have been successfully advanced especially by the American Legal Exchange Council (ALEC), a powerful corporate lobby financed by major utilities and the fossil fuels industry. (ALEC, not coincidentally, was also a crucial political force lobbying for the similar related Animal Enterprise Terrorism Act.) Many US states now have statutes on the books, reproducing key elements of model legislation proposed by ALEC, which rely on open-ended definitions of ecoterrorism. The statutes reject the usual view of terrorism as random violence against ordinary persons aimed at instilling fear, in favor of an open-ended view that includes targeted property damage potentially involving no harm to persons. Seemingly commonsensical, yet badly flawed, broad notions of violence as covering both harm to persons and property have morphed into misleadingly confused legal definitions of terrorism that encompass a wide range of property crimes.[71]

One might legitimately condemn green saboteurs who commit reckless attacks. Yet theirs remain very different from acts committed by Al-Qaeda or Hamas aimed at maximizing civilian deaths and generating widespread fear. Conflating them risks delegitimizing potentially justifiable modes of disruptive property disobedience. The repressive response is especially remarkable given much of recent ecotage's relatively modest challenge to property rights. In some contrast to the anti-capitalist Wobblies, many environmentalists seek mainly to minimize the existing property order's destructive contours: they challenge only the proprietor's right to engage in activities they deem ecologically harmful.

Nonetheless, as in the case of the vague criminal syndicalism statutes that neutralized the IWW, a major force behind the legislation has been privileged business groups that view sabotage as a nuisance and have sought to discredit it, even at the cost of exaggerating actual threats and generating public hysteria. Following the 9/11 terrorist attacks, the federal government relied in part on the broad measures of the Patriot Act (2001) to repackage ecotage as the country's biggest domestic terrorist threat and justify a fierce clampdown.[72] Even though the US Justice Department subsequently determined that the FBI overstepped its legal boundaries, federal "terrorism sentence enhancements" remain potent tools against eco-saboteurs.[73] The federal recommended sentencing guidelines add substantial incarceration time to those classified as eco-terrorists: the severe penalties meted out to Iowa Catholic Workers Montoya and Recznicek, for example, were based on them. The sentencing enhancements have also been used against other green monkey wrench militants who have received similarly harsh penalties and lengthy prison terms.[74]

The parallels to the Wobbly experience are striking. Although ecotage is understandably controversial, many public figures and media voices have accepted its framing by business lobbyists and state officials as "ecoterrorism." Revealingly, empirical research shows that only a minimal amount of environmental sabotage has resulted in harm or injury to persons; with some exceptions, ecotage has generated minor property damage.[75] The gap between the facts of ecotage and its media depiction and treatment by state officials is striking. Here as well, there are reasons for suspecting that militant "big talk," in this case among those who depict even limited property damage as akin to guerrilla warfare, has played into the hands of opponents. Revealingly, the authoritarian clampdown has encouraged erstwhile militants to rethink their tactics, with some prominent figures concluding that ecotage is politically untenable.[76]

One reason the parallels are suggestive is that the working class, anti-capitalist IWW and generally middle-class, anti-statist green militants influenced by the iconoclastic libertarian Abbey, despite their overlapping tactics, remain such different ideological and political creatures. Might sabotage's distinctive political dynamics help explain the surprising overlap?

Many years ago the political theorist April Carter observed that sabotage operates at the "borderline area between guerrilla war and direct action, since it may be an adjunct to paramilitary activities—for example, blowing up bridges."[77] Even when predicted on nonviolence vis-à-vis persons, sabotage's boundaries in relation to paramilitary activities blur because it "encourage[s] the type of organization and ethos conducive to full-scale armed attack."[78] By favoring elite clandestine units whose perpetrators are supposed to avoid capture, sabotage lends itself to a paramilitary orientation. That tendency is usually reinforced by repressive state policies that simply confirm in sabo-teurs' minds their sense of facing an existential foe against whom they have been forced to wage war. Unsurprisingly, a messy mix of nonviolence with paramilitary rhetoric and images results. That mix generates confusion and invites manipulation by powerfully situated opponents, especially when privi-leged capitalists decide that their property rights are at risk. Just as worrisome, it may contribute to misunderstandings among activists, whose nonvio-lent commitments risk taking a backseat to a paramilitary orientation. Like Abbey's *Monkey Wrench Gang*, which begins with key characters extolling the virtues of nonviolence but concludes with a dramatic battle scene, it may prove difficult to keep them apart.

*   *   *

Despite ecotage's rocky recent history, it is again on the agenda of militant green activists hoping to disrupt climate-killing industries and technolo-gies. Given both the necessity of dramatic action and the brief time span available to ward off massively destructive global warming, why not pur-sue property damage targeting the fossil fuels economic infrastructure and carbon-emitting technologies?

Significant internal disagreements notwithstanding, deep ecologists, green anarchists and Marxists, revolutionary environmentalists, and a growing number of allies have responded by settling on a shared approach that favors directly and immediately blocking global warming's human-based sources. They propose new forms of ecotage—for example, vandalizing automobile dealerships, SUVs, and luxury mansions, blockading and sometimes dam-aging gas pipelines, and attacking mining and petroleum operations. They sometimes condone doing so secretly to avoid legal sanctions.[79] Members of the diverse political club the political writer Naomi Klein labels "blockadia," today's climate militants are waging what they perceive as a defensive battle against the political and economic status quo's systemic assault on the planet and life.[80] Some appeal to the idea that not just human beings but also nature possess fundamental rights deserving respect. While occasionally accepting some role for conventional political tactics and nonviolent civil disobedience, what unites them is the belief that ecotage is better equipped to ward off envi-ronmental disaster and force an overdue green transition.

On this view, climate activists should immediately "announce and enforce the prohibition" on carbon-emitting technologies to "[p]ut them out of commission, pick them apart, demolish them, burn them, blow them up."[81] Doing so would assuredly involve property damage and destruction, but not necessarily harm to human beings. Smart ecotage might disincentivize those presently benefiting disproportionately from climate change. If the fossil fuel industry were to face a real prospect that major investments could be negatively impacted, non-carbon energy sources would look not only technologically but also economically more viable. In turn, governments might be better positioned to "ram through the transition" to an alternative green economy that we desperately need.[82]

It would be ungenerous to ignore this position's appeal: climate change cries out for a forceful political response. Nor does it make sense to view property rights as sacrosanct, especially when doing so endangers so many, and especially poor and vulnerable people in the Global South most likely to suffer devastating consequences.

Unfortunately, we can already discern evidence of a looming repressive backlash. Since 2016, many US states have approved so-called critical infrastructure laws designed to provide additional protections to oil and gas pipelines by dramatically increasing penalties on those participating in or even indirectly involved in acts of trespass or property damage.[83] Other countries are responding in kind, some even going so far as to follow the US example by branding climate militants "terrorists."[84] In Germany, officials have tried to link their efforts to those of the Taliban and the 1970s Red Army Fraction (RAF), a self-described revolutionary leftist group that engaged in kidnappings and assassinations of government officials and business leaders. Relatively minor legal violations by climate activists have resulted in harsh criminal sanctions.[85]

In this section, I briefly discuss the ideas of the Swedish environmental radical and Lund University professor Andreas Malm, who has gained a worldwide following, with his *How to Blow Up a Pipeline* (2021), translated into many languages and respectfully discussed in mainstream media venues. Editors of the leftist publisher Verso that has made his writings available report that *How to Blow Up a Pipeline* belongs among their bestsellers on an impressive list that includes the world's most famous leftist intellectuals.[86] Lamentably, Malm's oftentimes powerful reflections reproduce—and occasionally aggrandize—internal tensions plaguing earlier calls for sabotage.

Malm seems no less conflicted on the question of political violence than the Wobblies, Abbey, or Foreman. Correctly observing that "the similarity between breaking the bone of a child and breaking the bone of a table is deceptive," he initially suggests that we should delineate violence against persons from damage to or destruction of objects or property.[87] Human beings, but not inanimate objects, experience and suffer from hunger, extreme abuse, and other tangible injuries associated with violence. So, we should stop confusingly talking about "violence" directed against objects or property, as though a coal mine or SUV could suffer unwanted, painful violations or harms.

Regrettably, Malm abruptly abandons the distinction. Why? He thinks it a fool's errand to try "to convince the world" that protestors engaging in property damage are "practicing nonviolence—more than a conceptual stretch, a waste of rhetorical effort."[88] Pushing back against confused ideas of violence is apparently not worth the political capital.

This unfortunate concession proves consequential. To be sure, property damage can be used to intimidate and threaten political opponents. We often equate violence against persons and property damage because the latter sometimes *results in* or is causally *related to* the latter. But this hardly justifies sloppily conflating them. Malm's failure to separate violence against persons from property damage generates tensions within his analysis.

For example, Malm wants climate activists to gain inspiration not from Gandhi but Frantz Fanon, for example, the famous defender of organized anti-colonial and revolutionary violence.[89] With Fanon, he refuses to rule out violence against persons on moral or strategic grounds, and then oddly describes some groups (e.g., the German Ende Gelände) and protests (e.g., blockades and occupations of coal mines) as examples of the new and supposedly more Fanonian movement he wants—a claim that conflicts with the self-understandings of the groups he identifies, which continue to describe themselves as fundamentally nonviolent.[90] Occupations and blockades that result in limited property damage but no harm to persons are accurately viewed by most present-day climate activists as nonviolent.

Confused views of political violence also surface in his occasional idealization of heroic saboteurs, now tasked with warding off cataclysmic climate change. Malm is right to characterize our present situation as a climate crisis or emergency, if we define "emergency" as a rapidly unfolding, partly unpredictable, systemic, and far-reaching threat to human (and nonhuman) life. However, we know that crisis and emergency political discourse can easily undermine democratic politics.[91] Predictably, Malm's defense of ecotage reproduces the troublesome idea that effective emergency politics depends on rapid-fire decision-making among small numbers—in his case, a small band of clandestine saboteurs. Selective sabotage by a dedicated avant-garde, he suggests, is the best way to pull the emergency brake on the rapidly moving machinery of climate catastrophe. Since the fossil fuel infrastructure is especially vulnerable, anonymous attacks can immobilize its key components; only minimal know-how is necessary to disable gas pipelines or utility power lines. Because sabotage supposedly can be successfully conducted by a small elite, it potentially generates immediate results in ways that more familiar mass movement politics cannot, partly because it can quickly disincentivize additional investments in the fossil fuels-based economy.

To be sure, broad-based social movements only get off the ground when small groups first decide to act. But it would be wrong to read Malm as repeating familiar homilies about mass political mobilization: there is more than a faint echo here of the old—and unpersuasive—anarchist idea of the "propaganda of the deed," according to which some dramatic, attention-gaining, probably violent political act best ignites popular upheaval. The claim that a small elite of saboteurs might cripple our complex fossil-fuel economy is more science fiction than serious political analysis. Even if activists successfully disabled power lines, gas pipelines, and coal mines, it is improbable that their relatively isolated acts could effectively disrupt the worldwide fossil-fuel-driven economic infrastructure. If sabotage *were* somehow miraculously to do so, other problems would remain. A key takeaway from the social science literature on social movements is that only when followers are sufficiently *numerous* can a movement generate lasting, constructive change.[92] One source of this empirical pattern is clear enough: policy changes garner the necessary institutional "staying" power only when enough actors have internalized reasons or grounds for advancing or at least accepting them. A vanguard of green saboteurs seems unlikely to generate the broad-based, durable shifts in attitudes and behavior on which meaningful political and social change depends. Nor are there sufficient reasons to believe that dramatic acts of sabotage might successfully ignite mass support rather than discredit climate militants and simply make it easier for hostile state authorities to justify a clampdown.

Malm's confusions on violence lead to an unnecessarily hostile assessment of climate activists committed to nonviolent civil disobedience. He criticizes their (alleged) *absolute* nonviolence and "moral pacifism" before abruptly pivoting to attack *strategic* nonviolence.[93] Even as he is right to criticize some simplistic renditions, political nonviolence becomes a moving target in ways that confuse the issues at hand. The distinction between absolute and strategic nonviolence, for example, is significant. Those, like Gandhi, historically committed to spiritually motivated absolute or "perfect" nonviolence, in fact, have often been hesitant to condone property damage, whereas those, usually of a more secular bent, often favor it for tactical reasons and, in some cases, have accepted the possibility of limited property damage.

As a result, Malm obscures possible congruence between strategically motivated nonviolent civil disobedience and his own ideas. Sharply delineating his proposals from random or uncontrolled violence (e.g., terrorism), he thoughtfully insists on some restrictions and condemns extreme political violence, e.g., political assassinations.[94] "Intelligent sabotage" is supposed to minimize any harm to human beings and be "explainable and acceptable to enough numbers in some places."[95] It should not be random: "We would not want a situation where people went around throwing bricks into cafes and toppling school walls and slitting jackets on a whim, just for the hell of it."[96] Because climate change constitutes a terrible injustice and previous protests have failed to generate the requisite changes, is it legitimate. Sabotage represents a "last resort" justifiable given the "magnitude of what is at stake."[97] By day's end, his analysis occasionally echoes influential accounts of nonviolent civil disobedience.

Following the philosopher Henry Shue, Malm accepts the distinction between luxury and subsistence emissions and calls for eco-saboteurs to target the former but not the latter.[98] Since luxury emissions are responsible for a huge chunk of global warming, by disabling its sources we might mitigate the climate crisis. Malm's otherwise sensible recourse to Shue leads him to elide some tough issues, about which he has surprisingly little to say. Other Marxists, for example, distinguish personal from capitalist property in the means of production; they also delineate small or petty bourgeois from large-scale capitalist ownership. And, of course, private property in general can be delineated from common or public property. Is sabotage no less justified when directed against a gas station or auto dealership owned by a family that works and lives from it, for example, than a proposed gas pipeline owned by a multinational corporation?

My paternal grandfather briefly gained ownership of a small neighborhood gas station, though he quickly was forced to hand it back to Esso (ExxonMobil's predecessor company). He spent much of the remainder of his life as an auto mechanic working for others. Would sabotage be as legitimate when directed against his Esso station as a coal mine? What about individually owned SUVs versus gas pipelines owned by a multinational corporation?

To the extent that these examples all arguably contribute to luxury emissions, it is not clear that Malm's framework provides adequate guidelines. Property is not sacred. Yet it comes in a variety of forms, and attention to relevant differences between and among them seems apposite.

Malm's polemical tone, in conjunction with his decidedly orthodox—and sometimes unabashedly Leninist—Marxism, get in the way of acknowledging not only overlap with strategic nonviolence but also, more generally, familiar ideas about civil disobedience as a mode of lawbreaking that targets extreme injustice, rests on moral conscience, and seeks lasting political change.[99] Malm's overheated "big talk" overstates the novelty and political radicalism of some of his proposals. His misleadingly stylized contrasts between nonviolent protests and so-called "violent" property damage generate misunderstandings about both. Because of Malm's growing influence, such distortions may have real-life consequences.

It matters, for example, if we view sabotage as fundamentally a break with rather than potentially building on political nonviolence. There are many reasons why a principled commitment to nonviolence vis-à-vis persons makes sense in more or less democratic contexts. Malm is right that carefully selected acts of ecotage, in principle, can prove useful in the battle for climate mitigation. But it makes a difference morally and politically if we view them as part of an attempt to engage our political equals respectfully, rather than episodes in avant-garde or revolutionary violence. If the former, we will find ourselves obliged to avoid damaging property whenever doing so risks injuring or violating other persons. Only then do we demonstrate respect for others as political peers. Absent such evidence we cannot realistically hope to win the support of those with whom we may vehemently disagree. Nor perhaps should we expect democratic politics to flourish in a world that faces the looming specter of disastrous global warming.

*   *   *

This chapter has explored the case of sabotage, among the most controversial types of disruptive property disobedience, as a way of investigating its challenges. I have focused on conflicted ideas about violence among some of sabotage's prominent proponents, in part simply to make sense of the political backlash and severe legal penalties they have faced. My hunch is that similar internal tensions plague movements elsewhere that have favored sabotage.[100] I worry that without attention to them contemporary climate

activists may find themselves in the same boat destined to run aground. Sabotage's political logic may, unfortunately, invite precisely that confused mix
of nonviolent and paramilitary commitments that eases the way for opponents—and powerful defenders of existing property rights—to demonize its
practitioners.

Yet, acknowledging such dangers does not preclude the prospect of justifiable and politically appropriate acts of sabotage, though it does infer that
activists should reflect long and hard about possible consequences. The literature on ecotage already suggests fruitful ways to think about sabotage's necessary preconditions.[101] Militants should target only private or public property
directly involved in the most egregious wrongdoings, with any possible harms
or injuries to persons minimized. Such acts should typically represent a last
resort after more conventional modes of redress have failed. Lawful political
advocacy and more conventional modes of civil disobedience should ideally
"be attempted prior to the use of direct action, unless there are compelling
reasons to conclude that such tactics would be ineffectual."[102] Those engaging
in sabotage need to keep in mind that they are trying to persuade their political peers and generate durable change. Of course, saboteurs will sometimes
communicate their agendas in ways that are unfamiliar and unsettling; it
may be hard to disrupt wrongdoings without some subterfuge. Nonetheless,
disruptive property disobedience precludes neither public explanations nor
perhaps advance warnings, akin to that provided by recent "valve turners," to
avoid unnecessary harms to those not responsible for the targeted injustice.
Some effort to send a clear message to political peers, at any rate, is essential
if their support is to be earned.

Disruptive property disobedience—including sabotage—should always
be constrained, proportionate, and discriminating, with special efforts made
to respect the principle of nonviolence vis-à-vis persons and avoid property
damage that could prove harmful to people. When activists successfully
follow these general guidelines, their acts remain in principle respectful of
core democratic ideals, even as they break the law. Nonviolence infers basic
respect for others as political equals, as do conscientious efforts to address
and persuade them. When a last resort, their acts implicitly presuppose the
basic legitimacy of ordinary political and legal mechanisms, even as militants
ultimately pursue political illegality because they can plausibly claim that the
political process has failed or even broken down. Given massive inequalities
in political access and power, many of our peers now find themselves forced
to do so. We should not be surprised that they are engaging in disruptive

property disobedience where the stakes are so high, and overdue reform has been repeatedly stymied by privileged economic and political blocs.

More controversial is the question of whether those engaged in sabotage or other types of militant disruptive property disobedience should take legal responsibility for their acts. The obvious reason many seem reluctant to do so is that they frequently face the prospect of inordinately repressive legal sanctions. When political lawbreakers face a legal context in which there is "no right of public trial, and no possibility of using punishment for publicity, or . . . punishments [are] made draconian in order to prevent dissenters from publicizing their views," it is hard to see why evading legal sanctions is necessarily unjustified.[103] Willingness to appear before a tribunal makes sense when it remains independent of direct political pressure, and basic legal protections are secure. Those cooperating with kangaroo courts risk becoming complicit in the prosecuting regime's disdain for legality and basic norms of legal fairness. Under such circumstances, accepting legal sanctions has little if anything to do with showing respect for the rule of law or constitutional government, at least when conceived along minimally liberal and democratic lines.

Unfortunately, it would be wrong to see this sort of ominous legal scenario as only pertinent to openly authoritarian states. In an April 1918 Chicago mass trial targeting the Wobblies, for example, more than a hundred defendants shared four overworked defense lawyers, with indictments based "solely on words they had spoken or written."[104] Exploiting wartime hysteria and fears of left-wing radicalism, state officials, egged on by President Woodrow Wilson, made mincemeat of basic legal protections. The political writer Adam Hochschild describes the haphazard proceedings as a show trial, with an unsympathetic judge regularly making a mockery of basic judicial procedures, and prosecutors going out of their way to emphasize the "alien" nationality or "racial stock" of defendants, "particularly looking out for those who were German or Jewish."[105] According to Hochschild, the "deliberations, if they can even be called that, were so swift that only a single lawyer from the defense's legal team had made it back to the courtroom," before the judge announced that all the Wobblies had been found guilty on all counts, many of whom received exceedingly harsh prison sentences and whose lives were essentially ruined.[106]

Recent efforts in the United States and elsewhere to brand eco-saboteurs eco-terrorists, and subject even limited property damage to extreme penalties with recourse to dangerously vague statutes, hardly incentivizes activists to take legal responsibility for their acts. Commitment to the rule of law normally demands of those breaking the law for political reasons that they try to do so. However, that requirement is predicated on democratic states treating politically motivated lawbreakers according to basic norms of legal fairness. It also usually means recognizing their *political* aims and treating them differently from run-of-the mill, self-serving criminals. Existing statutes and sentencing guidelines that call for punishing property disobedients *more* severely than burglars or fraudsters fail those tests. They send precisely the wrong message that politically based property disobedience is less worthy than a host of ordinary crimes. That approach is unlikely to discourage otherwise nonviolently inclined activists from succumbing to irresponsible martial and paramilitary illusions, something no democracy can possibly desire. Authoritarian state responses tend to embolden militants advocating the most extreme—and violent—protests.[107] Calling saboteurs "terrorists" may simply boomerang back on liberal governments: misguided militants may soon embrace the term and start, in fact, modeling their activities on terrorism. Draconian laws and criminal sentencing guidelines surely cannot be the right way to respond to disruptive property disobedients who profess nonviolence and contribute constructively to democratic political life.

CHAPTER 5

Property Seizures

P rotest-related property *seizures* occur when people take property legally belonging to someone else, with participants frequently claiming that they are the rightful—or at least more suitable—owners. They may even assert that those with enforceable property titles misused or forfeited them because they failed to abide legitimate ownership's necessary presuppositions. Seizures directly challenge existing property claims and, in some cases, the ideas of ownership that undergird them.

To be sure, other property disobedients also consciously target existing property relations. The Wobblies, for example, justified workplace sabotage by appealing to a labor-based concept of property and positing that the means of production were properly theirs. Radical green saboteurs challenge our fossil fuels-driven economy. But many who pursue symbolic or disruptive property disobedience seem uninterested in raising critical questions about property per se. BLM-related activists who vandalized Confederate monuments, for instance, aimed to undermine racism, not challenge the statues' status as public property. In contrast, participants in politically motivated seizures foreground key questions about property and its present-day organization. Their acts sometimes culminate in real-life enactments of an alternative, ostensibly improved property regime, in part to demonstrate concretely why and how existing state-backed property claims are unjust.

Poor farmers who occupy lands owned by large absentee landlords occupy, use, and labor on "their" land, envisioning their squats as tangible evidence that they best satisfy the preconditions of lawful ownership, properly understood. Unhoused activists inhabit vacant buildings and rehabilitate them based on ideas of "sweat equity" to pave what they often hope will be a road to formal ownership. Similarly, Indigenous peoples reclaiming land stolen by colonial settlers assert not only that they are retaking what is rightfully theirs, but also that they are better suited to treating it according to a superior spiritually oriented vision of property in which land and other natural resources are no longer passive, lifeless objects. Their reclamations *prefigure* the property system they hope to see realized.

Many who engage in seizures are "property outlaws" in the strict fashion described by Peñalver and Katyal, that is, they seek chiefly to change existing property relations. However, property seizures can prove vital to protests about a wide variety of concerns.[1] Those repurposing land or buildings, for example, often link their efforts to broader agendas and visions of social change. North American Indigenous groups that participated in the 2016 Dakota Access Pipeline protests were part of a diverse coalition opposing environmental degradation, even as they justified their reoccupations of public and private lands by claiming that existing ownership patters were illegitimate, and that US government officials had failed to abide binding treaties between sovereign American Indian nations and the federal government.

Property seizures also have clear symbolic as well as disruptive contours. Property is selected to communicate some message about an alleged wrongdoing, with the resulting seizure functioning to put an end to it. Politically motivated urban squatters occupy vacant, neglected properties to message their critical take on existing housing policies. By doing so, they disrupt the business-as-usual of a housing market that leaves many people under- and unhoused. However, such protests also entail, more clearly than in property disobedience's other ideal-typical variants, efforts to seize and reuse and not just damage—or, in extreme circumstances, destroy—property complicit in or tied to some injustice. Here again, in social reality the boundaries between and among ideal types get blurred. From the proprietor's perspective, the distinction between an act of sabotage that damages or destroys property, and efforts to seize and reuse it, may seem irrelevant. Yet, in most cases, the divergences remain consequential: most of us would probably distinguish, for example, between poor people squatting and cultivating an unoccupied building from burning it to the ground and making it uninhabitable.

These general claims about property seizures can be made clearer by examining its three main types, namely: property *repossession*; *repurpose* and/or *reuse*; and more or less outright *consumption* or *use*. Each type, as we will see, raises tough normative and political questions. Property seizures involving the taking of ordinary consumer goods, what we usually refer to as looting, are the hardest to justify because they tend to fuse with violence.

I start by discussing repossessions, in part because of their growing political prominence, and in part because of their especially far-reaching challenges to the existing property order. If one of property seizure's most striking traits is its tendency to highlight the social contingency of existing property relations, repossessions do so most vividly.

*   *   *

Indigenous people are now routinely involved in protests worldwide aimed at protecting land and water supplies, often in response to aggressive attempts by large corporations with well-placed political allies seeking control over the planet's increasingly scarce natural resources. According to the World Bank, Native peoples worldwide safeguard about 80 percent of the planet's "most biologically important land and waters," many of which have been earmarked for what critical commentators call "land grabs" by large extractive industries.[2] Recent decades have witnessed an explosion of Native "extractivism," as Indigenous groups working alongside non-Native environmentalists aim to thwart mining, forestry, and nuclear and petroleum industries from gaining access to land and waters Native peoples often view as lawfully theirs.[3] Many of the world's most prominent environmental protests have involved substantial Indigenous representation. Participants have faced drastic repercussions, with their critics and some government officials in the United States, for example, branding Native activists "eco-terrorists."[4]

The Dakota Pipeline protests, in which a significant number of North American Native peoples coalesced in opposition to utility companies claiming control over ancestral lands, offers an illuminating example of this pattern. There, as in many similar protests elsewhere, activists tried to stop a planned extractive industry project via a series of blockades, encampments, and occupations.[5] Displaying symbols of Indigenous culture and aiming to halt a project they viewed as destructive and potentially life-threatening, the protests had manifest symbolic and disruptive contours. Self-described "water protectors," they highlighted the centrality of water to Native ideas about life. Beyond such symbolic and disruptive dimensions, Indigenous activists claimed to be stewarding resources over which they asserted proprietary rights. Their acts were not merely symbolic and disruptive but also entailed concerted efforts at property repossession.

Native activists made use of an impressive array of political and legal arguments. Crucially, they claimed that the planned Dakota pipeline threatened not only existing Native lands but also previously controlled territory that had been unfairly taken from them. Militants accurately noted that pipeline planners had consciously rerouted it away from the largely white city of Bismarck, North Dakota, because of worries about its environmental consequences, to an area less than a mile from the Standing Rock Reservation that extends across the border of South and North Dakota. Its construction was slated for ceded tribal lands on which tribes still claim hunting, fishing, and some cultural rights, as per the Treaty of Fort Laramie (1868).[6] Although those rights have long been systematically violated, they minimally required—activists insisted—a comprehensive environmental study of the pipeline's expected impact on disputed territory.[7]

In effect, protestors reasserted and reclaimed property rights, as codified in treaties between the US federal government and sovereign Native peoples, in opposition to a long history of failures to abide them. From their perspective, the proposed pipeline represented yet another attack on Native property by white settlers, a worry soon corroborated by at least one and probably more desecrations of Native cultural and burial sites by the pipeline developer, Energy Transfer Partners, which activists accused of ignoring the National Historic Preservation Act and federal rules requiring proper consultation with Native tribes.[8] They viewed the alliance between Energy Transfer Partners, government officials, and public and private security forces as the latest chapter in the terrible history of dispossessing Native rights and property, a history plagued by horrific violence. In fact, in the Dakota protests, as in many preceding conflicts, violence was deployed against nonviolent Indigenous protestors.[9]

Recent property *reclamations* by aboriginal groups, even when chiefly focused on warding off environmental destruction, proffer a vivid reminder of the historical contingency of contemporary ownership patterns, and their all-too-frequent sources in deceit and violence. I cannot recount the specifics of those histories; others have already done so.[10] Even libertarian defenders of strict property rights recognize the problem.[11] In states founded by settler colonizers we cannot plausibly trace contemporary "land titles to a just origin, and we should stop pretending we can. Our titles come from a combination of military conquest of sovereign nations and forced relocations of free peoples. Not a pretty picture and we should stop denying it."[12] Nor can we ignore the ways in which this legacy contributes to present-day inequalities and injustices between Natives and non-Native settlers and their descendants. The dispossession of Native peoples is not simply a sad historical fact:

it continues to shape, in far-reaching ways, social and political relations between settler communities and Native peoples.

One immediate takeaway is that we should not categorically deny the potential legitimacy of property disobedience. Because we cannot presuppose the fundamental moral soundness of existing property relations and patterns of ownership, we are obliged to provide some space for illegal but nonviolent protests impacting property. Of course, there are good reasons why we typically seek a measure of predictability and security in economic affairs; no property system can thrive if subject to constant upheaval. However, we do not need to go so far as to embrace Pierre-Joseph Proudhon's axiom "property is theft!" to recognize that existing property relations are too often founded on historical injustice, and that they will require far-reaching modifications if some measure of corrective justice is to be achieved.[13] Those opposed to even relatively harmless forms of property disobedience cannot simply decry them as violent attacks on sacrosanct property rights: they need to provide stronger justifications for existing property rights and their real-world distribution. Doing so is likely to prove difficult for reasons identified by Native political activists who have forcefully recalled the sordid real-life historical contours of property acquisition and wealth accumulation.

The point is not that anything goes in protest-related property disobedience: we can legitimately expect of those engaging in it to meet some basic standards and practice nonviolence vis-à-vis persons. However, property disobedience can fruitfully highlight injustices that require correction, and thus play a positive role in generating necessary political contestation. Without Native protests that evoke the long history of broken promises and violated treaties, how many of us would reflect on the possibility that we have regularly benefited from resources robbed from or ceded under duress by aboriginal peoples? Absent militant political acts that jolt people to reconsider frequently naturalized premises about existing property relations, change seems unlikely to occur. Native reclamations and repossessions have generated fiery political backlashes. Yet they have also invigorated debate and sometimes opened the door to constructive change.

Simply leaving things there, however, risks obscuring the *specific* claims made by Native peoples in favor of property reclamations. How might we begin to evaluate them?

Jeremy Waldron has faulted Indigenous movements for relying on ideas of *first* and *prior* occupancy to reassert control over land and resources seized by settler populations.[14] As Waldron points out, those two ideas are frequently

conflated: first occupancy infers that those who originally occupied a territory have legitimate property claims, whereas prior occupancy favors claims
made by previous or preexisting occupants. The latter is a conservative principle favoring existing property owners and discouraging endeavors to over-
turn de facto ownership patterns, even when unfair or unjust. Although prior
occupancy might have delegitimized acts of dispossession committed by white
settlers during colonization, it now sanctions the property status quo. In contrast, first occupancy suggests the necessity of potentially massive compensa-
tory measures favoring original property owners forcefully dispossessed. Its
application would require difficult and probably impossible efforts to identify
not only the original owners, but also subsequent generations of disadvantaged heirs.

More fundamentally, claims based on first occupancy ignore that property entitlements should sometimes be superseded by changes to political and
social background conditions. Despite his sympathies for attempts to address
historical injustice, Waldron worries that calls to recalibrate property according to the principle of first occupancy downplay the vastly different conditions
(e.g., increased population, changes in production) between original Native
and contemporary economies. If a fertile, populous territory once occupied
by a small aboriginal nation were repatriated to descendants of its heirs, new
injustices would result. Reestablishing exclusive rights based on the idea of
first occupancy would now "mean many people going hungry who might otherwise be fed and many people living in poverty who might otherwise have an
opportunity to make a decent life."[15] First occupancy is a backward-looking
view of property that fails to pay heed to changing conditions and contemporary exigencies: it should carry little independent normative weight, in
part because it presupposes a preexisting property order that itself requires
justification.[16]

Waldron's intervention has generated a heated debate.[17] Whatever its
philosophical merits, his view seems disconnected from real-life Indigenous
protests in which more nuanced ideas about property reclamation surface.
In the Dakota protests, for example, some participants undoubtedly believed
aboriginal peoples to be the rightful, exclusive owners of lands robbed by
European settlers; some might even have fantasized about settler offspring
packing up their belongings and returning to their ancestral homelands. Yet
they recognized that such ideas belong to the realm of political make-believe.
Accordingly, their key claims focused on alleged violations of treaties between
Native peoples and the US government, according to which Indians should

retain *some* proprietary rights over ceded territory: a call for enhanced Native participation was the main political takeaway. I cannot evaluate the legal and constitutional merits of these and related claims, some of which remain controversial even among Native activists and intellectuals.[18] Whatever their legal virtues, they highlight the extent to which Indigenous protestors reference a wide range of ideas about property and their rights to it. Dakota activists appealed to US federal law concerning environmental protection and historical preservation; similar movements elsewhere have tapped domestic laws, treaties, and the UN Declaration on the Rights of Indigenous Peoples.

This more sympathetic interpretation is corroborated by the iconic, extraordinarily influential November 1969 reoccupation of Alcatraz Island in San Francisco Harbor by the self-described "Indians of All Tribes." Lasting about eighteen months, the repossession gained global attention and generated worldwide sympathy for Native peoples struggling to reassert their rights. It is also widely credited, despite its eventual failure, with initiating positive changes in US federal policy.[19] The intricate details of the Alcatraz occupation have been retold elsewhere. For our purposes the occupation's deployment of a diversity of political and legal claims stands out. Alcatraz militants appealed to the Fort Laramie Treaty, interpreting it as granting Native peoples rights over unused or abandoned US federal lands.[20] Public statements by the re-occupiers referred to notions of Native self-determination and cultural preservation, with their proposals for the island including a new Native cultural center, schools, and a "viable program of higher education serviceable to the needs of the Indian people."[21] Activists asserted that Alcatraz, like other territories in North America, had been stolen from the American Indians. Thus, they were merely reclaiming "the right to use the land for their benefits," while insisting that doing so was congruent with humanity's shared interests.[22] Mohawk militant Richard Oakes reported that he and others originally planned only briefly to reclaim Alcatraz symbolically by making a statement from a boat in the harbor, "but a lot of us were sick of doing things [simply] for the public; so when they [sic] sailed around the island, we decided to jump off the ship and when it got close to Alcatraz, swim out to the island and claim it."[23] Even so, their act possessed symbolic and communicative features, with Oakes pointing out in a public statement that desolate conditions on the island (which until 1963 had housed a federal prison) illuminatingly reproduced those found on Indian reservations: Alcatraz had no running water, adequate means of transportation, or access to valuable natural resources Native Americans had controlled prior to colonial dispossession.[24]

While referencing ideas of first occupancy, Oakes satirized their cynical use by European colonists. Drawing parallels to the acquisition of Manhattan by Dutch settlers, Oakes ironically announced that

> We, the native Americans, re-claim the land known as Alcatraz Island . . . by the right of discovery. We wish to be fair and honorable in our dealings with the Caucasian inhabitants of this land, and hereby offer the following treaty: We will purchase said Alcatraz for 24 dollars . . . in glass beads and red cloth, a precedent set by the white man's purchase of a similar island about 300 years ago . . . We know that $24 in trade goods for these sixteen acres is more than was paid when Manhattan Island was sold, but we know that land values have risen over the decades.[25]

In this and subsequent reoccupations inspired by Alcatraz, Native militants claimed that they would prove better stewards of neglected land and resources that could be put productively to serve Indigenous peoples whose economic, cultural, and political rights had been systematically violated. Bleak Alcatraz, for example, could be transformed into a thriving cultural site where Native Americans might realize their ideas of self-organization and self-education. The "illegal" occupiers, in other words, could enact a political and economic alternative to a status quo that so far had systematically disadvantaged Native peoples. By selecting Alcatraz, militants implicitly signaled that they might do so without incurring harms or injuries to the descendants of white settlers: the island's only resident, they pointed out, was the island's official (white) caretaker, with whom they hoped to maintain cordial relations. As Oakes humorously commented, if the caretaker played his cards right he might be installed as the new director of a proposed "Bureau of Caucasian Affairs," a spoof on the paternalistic federal Bureau of Indian Affairs overseeing American Indians.[26]

In a related vein, recent Dakota Indigenous protestors obviously recognized that their protests challenged large corporations engaged in resource extraction. Yet they sought alliances with white farmers, ranchers, and others negatively affected by the pipeline, making concerted efforts to identify common interests with some white communities. Those efforts partly paid off, with a broad coalition of activists scoring some victories: though the pipeline went into operation in 2017, tribes and environmentalists successfully forced a comprehensive environmental impact review that eventually may still block some of Energy Transfer Project's plans.

Admittedly, robust Native claims for property reclamation potentially challenge a wide range of existing property owners and not simply large corporations. Waldron is right that appeals to first occupancy provide an insufficient basis for resolving the heated conflicts that inevitably result. In the final analysis, such disputes will need to be negotiated in the political arena; they will likely embroil groups with sharply diverging interests and aims. It would be naïve to posit that they can always be resolved without winners and losers. Yet, both the Alcatraz and recent Dakota examples suggest that property repossessions can play a constructive role in pluralistic political communities. In some hypothetical polity in which democratic institutions responded effectively to minorities and disadvantaged groups, relations between settler and Native communities were based on mutual respect, and property relations were equitably structured, we would not need illegal property reclamations. Yet, that ideal world is remote from real-world experiences—particularly those of Indigenous peoples.

Like other types of property disobedience, recent Native reclamations have regularly reproduced familiar elements of civil disobedience. They are for the most part open and public, with activists seeking not only to cement backing from Indigenous communities but also to persuade broader publics. They rely on legal and constitutional appeals, positing that those who violate treaty and property rights are, in fact, the *real* lawbreakers. Dakota protestors endorsed political nonviolence; the Alcatraz occupation initially possessed nonviolent credentials, though some re-occupiers ultimately embraced armed self-defense and began carrying weapons.[27] Many familiar normative and political reasons favor property repossessions that follow the civil disobedience playbook.

However, political theorist Burke Hendrix is probably right to argue that some leeway should be provided for more militant, illegal protests that aim to reshape the profoundly unjust, unequal relations between Indigenous communities and settler states. The deep and persistent injustices suffered by Native peoples reduce the usual general obligation to preserve legality and uphold the law.[28] In the US, for example, Native tribes are subjected to a "morass of incoherent and self-defeating laws that currently block Aboriginal peoples from managing their own territories and properties."[29] Even as we acknowledge general fidelity to the law as a desirable trait of any worthwhile democracy, those subordinated to pervasive injustices possess reasonable grounds on which to engage in political illegalities that potentially transcend the standard civil disobedience playbook—for example, they might seek to evade legal punishment. In its standard liberal rendition, that playbook commonly assumes a unified political community where near-universal political and legal equality obtains, with some vestigial injustices requiring correction, not quasi-colonial relations between a hegemonic political community and Native peoples still unfairly subjected to its whims. Given such far-reaching asymmetries, it seems inapposite to deny Native peoples the possibility of engaging in militant acts otherwise generally viewed as unacceptable.

What boundaries should they abide? In the US, any sound answer must grapple with the messy, historically poisoned legal and constitutional ties between tribes and federal institutions, which already, to be sure, provide Native peoples with opportunities for self-government. Legitimately, many American Indians want more sovereignty and remain frustrated with overbearing, frequently unjust federal policies. At the same time, they aim to *renegotiate* the relationship to federal (and other) institutions and laws, not get rid of it. For the foreseeable future, Native and non-Native peoples will likely abide a relatively extensive set of *common* laws and political institutions, even as many Natives hope to reconfigure them.

Why does this matter? The political defense of nonviolence vis-à-vis persons sketched in Chapter 2 still possesses some bite: to the extent that both Natives and non-Natives aspire to participate in a (substantially) shared *democratic* political project, violent acts that reduce political peers to mere objects, to "things" potentially subject to harm or even annihilation, should remain out of bounds. Respect for others as political equals precludes denying them possibilities for sustained cooperation by committing severe bodily and psychological injuries. If you aim to deliberate with and govern alongside others, it does not make sense to fire a gun at or hit them over the head with a club. Doing so means rejecting their status as political equals worthy of proper consideration and equal dignity. Despite understandable historical reasons why Native militants might prefer organized political violence, to the extent that they hope to contribute to some superior, more equitable shared political order they would be well advised to avoid embracing it. Of course, it goes without saying that the long and shocking history of frequently quasi-genocidal white settler violence against Natives must finally end.

When militants embrace ambitious views of Native independence and perhaps seek secession, matters get more complicated. Yet, interestingly, some

Native political thinkers have sketched creative defenses of nonviolent political resistance.[30] For his part, Hendrix leaves room for violent resistance, though he rightly worries about the ways in which it negatively disfigures Native activists and may result in political exhaustion.[31]

As King noted in response to Black Power militants who condoned potentially violent self-defense in the struggle against American racism, its deployment was not only morally suspect but likely to prove politically counterproductive. King's reflections from the 1960s seem eerily relevant to debates about armed Native resistance.

King worried that calls for violent, organized self-defense aggravated racist animosity and made repressive backlashes morally and politically less costly for defenders of the status quo. In the United States, they inadvertently invited massive casualties "to a minority population confronting a well-armed, wealthy majority with a fanatical right wing that is capable of exterminating the entire Black population and would not hesitate such an attempt if the survival of white Western materialism were at stake," a prediction that seems equally prescient in reference to Native Americans, who have repeatedly faced horrific violence by white settler communities.[32]

Too often, King argued, those endorsing violence confuse potentially legitimate calls for *individual* or *personal self-defense* with *organized, collective violent self-defense*, two very different phenomena that follow competing logics.[33] It is one thing to forcefully resist a violent intruder's entry into one's home; it is something quite different when people set up paramilitary units and undertake military training with the hope of advancing social change. Movements espousing organized violence, even when conceived as defensive *counterviolence*, tend to scare away possible participants and sympathizers, an astute prediction that has been confirmed by recent empirical research on social movements.[34] Moreover, people tend to have a hard time discerning the boundaries between defensive and organized violence; movements may find it difficult to maintain them. Too often, the media and movement critics will successfully focus public attention on isolated acts of violence, rather than the injustices targeted by activists. By accepting organized violence as a legitimate political tool, even the most well-meaning movements risk obscuring what is at stake politically. Their likely failure leaves behind what King called "a long desolate night of bitterness" among frustrated activists and future generations forced to live in the shadows of violence and political defeat.[35]

Whether property reclamations can be linked meaningfully to violence depends on whether they pose clear, tangible threats to persons' bodies and psyches. When pursued responsibly by activists committed to nonviolence vis-à-vis persons, many of them will *not*, especially when militants avoid harming property owners whose existence depends directly on the reoccupied property. Different types of property ownership also matter.[36] It is one thing to occupy federal property, or even privately owned lands to block a large corporation from building a controversial, potentially life-threatening pipeline. It is something quite different to seize a modest private home or business and deny somebody their abode and livelihood. Whether property is neglected or instead actively used to support persons matters. At any rate, there is no a priori reason to describe all property reclamations or repossessions as violent. Of course, when militants reoccupy property by attacking or threatening its inhabitants or owners, or the protests in question pose an existential threat to some person or group of persons, the boundaries between violence and property disobedience blur. But many and probably most Native property reclamations and repossessions have rightly avoided doing so. In North America and elsewhere, it has been settler populations, of course, that have been responsible for systematic, sometimes genocidal violence against Native peoples.

*   *   *

Politically motivated property *repurposing* or *reuse*, whose most common forms are usually called *squatting*, manifests itself in an astonishing variety of ways throughout history.[37] Despite its ubiquity, contemporary philosophers and political theorists have had little to say about it.[38] In the Anglophone world, any list of renowned squatters would have to include the seventeenth-century English Levellers and Diggers, with the latter gaining their name from efforts to "dig" (or farm) on enclosed private lands. Especially in the Global South, property repurposing and reclamation overlap since many squatters tend to be Indigenous. For reasons of analytic clarity, however, I distinguish them.

Repurposing's myriad types and messy real-life contours risk obscuring general patterns. Some protests chiefly target property-based inequities; others are linked to movements that pursue a variety of causes.[39] The unwieldy empirical haystack with which squatting presents us means that the relevant normative and political needles easily get lost.

Present-day pundits delight in ginning up popular anxieties by highlighting isolated cases of shocked homeowners returning from vacation to meet squatters who occupied their residences and refuse to leave.[40] Social media postings are replete with horror stories of ostensibly conscientious landlords faced with clients who fail to pay for and vacate their premises, with critics frequently dubbing the squats *home invasions*. The obvious flaw with this framing is that it suffers from historical amnesia: most US Americans (and many people elsewhere) forget that their wealth partly stems from European settlers who seized, in open defiance of the law and countless treaties, Indigenous and public lands. A great deal of antebellum US political debate involved fierce battles between defenders and critics of (white settler) "squatter rights" in the context of what historians accurately call our early "squatter's republic."[41]

Even as critics exaggerate its scope, the obnoxious squatting of private residences remains real enough, particularly where housing shortages prevent people from acquiring a decent place to live, and they come to see short or long-term squatting as a viable option. Of course, there are understandable reasons why anyone returning from a hard-earned vacation would prefer not to encounter strangers comfortably camped out in their bedrooms. Generosity is a moral virtue, yet it has its limits.

Overblown reports of isolated home invasions unfairly discredit distinctly *political* types of property repurposing and reusage. Even if individual squatters who occupy private residences may do so because of economic exigencies, this does not necessarily render their acts political in the sense used here. Squatters often simply want a place to sleep and be left alone; they would prefer remaining undetected. Most do not want their squats to become objects of political contention. They may assert some right to stay on, at least temporarily. But they neither intend to challenge the property status quo nor envision their efforts as part of a wider call for political change.

Historically, a great deal of land squatting by (overwhelmingly poor) rural dwellers, and countless illegal seizures of residences in towns and cities, has taken place below the political radar, with most squatters simply wanting a roof over their heads, or a small plot of land to eke out a living.[42] A well-nigh universal phenomenon, it approximates what James Scott calls *hidden resistance*—in other words, covert, frequently individualized, endeavors to push back against the social and political status quo, in ways that fall short of open, self-consciously ideological, organized, collective political action. As Scott has observed (and many examples corroborate), hidden resistance *sometimes* paves the way for open political protest, though in many instances it will not.[43] In cases of the former, initially apolitical squatters recognize that others face similar existential challenges, and that their shared plight has deeper roots that need to be addressed collectively. The personal then becomes political.

Such complexities notwithstanding, we need to acknowledge politically motivated property repurposing's distinctive traits. Political movements that pursue land seizures or urban squatting do not call on participants to occupy Grandma Smith's modest abode or Grandpa Jones's working farm. On the contrary, they openly acknowledge the harms likely to result for individual proprietors who bear little responsibility for homelessness or rural poverty.[44] Beyond fears of the predictable political backlash, they reject such squats for a principled reason: many of them endorse, implicitly or otherwise, notions of legitimate proprietorship as resting on direct possession, labor, and use. When their squats are stabilized and participants prove able to enact their own ideas about property, they often mimic Grandma Smith or Grandpa Jones. To a surprising extent, some appear eager to join the ranks of self-respecting property owners who gained their possessions through hard work. They claim to be making productive use of resources otherwise likely to be wasted. They justify property seizures and, in the process, condemn the existing distribution of property for violating some common normative intuitions. By taking care of and working otherwise neglected properties, they aim to position themselves as *better* proprietors than those the law views as rightful owners. Squatters prefigure an improved property order, with property repurposing deemed necessary to gain a fair chance at properly "doing" property in ways hitherto denied them. It seems odd and perhaps obtuse to characterize their efforts as a frontal attack on property as such.[45]

Urban movements rarely target temporarily vacant buildings owned by conscientious individual proprietors, usually leaving small-scale landlords—so long as their properties are kept up and tenants treated decently—in peace. Squatters engage in what are oftentimes surprisingly deliberative, thoughtful internal debates about *which* properties constitute legitimate objects for repurposing, and *why* the properties targeted should serve symbolic functions and help them gain public sympathy.[46] They focus on long vacated, badly neglected buildings, some in public hands as a result of a previous owner's malfeasance or tax-related arrears, and others owned by large, typically absentee private landlords.[47] Squatters point out that neglect by either public or private owners tends to aggrandize criminality, reduce the value of nearby properties, and contribute to an overall lowering of the quality of life for neighbors. So-called "blighted" neighborhoods are filled with boarded-up, vacant buildings. One lawyer sympathetic to the US-based activist

group Occupy Our Homes—an organization that supports squats of buildings foreclosed by large banks—puts it nicely: "banks are bad neighbors,"
given their widely documented failure to maintain rudimentary upkeep on
residential properties.[48] Absentee owners and stockholders—many of whom
may not even be aware they are profiting from foreclosed residences—do not,
of course, live in or take care of the homes. They "possess" them legally but
not in person.

By zeroing in on derelict properties owned by public or large private businesses, activists highlight the injustices of a system that allows some to remain
unhoused while privileged proprietors misuse their assets in harmful ways.
They also hope to disrupt—or at least unsettle—a housing economy that often
serves large economic interests but not the unhoused, poor, or young people.
Others repurpose neglected buildings acquired by large-scale property developers slated for destruction but, in the squatters' view, eminently deserving
of historical preservation.[49] Then conservationist appeals fuse with existential claims to affordable housing. By improving and refurbishing decaying
building structures, squatters provide themselves with a home while hoping
to bring attention to their architectural and aesthetic merits.

Similarly, successful politically motivated rural squatter movements target unused lands controlled by large, frequently absentee landlords, not small
or medium-sized working farms. The Global South's most prominent land
occupation movement, Brazil's Landless Workers Movement (MST), takes
advantage of Article 184 of the Brazil Constitution and its provisions for
expropriating unused lands controlled by large landholders.[50] MST activists
first identify properties deserving of expropriation. After doing so, they coor-
dinate organized seizures by sizable contingents of landless peasants, many
of whom face dire existential prospects, then proceeding to set up temporary housing and start working previously unworked land. Although initially
covert (to avoid detection by police or private security agents), their squats are
then usually publicized, with formal appeals directed at government agencies
tasked with transforming the peasants' de facto possession into legally sanctioned property.[51] The battle to do so is rarely easy. Even as public authorities are legally required to compensate owners, absentee landlords usually do
whatever they can to remove squatters. MST-related peasant land occupiers
have often encountered violent reprisals.[52]

Nonetheless, since the late 1980s the MST has scored impressive victories and successfully reused thousands of properties by redistributing them
to poor rural dwellers who had previously suffered the ravages of extreme

poverty. In a political setting plagued by shocking inequalities, where overdue land reform has been blocked by powerful agrarian elites, poor, landless peasants reusing unused lands makes for powerful political symbolism.
Interestingly, the MST takes advantage of a legal gray zone: it illegally trespasses on and occupies private and some public lands while appealing to
constitutional clauses requiring that property must serve social purposes.
MST aggressively disrupts Brazil's unequal agrarian economy but taps the
Constitution to do so.

In India, in Mumbai's legendary Dharavi "slum," where poor people have
long set up so-called "informal" settlements, since the 1970s community
based organizations and activists (including PROUD, People's Responsible
Organization for a United Dharavi) have worked alongside local residents to
pursue a messy mix of strategies aiming to legalize their otherwise insecure
property claims, often by gaining documentary evidence squatters deploy to
give their settlements some sort of more or less official status. Residents hope
to acquire survey slips or "photo passes" to demonstrate not only that they
have taken possession of some site but that they are "doing" or practicing
property. Many of their activities elide the conventional boundaries between
informal possession and formal ownership: "doing" ownership involves syn-
thesizing what the sociologists Varun Patil and Martin Fuchs call "rights-in-
practice" with "rights-in-normative law," in a rich variety of complex, highly
strategic ways.[53] While not strictly parallel to Brazilian land squatters who tap
their country's constitution, Indian squatters also take advantage of a variety
of legal grey zones to thicken and thereby substantiate their property claims.

Some major differences notwithstanding, parallels to urban squatting
movements in the Global North can be identified. The US-based Homes Not
Jails movement, for example, has targeted neglected, unused properties, some
of which it squats covertly to avoid police detection, while others are chosen
for immediate open, public squatting to relay symbolic messages. This "dual
covert and political strategy" has allowed the organization "to immediately
provide housing for homeless people, while at the same time using the media
to educate the public and pressure politicians."[54] Rarely facing the brutal
violence experienced by land squatters in the Global South, they and other
urban squatters have nonetheless encountered their share of harsh official
responses.[55] Like the land squatters, they combine politically savvy, symbolically effective repurposing with nuanced legal strategies. When operating in
contexts where legally permissible evictions are restricted, or housing rights
are legally secured, they rely on legal appeals to legitimize their efforts.[56]

In this spirit, some legal advocates encourage squatters to use the old common law idea of *necessity,* according to which nonowners, under some circumstances, can trespass on and appropriate others' property to circumvent greater harms.[57] Squatters sometimes tap the legal doctrine of *adverse possession,* which allows for open possession of another's property without consent, with those squatting obliged to maintain the property for a designated period as a pathway to formal ownership. Crucially, the adverse "possessor must exercise his dominion and control over the property such that there are visible signs of the possessor's occupation," as well as tangible evidence that those who have taken possession take care of the property.[58] They are expected, in other words, to practice or enact property, understood as control over objects necessary to basic well-being and thus requiring proper maintenance. Squatters show that by doing do they, in fact, are the "real" property owners. Implicit here is the intuition that property rights and obligations are necessarily intertwined: those who responsibly maintain a residence gain proprietary rights, so long as their occupation is open and the existing owner, in principle, has thereby received fair notice.[59]

Of course, squatting remains controversial, even if specific incidents sometimes gain public support. Who could fail to sympathize, for example, with hungry people occupying unused buildings or lands to support their families? Or the thousands of unhoused people who, in the aftermath of the Second World War and a sudden housing shortage, occupied recently vacated military barracks and empty public buildings in France, the United Kingdom, and elsewhere?[60] They and many other squatters break the law, something undesirable in well-functioning democracies that take general fidelity to the law seriously. The problem, unfortunately, is that our democracies are not always well-functioning or sufficiently just. Moreover, some injustices are so momentous that they cry out for an urgent response. When political authorities regularly fail to address their concerns, what else can ordinary people faced with hunger or homelessness be reasonably expected to do?

It seems morally perverse to tell a hungry farmer or unhoused person that they must wait on legislative or policy changes, particularly when previous reform efforts have regularly foundered. Even in many longstanding democracies, well-heeled landed or real estate interests and large financial firms often possess disproportionate influence over political authorities, especially at the local level; housing policies potentially favorable to the poor and working classes face massive roadblocks. So-called, ostensibly temporary housing "crises" constitute a more or less permanent feature of every social order where housing becomes a commodity whose exigencies are determined by capitalist profit-making and, increasingly, financial speculation.[61]

In the Global South, overdue land reform has been regularly stymied by landed elites and political systems that grant them extraordinary influence. The economist Albert O. Hirschman pointed out many decades ago that land seizures constitute an essential ingredient of effective reform measures: seizures entail not only *"protest* and *pressure* on problem-solving authorities, but also *direct problem-solving activity."*[62] For example, a "Colombian peasant [not only] satisfies his cravings for a piece of land when he squats," Hirschman observed, but also signals to policymakers the need for decisive state action, while simultaneously reducing "the size of the problem" to be solved by directly expropriating land. Land reform often proved unachievable in Latin and South America absent mass illegal action by peasants who occupied and repurposed large agricultural estates.[63] Only in the aftermath of illegal land seizures are governments sufficiently well positioned to neutralize landowners.

Squatters inconvenience property owners. Crucial to any property system is the owner's right to exclude nonowners from using or controlling property. Property seizures obviously violate that right. Yet, all modern legal systems *already* contain significant exceptions to it; it does not make sense to interpret the right to exclude absolutely, or to see it as the sine qua non of private property.[64] A decent legal system obviously prefers predictability and relatively secure property rights. Yet it remains difficult to grasp why legal predictability and strict fidelity to existing ownership patterns should always trump illegal protests that challenge extreme injustices. One sensible response to Anatole France's legendary quip that the "majesty of the law . . . . forbids rich and poor alike to sleep under bridges, beg in the streets, and to steal their bread" is that a legal system that fails to tackle gaps between rich and poor is unlikely to thrive.[65] Squatters do not challenge the necessity of legality or constitutional government per se. Rather, they recognize that some (typically minor) violations of property rights can help create a political and legal order that reduces material inequalities. In many and perhaps most cases, harms to proprietors seem relatively limited, especially when contrasted to those suffered by people otherwise forced to live on the streets or go without food. What realistic alternatives do they have, with governments now cynically competing to pass statutes prohibiting the unhoused from sleeping in public places or in the open?[66]

We should not sentimentalize squatting or ignore its unpalatable forms. Still, it remains difficult to see what tangible harms result, for example, when property disobedients take over neglected public properties that otherwise threaten to drain public resources. The common good is then often best served by authorities working with squatters to improve properties and helping them gain ownership, in the process revitalizing residential areas otherwise potentially doomed to decline.[67] Many once declining urban areas in Europe, North America, and elsewhere in which politically militant squatters were once active are now booming, vibrant, and—yes—oftentimes gentrified, sometimes to the chagrin of radical militants who originally squatted them.

Matters are perhaps more complicated when private rather than public property is impacted. However, when squatters target well-resourced multinational banks or real estate firms, or wealthy, absentee landowners, the resulting harms often seem limited. Meaningful links between squatting and tangible, physically or psychologically debilitating violations to proprietors will be difficult to trace. Occupying a foreclosed home hardly entails violence against a bank's stockholders or investors. It seems farfetched to claim that it has necessarily undermined their status as political equals deserving of respect. Given the complexities of corporate ownership, it will often prove difficult to figure out which if any "natural person" has suffered negative consequences.[68]

Nonetheless, some scholars critical of the MST, for example, worry that its efforts have destabilized Brazil's system of property relations: militants have perversely disrupted ordinary market mechanisms and thwarted economic development. MST's otherwise well-meaning protests, they say, are not only economically counterproductive but also culpable for the violent contours of Brazilian rural life, whose sources alleged lie in legal uncertainty and excessive battles over property rights.[69] Parallel arguments have been directed against urban squatters who allegedly interrupt ordinary market mechanisms, contributing to irrationalities best corrected by secure property rights. In this vein, the conservative *National Review* has blamed squatters and the urban policy makers who treat them leniently for lawless "states of nature" in US cities.[70]

Beyond its fidelity to contestable economic theories, this critique obscures the harsh realities of substantial material inequalities and many effectively propertyless people. Too often, strict respect for existing property rights means that many people will go to bed—if lucky enough to have one—destitute or hungry. It also makes light of the fact that most squatters regularly appeal to old-fashioned ideas of property, according to which rightful ownership requires possession, use, and mixing one's labor with an object. If

property is viewed as a universal right, squatting helps ensure that more people gain and benefit from it.[71] Although "wrong to take all of a person's property away from him," on this view it is similarly wrong "that some individuals
should have had no private property at all."[72] To the extent that squatters
redistribute property that otherwise would be inappropriately concentrated,
without rendering those impacted propertyless or disabling their capacity to
participate as equals in political affairs, it seems justifiable.

The literature is replete with quotes from squatters who say they simply
want to gain their own bread with their own hands, or because they believe
that every person deserves a "home of their own," and that such homes have
to be earned on the basis of what squatter movements usually dub "sweat
equity," in other words, the hard work that goes into renovating neglected
buildings.[73] Squatter organizations typically require of residents that they
put in the requisite labor: loafers are not welcome. Philosophers criticize
Lockean and other labor-based ideas of property by highlighting their potential *contingency*: since only those who labor gain legitimate ownership, property potentially becomes a special right enjoyed by some but not everyone.[74]
Yet, precisely this conceptual Achilles' heel works to the advantage of squatters who claim property rights by pointing out that they—not large absentee landlords, for example—have mixed labor with, and then made tangible
use of, their squats. With strikingly Lockean overtones, squatters often point
out that they are using resources that would otherwise remain unused, and
that any legitimate property order needs to leave "still enough . . . [that]
the yet unprovided can use."[75] Nor can it be viewed as justified if some are
denied access to uncultivated or neglected resources essential for individual
self-preservation.

It would be silly to attribute deeply considered theories of property to
squatters who are often scrambling to make ends meet. Still, they often appeal
to recognizable, sometimes venerable notions of property. Anders Corr has
demonstrated that a great deal of squatting can be squared not only with
instrumentalist views of property but also with accounts that envision it as
essential to self-development and autonomy, and thus as inextricably tied up
with our persons.[76] Homelessness is inconsistent with any but the meanest
understanding of personal liberty.[77] On the personality theory, for example,
property "is necessary to give people 'roots,' stable surroundings, a context
of control over the environment, a context of stable expectations that fosters
autonomy and personality."[78] This intuition syncs with the self-understanding
of many squatters who typically do not seek to get rid of property in toto, but

only hope to point out that absent squatting they have no chance to enjoy its essential benefits.[79] They recall property's most basic and perhaps original association with "no more or less than to have one's location in a particular part of the world."[80] Squatters violate the present owner's right to exclude nonowners, but only because they deem some facets of the existing property order unfair. Those seeking a legal imprimatur for their squats presumably still hope to enjoy some version of that right. By using and improving otherwise neglected properties, they also endorse the old idea that ownership requires the use of objects, and that those not meaningfully involved with them should not be viewed as legitimate owners.[81]

Given substantial inequalities worldwide in land and residential ownership, these claims deserve a fair hearing. Squatters, in effect, call on their political peers to hear them out and consider whether the specific property repurposing they have endeavored is justifiable. In a pluralistic democracy, disagreements will inevitably result. However, it will simply not do to dismiss squatters' claims by dubbing them a priori violent or raising the banner of property rights without considering how squatters themselves thoughtfully address property's normative bases.

Successful squats effectively put into *practice* powerful ideas about property that arguably have been violated by the economic status quo. Squatting's most valuable implicit intuition may be that the existing economic order does not consistently mesh with deeply rooted, sometimes hallowed ideas about property; property theorists have highlighted the same gap. Proponents of the personality theory, for example, note its incomplete realization in contemporary society: it provides no ready justification, for example, for large-scale corporate ownership.[82] Likewise, the labor theory of property is hard to parse with an economy in which some people labor a great deal but own little or nothing, whereas others possess wealth (by inheritance, for example) without much evidence of labor having been exerted.

Most squatters are not in principle opposed to property or legal protections for it, but instead to elements of the economic system that deny them possibilities to gain what they view as legitimate ownership. On their view, property repurposing and reuse, even when contravening the law, constitutes an appropriate and oftentimes necessary corrective.

Squatting comes in many shapes and sizes. Not all politically motivated squatters are otherwise impoverished; some are preoccupied with nonexistential concerns—for example, historical or architectural preservation. Many are committed to radical political and social ideas of anarchist or socialist provenance and view their squats as attempts to prefigure a novel postcapi-talist order, not join the socially respectable working class or petty-bourgeois world of Grandma Smith or Grandpa Jones.[83] When their squats prefigure an alternative property order, they take on different contours from those resting on mainstream views of private property.

It makes sense to delineate existential or survival-based property repur-posing from cases in which activists squat to experiment with alternative modes of collective life, along the lines of the ideologically self-conscious squats found in many parts of the world. Similar tensions plague land squat-ters: the MST, for example, favors cooperative farming as a stepping stone toward a socialist Brazil, whereas many peasants making up the movement prefer small-scale, individual farming.[84] The peasants want to be Grandma Smith or Grandpa Jones, whereas their more ideologically inclined leaders tell them to read Karl Marx. There are differences between materially precari-ous people who participate in squats with the hope of gaining a home or piece of land and ultimately private property, and those from a variety of social backgrounds creatively testing forms of common life that prefigure a different world. Given my discussion thus far, the former is most readily justifiable: when otherwise denied a roof over their heads or food for their children, and ordinary political channels seem badly clogged, their typically limited violations of property rights should be treated leniently by state authorities.

Yet it seems misleading to overstate the differences. Even anarchist and radical leftist squats, for example, are frequently established by single, young, economically vulnerable people disadvantaged by private housing markets and systems of public housing that prioritize conventional families, gender roles, and views of sexuality. They have turned to squatting because their needs have been ignored by the housing status quo. Some forcefully reject capitalism, perhaps aiming for something along the lines of a *commons* tran-scending existing modes of both private and public property.[85] Yet, while giv-ing them a radical gloss they often appeal to familiar ideas of ownership as based on labor, possession, and use. They demand sweat equity: loafers are no more welcome in anarchist or communist squats than elsewhere. While prefiguring utopia they inevitably revisit familiar questions, e.g., whose turn is it to do the dishes or clean the toilets? Both Grandpa Jones and Grandma Smith would surely be able to make sense of many of the ensuing responses.

Even if perhaps more difficult to justify property repurposing by small, by no means economically disinherited groups experimenting with alternative modes of life, we would do well, in the spirit of John Stuart Mill, to recall the virtues of a social order that not only tolerates but celebrates such experiments, so long as harms to others are minimal.[86] To the extent that radical squatters target neglected, unoccupied properties owned by large-scale proprietors, with only marginal economic losses and no identifiable violence resulting, they potentially meet the requisite tests.

Nonviolence vis-à-vis persons remains essential here as well, at least in more or less democratic political contexts. In fact, contemporary squatter movements—including a surprising number operating under non- or semi-democratic political conditions—often interpret their endeavors as basically nonviolent.[87] Only when confronted with punitive police crackdowns that leave them reeling do they start to entertain doubts about their nonviolent proclivities. The resulting shifts can prove politically counterproductive.

Property seizures always risk generating harsh official responses. So long as existing property relations are viewed as legitimate, and the economically privileged possess inordinate political influence, this unfortunate pattern is likely to continue. There are no pat answers for squatters faced with repressive, violent clampdowns. Nevertheless, existing scholarship suggests that those embracing counterviolence usually undergo a radicalization that scares away participants and possible sympathizers. Amsterdam squatters who did so, for example, jettisoned democratic, consensus-oriented for top-down, secretive, increasingly authoritarian decision-making. As we similarly observed among militant *saboteurs*, a paramilitary mindset and martial logic tend to replace the hard work of day-to-day democratic politics and movement building. When political movements decide they face an existential crisis or need to go on a wartime footing, time-consuming, inclusive deliberation suffers. Even squatter movements that hoped to undermine conventional gender hierarchies take on increasingly masculinist traits. In Amsterdam, public sympathy for squatters evaporated as their efforts increasingly focused on ritualized battles with the police, waged by an increasingly isolated band of macho militants hellbent on holding down the squat-cum-fort.[88]

It is worth pointing out that squatters faced with inordinate state (and private) violence have sometimes responded responsibly. Brazil's MST, for example, draws on Marxism and Christian liberation theology and rejects pacifism. Partly because of a long history of brutally violent clampdowns, and partly stemming from its radical leftist aspirations, it permits squatters to engage in self-defense via agricultural tools (e.g., shovels, machetes) when attacked.[89] It seems, at any rate, misleading to dub their acts violent land *invasions*, as though otherwise peaceful peasants using pruning hooks to defend

themselves against heavily armed security forces were equivalent to organized, trained paramilitary troops.

When squatters are unarmed, with "force" used only to break open a front
door or tear down a fence, and no tangible bodily or psychological violations
to persons result, land seizures and building squats remain nonviolent. Quite
correctly, the nonviolent theorist Gene Sharp described land occupations
as, in principle, nonviolent.[90] It does not do to pose the misleading rhetorical question, along the lines of a former Brazilian Minister of Justice who
asked, "Isn't an invasion [of land by squatters] in itself violent?"[91] The answer
is oftentimes "no." Only overly broad, conceptually confused notions of violence sloppily infer that squatting-based disruptions to the agricultural or
housing market are inherently violent.

Given my discussion so far one might ask why some types of squatting
should not be categorized as nonviolent civil disobedience. Even those squatters who first covertly occupy land or buildings soon publicize their acts and
remain basically nonviolent. They make public appeals to their peers and view
their efforts as congruent with the common good. Moral conscientiousness
is also at play: squatters offer a range of not just political but also identifiably
moral arguments. The Diggers were inspired by radical Protestantism; the
MST has roots in liberation theology. Squatters will typically be charged with
legal violations (for example, trespassing) and violating property rights. Yet
they appeal to a range of legal principles and even, when available, appropriate constitutional norms: they break the law while implying "higher respect"
for it. Admittedly, their lawbreaking involves violations of property rights
and conflicts with restrictive liberal accounts of civil disobedience as focused
exclusively on basic civil and political liberties but not economic injustices.[92]
Yet such interpretations have been widely criticized, and there is no reason
why civil disobedients cannot target material inequities.[93]

Some property repurposing should indeed be interpreted by state authorities and others as closely akin to nonviolent civil disobedience, not as ordinary criminality. It deserves some measure of respect and prospectively more
lenient treatment from officials. Regrettably, legal developments have moved
in the opposite direction. Bolsonaro's extreme right-wing Brazilian government set up a parliamentary commission filled with voices hostile to the MST
who used it to discredit the group.[94] In Europe, recent housing crises have
generated not increased official toleration of squatters but rather new legal
weapons against them. Since 2010, legal changes in France, the Netherlands,
Spain, and the United Kingdom have made it easier to evict squatters and

subject them not only to fines but prison sentences. In the United States, states have further tightened adverse possession rules to make it more difficult for squatters to tap them.[95]

Squatting advocate Alexander Vasudevan observes that it is hard "not to see the new wave of anti-squatting legislation as an attempt to protect the ongoing commodification of housing" precisely as "many people are looking to . . . reassert the cultural, social and political value of housing as a universal necessity and as a source of social transformation."[96] Squatting's intensified criminalization belittles ideas of a universal basic right to housing, as promulgated in some national constitutions and international human rights agreements. Appeals to that right have long been commonplace among residential squatters and their defenders.[97] Punitive legal trends also corroborate King's observation that we live in a society where "profit motives and property rights are considered more important than people," especially when the people in question tend to be poor and unhoused.[98]

To be sure, some squatting does not fall under—or in the proximity of—the usual civil disobedience rubric. During the summer of 2020, BLM-inspired activists occupied streets and districts of some big US cities, declaring them autonomous no-go zones for the police in order to protest police brutality. Seattle's Capitol Hill Autonomous Zone (Chaz), for example, began for the most part nonviolently, with activists using a local park as a combined public gathering space, campground, and community garden. Initially, local Seattle and state-level Washington officials responded cautiously, despite vociferous calls by President Trump and his allies to evict the occupiers forcefully. However, there were soon reliable reports of assaults, rapes, and robberies. Residents and local businesses were increasingly worried by what they viewed as a general climate of lawlessness.[99] Protestors permitted the open carrying of firearms, in part because of concerns about police violence, and in part because of counterprotests by armed right-wing extremists. Local businesses rushed to hire private security forces to protect their property. After five shootings in June 2020, local police used tactical vehicles to remove the occupants, arresting about seventy-five people involved in the occupation, charging a number with felonies relating to violent crimes.[100]

When repurposings of either private or public property rely on or invite violence against persons, or they produce a perilous climate in which it is only a matter of time before serious injuries to persons transpire, public authorities will be forced to act. Their responses should always minimize violence and reduce rather than aggrandize political tensions. Militarized police responses are unlikely to meet the requisite tests.

Most cases of repurposing are more ambivalent. At a minimum we should expect of authorities that they not simply dismiss squatters' claims by appealing to sloppy ideas about political violence or tired defenses of existing property relations. As many squatters infer, there is tangible evidence that those patterns do not conform to normatively appealing, longstanding ideas about property.

Squatters can select inappropriate targets or embrace violence and thereby communicate disdain for their political peers. Any list of such negative cases would have to include the 2016 occupation of Oregon's Malheur National Wildlife Reserve, coordinated by Ammon Bundy and other far-right extremists who question the legitimacy of federally owned lands and seek their privatization. Their protest, at first glance, seems roughly parallel to others we have discussed, despite some obvious ideological differences. Bundy and his allies appealed to divine law and the US Constitution, which they interpreted as incongruent with public ownership of lands previously controlled by farmers and ranchers. Tapping widespread discontent with federal land management, the Malheur occupation was designed to gain public attention and drum up support. It may have presupposed a nascent ranchers' "labor theory of grass," according to which families that had previously grazed on public lands had acquired "rights to the grass on those lands," despite federal laws denying them legal title.[101]

At closer look, things become more worrisome. Bundy and his followers embraced not only unusual readings of divine law and the US Constitution, but ones steeped in racism: they have been outspoken in embracing white supremacist ideology. Modern US democracy, and its unfinished quest to include previously excluded voices, in their eyes is an apocalyptic story of decay and decline. Their criticisms of alleged federal dispossessions of private lands ignore the harsh facts of white settler dispossession of Native peoples. Their grasp of the main reasons for federal land control and policies pertinent to its regulation is, at best, incomplete and, at worst, dangerously misleading.[102] There are numerous substantive reasons for rejecting their views and condemning their acts.

In a pluralistic democracy we should provide a wide berth for protests that rest on views many of us are likely to consider unpalatable. Nonetheless the Malheur occupation remains beyond the pale. No existential danger

linked to the disputed federal land policies plausibly threatened participants'
well-being. (The group's ringleader owns an Arizona-based business that
rents and repairs trucks; he and most of his followers would be hard-pressed
to characterize themselves as disenfranchised farmers or cattle ranchers.) Yet,
their recourse to organized violence *did* directly threaten political peers and
federal agents, with protest participants providing clear evidence that they
sought violent confrontation with government representatives. Bundy told
his comrades to bring weapons to the occupation; many did just that. Public statements implied that they were eager to provoke a conflagration with
government officials.

In an earlier 2014 run-up Nevada protest, "Bundy and his supporters
pointed weapons at the rangers, kicked a police dog several times, and refused
to stand down."[103] Ammon's father, Cliven Bundy, told supporters that they
should get ready for civil war if their demands were unmet.[104] Possible boundaries between defensive and offensive vanished. Aiming to intimidate opponents, the group vandalized the Wildlife Reserve's headquarters. Based on
their reactionary originalist interpretation of the US Constitution, they envisioned the Malheur occupation as a launching pad for an organized armed
"retaking" and refounding of the American republic. Property repurposing
served chiefly to launch a violent counterrevolution aiming to roll back democratic political achievements.

Tellingly, the Bundy family and their followers have faced few legal sanctions. Despite their key roles both in the 2016 Malheur occupation and other
armed stand-offs with government officials, the Bundys have been acquitted
by juries and benefited from mistrial declarations by judges.[105] Unlike nonviolent poor and previously unhoused squatters who face increasingly harsh
legal penalties, racists and white supremacists who engage in violent occupations, it seems, can get a free pass in twenty-first-century America.[106] Based
on the analysis I have provided, this is precisely the *wrong* way to distinguish
legitimate from illegitimate property repurposing.

*   *   *

Politically motivated seizures of ordinary goods typically get grouped under
the imprecise term *looting*. Looting can refer to systematic banditry by armed
groups during warfare, opportunistic robbery amid natural disasters or other
emergencies, or even the coordinated appropriation of society's resources
by corrupt elites and government officials. Its objects, ranging from basic

foodstuffs to high-value consumer goods, vary. Some types fall outside the scope of our discussion, since they seem tangentially, if at all, political. Admittedly, the boundaries between political and nonpolitical looting can be hard to draw: it would be silly to gloss over the difficulties. Hungry people throughout history have participated in bread and food riots involving extensive looting. In the contemporary Global South they remain commonplace.[107] Although seemingly spontaneous and unorganized, they can quickly take on political coloration. We also can find historical examples of individuals or small groups of desperate people, having no recognizably political goals or organizational links, who opportunistically steal, usually in the context of economic instability.[108] It is unclear whether it makes sense to classify such episodes as politically motivated property seizures.

Finally, regimes have often invited—and even egged on—people to loot as part of coordinated attacks on so-called "enemies." In 1938, the Nazis orchestrated the heinous antisemitic Kristallnacht, in which armed thugs plundered Jewish businesses and private residences. Violence went hand in hand with property seizures. The Nazis had learned from previous experience that looting Jews was a powerful mobilizing device: as early as 1923, they and other right-wing movements unleashed a nationwide campaign that combined looting with violence against Jews to scapegoat them for Germany's economic troubles.[109] Kristallnacht fused elements of far-right movement politics with top-down coordination. The Nazis' bureaucratically organized yet simultaneously quasi-grassroots looting directly paved the way for mass murder. By any account, its role in impoverishing European Jewry was crucial to the Holocaust.[110]

Despite its significance, state-organized looting falls beyond the scope of our discussion, even as the Nazi case remains ominously pertinent. Too often, looting targets minority ethnic, racial, or religious groups. In US history, the most extreme incidents have occurred during shockingly numerous "white riots," in which racist white mobs looted and destroyed Black-owned businesses and homes.[111] Looting often serves as a weapon for those eager to denigrate and humiliate precarious groups. When aiming to degrade, violate, and ultimately exclude people from political life, it is both morally heinous and incongruent with basic democratic commitments to political equality and mutual respect.

In this volume, I have insisted on delineating property damage from violence, arguing that many familiar cases of the former are in principle unrelated to the latter. By doing so I hope to show how property disobedience can sometimes be justified even in more or less democratic political contexts. However, in the vast majority of real-life scenarios involving politically motivated looting, the conceptual distinction between violence and property harms breaks down. One aim of this section is to try to make sense of the reasons why. As I hope to demonstrate, there is solid ground on which to condemn looting. Property seizures are always controversial. Yet looting poses exceptional challenges and only in the rarest of circumstances seems prospectively justifiable.

For our purposes, identifiably *political* looting refers to the widespread appropriation of goods, usually undertaken by a group of people acting openly, in the context of some emergency or breakdown of civil order that has political overtones.[112] One of looting's appeals is that it "gives large numbers of people something to do," and thus encourages mass participation, even if usually spearheaded by a "small elite at the front" first to smash storefront windows and rob businesses.[113] Some participants usually justify their endeavors in vaguely political terms, even as ideologically more sophisticated activists and movement leaders commonly condemn them. Looters rarely if ever seem to give voice to a shared political agenda or list of demands. Nonetheless, there may still be some "hidden morale" or protest-related message to their acts.[114] Arguably a borderline case of property disobedience, looting fuses with opportunistic criminality.[115] It often emerges in the context of seemingly spontaneous rebellions, in which some "desire to exploit the system opportunistically" merges with identifiable albeit inchoate political frustrations.[116] Its messy contours notwithstanding, it is wrong to view it as inevitably nothing but "dangerous . . . group criminal activity."[117]

Under the rubric of political looting, we can group myriad well-known incidents that devastated US inner cities between 1964 and 1969. Widely interpreted by contemporaries as motivated by frustration with racism and economic inequality, the looting that shook hundreds of both large and small cities proved massively costly and destructive. Contemporary civil rights leaders, including King, condemned it.[118] Looting that transpired in the shadows of the 2020 BLM protests also falls under this rubric. BLM leaders and activists, similarly, distanced themselves, accurately highlighting the role of *agents provocateurs* in some episodes.[119]

As with other property seizures, there is no denying political looting's symbolic and disruptive contours. During the 1960s US ghetto riots, for examples, mostly African American looters initially targeted white- and often Jewish-owned business they claimed had been charging local (mostly Black) customers bloated prices.[120] In some contrast to America's ugly "white riots" or Germany's antisemitic looters, they did not target private residences. In the 1992 Los Angeles riots (following a jury's acquittal of white police offi- cers who had deployed excessive force arresting Rodney King), looters zeroed in on Korean immigrant–owned small businesses similarly accused of price gouging and mistreating African American and Latino customers.[121] Looters customarily earmark not only specific businesses but also definite consumer goods.[122] More generally, "[t]he looted item or items may embody a regime, group, or individual, and so their seizure may send a message of changing power relations."[123] Frequently, looting "will have an expressive quality, per- haps related to wider social or political change."[124] As in other variants of property disobedience, the symbolic messaging may be poorly conceived and ineffective, but looting usually broadcasts *some* message, even if it often seems *retaliatory* rather than prefigurative: looters seem eager to punish those allegedly responsible for wrongdoings committed against them.

Looting is also disruptive. It usually happens during a breakdown of public order, what the sociologist Randall Collins describes as "moral holidays," or temporary collapses of ordinary social controls and norms.[125] Targeted busi- nesses will be unable to operate normally. Many of society's everyday activi- ties come to a halt. When incurring extensive losses, impacted businesses may close and never reopen, while others relocate to more hospitable locales.

There is no reason to deny that, as in other versions of property disobe- dience, looters sometimes think "that the legitimate channels are inoperative [and] . . . existing institutions are unresponsive," often with good cause.[126] People engage in looting because they doubt that their political representa- tives—or even protest leaders—listen to or care about them. Looting's ranks tend to be drawn from politically disadvantaged, socially marginalized, and economically precarious communities, even if not all individual looters are necessarily poor or disenfranchised. Socially respectable, upper-class people generally look down their noses at looters.

Nonetheless, crucial differences delimit political looting from other prop- erty seizures. First, it involves taking commodities such as foodstuffs, cloth- ing, or prestige consumer goods—for example, the color televisions looters apparently favored during the 1960s US riots. Even if buildings and land are commodities bought and sold on the marketplace, they possess a durability and relative permanence that food or even high-end luxury goods are unlikely to match. One reason, as we have observed, that squatters occupy residential structures is that they hope to gain some relatively stable, secure place in the world. While looters may claim some right to the goods they steal, they consume or "use them up." The goods in question are not designed to house anybody; they are unlikely to last or survive very long. In contemporary society, in fact, many useful objects are nothing more than rapidly obsolescent consumer goods destined to be used "almost as quickly as food" and unavoidably subject to rapid decay.[127] Looters may see their seizures as essential to gaining respect. In consumer capitalism, where possession of high-end consumer goods helps define personal success, there is an undeniable logic to doing so. Yet looters' relationship to the appropriated goods remains short rather than prospectively long-term. Even if we interpret looting as motivated by some implicit view of property as essential to personhood, the goods in question offer only limited possibilities to serve the requisite symbolic functions. Not surprisingly, observers often find it difficult to understand why seizing consumer or luxury goods—in contrast to land or a home—is anything more than, at best, an act of desperation, or, at worst, sheer criminality.

Second, property reclamations and reuses, as already noted, entail *enactments* of alternative ideas about property, for example, a property system more in sync with Native ideas of nature and spirituality, or building on the idea that labor constitutes its rightful basis. We can identify parallels to looting. In the immediate aftermath of the 1960s US riots, two sociologists observed that looting involved a "temporary redefinition of property rights," with those suffering from economic duress taking consumer goods otherwise denied them to make "a bid for the redistribution of property."[128] In King's remarks on the same incidents, looting was part of the "language of the unheard," a product of "the gulf between the affluence" its participants "see . . . in the mass media and the deprivation he experiences in his everyday life."[129] Looting constituted a confused yet still palpable protest against the harsh "fact of poverty amid plenty."[130]

Despite overlap with other property seizures, major differences remain. Vacant land or a neglected building can not only be seized but then also subsequently "worked on" and refurbished, with squatters often proudly pointing out that they are doing so. In contrast, food or televisions cannot be restored or improved; they are simply consumed, resold, or used up. Looting does not typically offer analogous opportunities for staging some sought-for alternative property order. Unlike many squatters, for example, those who take TVs or Nintendo games rarely use the seized goods to illustrate the possible contours of a revised economic system. It is hard to see how their acts might meaningfully prefigure some alternative social order. Looters usually add no labor to or improve seized property. Opportunistic looters do not care very much about combatting existing inequalities or injustices: they simply want to get their piece of the pie, which they hope to enjoy, if only briefly, before the supply runs out. In the words of one 2011 London looter, "I felt how rich was meant to be. I felt how to be rich."[131] Or a 2020 Californian looter: "We're doing it because we can . . . We're just trying to provide and take up the opportunity we are getting right now. That's all."[132] Looting often seems akin, as King correctly observed, to "a kind of stormy carnival of free-merchandise distribution," something that potentially resonates in a society that values consumption, but not in a way that typically allows participants effectively to anticipate the outlines of some political or social alternative.[133]

Looters rarely prove able to justify their acts in the ambitious fashion we find among property re-occupiers or squatters. In part because they take and use up consumer goods, their acts seem poorly designed to communicate much more than frustration with and anger about the status quo. In the words of another recent looter: "We've got no other way of showing people how angry we are."[134] Theirs is often, as King commented, "the desperate, suicidal cry of one who is fed up with the powerlessness of his cave existence that he asserts that he would rather be dead," or at least risk being killed by the police or military "than ignored."[135] This is probably why looting is more controversial than other property seizures, even as it arguably poses a less fundamental challenge to the property status quo. Looters hope to shock a broad audience and generate a concerted political response. Yet when queried by journalists and scholars about their motives, their remarks are frequently diffuse and apolitical.

While commenting on the '60s US riots, King described looting as serving "many functions. It enables the most enraged and deprived Negro to take hold of consumer goods with the ease the white man does by using his purse. Often the Negro does not even want what he takes; he wants the experience of taking it. . . . Alienated from society and knowing that the society cherishes property above people, he is shocking it by abusing property rights. There are thus elements of emotional catharsis in the violent act."[136] During the 1960s riots, looting symbolized a desire among the most estranged and worst-off African Americans to participate in a consumer society whites could take for granted. As King continued, a "curious proof of the symbolic aspect of the looting for some who took part in it is the fact that, after the riots, police received hundreds of calls from Negroes trying to return merchandise they had taken. Those people wanted the experience of taking, redressing the

power imbalance that property represents. Possession, afterward, was secondary."[137] In Watts and elsewhere, some looters did not even seek to hold
onto the goods they had stolen, even as their acts shocked whites who probably did value their property more highly than poor people of color.[138] King
did not think it made sense to smugly fault the economically desperate from
trying to gain goods enjoyed by the better off. Yet, looting remained congenitally flawed as a tactic for social change. While calling on critics to make sense
of its sources and emphasizing that most riot-related violence transpired at
the hands of police and the national guard, he rejected it, seeing in looting a
futile "violent act" likely to strengthen the hand of those opposed to overdue
social change.[139] Participants who expected it to generate constructive political change would be sorely disappointed.[140]

King's remarks highlight why it is far-fetched to interpret looting as an a
priori rejection of "the legitimacy of ownership rights and property" under
"cisheteropatriarchal racial capitalist society."[141] Many and probably most
recent looters simply hope to participate in the existing economic order. They
do "not attempt to undermine property rights in general."[142] Not surprisingly,
they take looted goods home, sometimes sell or trade them, but do not—for
example—announce that they are now commonly or jointly owned, as a stepping stone to an alternative property order. Much and perhaps most incidents
of looting end up harming vulnerable and disadvantaged minorities—in US
history, especially Blacks, Latinos, and recent immigrants. Politically motivated looting targeting racialized capitalism, in fact, has been the rare exception to the rule.

King was also probably right to describe looting as *violent*. Property reclamations and reuses *may* open the door to—or *sometimes* be accompanied
by—violence or acts of intimidation. But there is no necessary relationship
between them. Looting's political and historical record paints a different
portrait: "While an actual act of looting may not involve direct violence, it
will be precipitated by direct or indirect violence."[143] Episodic looting begins
by raising tensions during what are sometimes initially nonviolent protests,
provoking a fierce backlash from police and other security forces.[144] The subsequent breakdown of public order that precedes generalized looting is frequently set into motion by violent clashes between rioters and police. Even
if rioters bear the worst brunt of the initial round of violence, it is habitually
followed by an atmosphere of "threats and intimidation" and the lurking possibility of violence "should the goods' owners or custodians of goods resist
the efforts of looters."[145] Opportunistic elements get in on the game and use

or threaten to use violence. Targeting local businesses, that violence becomes disturbingly akin to intimate and fratricidal violence commonplace during civil wars, with looters targeting businesses and owners with whom they daily interact.[146] Not surprisingly perhaps, men have been more likely to participate, whereas women tend to stay home. In most real-life scenarios, "Looting either requires violence or the threat of violence to take place. That is to say, the *context* of looting is violence."[147]

Looting is frequently accompanied by arson. Of course, fires can quickly rage out of control, threatening both persons and property. Looting also tends to be accompanied by the outright destruction of goods and businesses. Looters, as noted, may start by targeting carefully selected businesses and goods. However, there is a tendency for their acts to become less selective, as onlookers join the moral holiday with the hope of getting in on the fun. By day's end, looters will have taken and destroyed goods not only from those businesses identified with or perhaps partly culpable for some injustice, but others as well.[148] In the United States, since many national retailers avoid poor inner-city neighborhoods, affected businesses are often small and medium-sized. For a host of reasons, they are also disproportionately minority-owned—for example, the Jewish-owned businesses devastated in the 1960s riots, or Asian American shops during the 1992 LA riot. Looters start by targeting big chains in search of luxury goods, but they often end up going after Mr. Goldstein's appliance store or Mrs. Kim's corner grocery.

Looting's "stormy carnival" atmosphere is hardly conducive to making basic normative distinctions or smart political strategizing. As a moral holiday it invites indiscriminate and probably irresponsible attacks. Only on the most tendentious logic can we interpret looting as basically nonviolent. What one legal scholar dubs "'pure looting,' in which no direct threat to persons is present," seems, at any rate, relatively rare.[149]

For example, during the 2020 BLM protests in Minneapolis and Saint Paul, participants not only burned down a police station but then—absent evidence of any real deliberation or advanced planning—looted small immigrant-owned businesses and even the offices of nonprofits that support Native American youth and other worthwhile causes.[150] Theirs were attacks on businesses and nonprofit organizations that directly supported individuals and families and unrelated to systemic racism or racist policing. Many BLM sympathizers were justifiably alarmed by looting in which family-owned restaurants and the shelves of small retail shops were ransacked. Such political acts can have disastrous, potentially existential consequences. Too often, the "small fry" but not perhaps CEOs or stockholders in national chains will pay the highest price. Even if those stealing from local businesses may never have sought to harm or endanger anyone, their acts risk becoming links in a traceable chain of events that prospectively culminates in material distress and its all-too-familiar negative bodily and psychological effects.

The philosopher Tommie Shelby is justified in claiming that extreme conditions of injustice in America's urban ghettos require relaxing the usual expectation of general fidelity to law among residents. In principle, a wide range of illegal activities constitute justifiable responses to institutionalized racism and systemic oppression. Tapping Rawls, Shelby describes ghettos as resting on basically unjust rather than nearly just political and social conditions. Accordingly, the relatively strict standards for principled political law-breaking (e.g., nonviolent civil disobedience) that Rawls linked to the latter but not the former no longer obtain. So we should provide normative space for property damage and destruction. However, for moral and political reasons, Shelby correctly adds, ghetto conditions do not justify cruelty, reckless violence, or causing unnecessary suffering.[151] Even the worst off and most exploited have some duty to help construct a more just political and social order, and thus "not to do things that would clearly make a more just society more difficult to achieve."[152] Since social change is almost always brought about by the oppressed, without their efforts to try to do so it will simply not happen.

In the final analysis, even when engaged in by the oppressed, and linked to an admirable cause, looting tends to be intimately related to violence, often counterproductively increasing "the burdens of injustice on those in ghetto communities or others similarly situated."[153] How it could constructively contribute to political and social change is very hard to fathom.[154] This should not surprise us: many looters seem at most marginally interested in political causes.

Admittedly, our planet's many desperate and downtrodden people are still likely to decide occasionally that looting is how best to draw attention to their plight. Mine is *not* a blanket, moralistic rejection of their decision to do so. As King correctly noted, however, such acts usually represent a "desperate, suicidal cry." It is difficult to envision looting as part of a well-conceived political strategy, especially in more or less democratic societies. In those exceptional cases where contemporary political movements *have* advocated looting, they have faced a backlash.[155] To be sure, political authorities should be expected to respond proportionately and responsibly, minimizing any loss of life, something they far too rarely manage to accomplish. The approach advocated by President Trump amid 2020 BLM-related looting—"when the looting starts the shooting starts"—hardly seems like the right answer.[156]

One possible exception to this general pattern is suggested by some rare incidents of politically oriented, nonviolent "pure looting," or *robinhoodism*, in which economically vulnerable people steal from carefully selected targets while limiting possible damages and harms. In such cases, looting—its many perils notwithstanding—may prove tragically necessary to prevent otherwise avoidable misery and loss of life. Even if subsistence-based looting does not allow participants to prefigure an alternative property order, there are identifiable parallels to squatting by the unhoused and materially desperate.

Some recent food riots and other incidents of looting by the poor in the Global South possibly fall under this rubric. In the Global North, some shoplifting and so-called "dumpster diving," when existentially motivated, may as well.[157] In early twentieth-century Europe, visibly hungry women, with the involvement of labor unions and leftist organizations, occasionally resorted to looting food suppliers, declaring that otherwise they would be unable to feed their families. One historian points out that conventional political instruments for registering discontent either openly excluded women or were badly "geared to the problems of mothers," and thus looting seemed to many of them the only feasible alternative, particularly given the imminent food emergency they and their loved ones faced.[158] During the 1930s, opportunistic looting was widespread among desperate people; some episodes took on unambiguously political hues. In the United States, radical leftists coordinated the looting of chain stores and supermarkets and bootlegging of coal so that poor people could eat and heat their apartments and homes. A labor historian notes that by 1932, organized looting, sometimes linked to radical groups, "was a nation-wide phenomenon."[159] These and related incidents of robinhoodism targeted nationally based chain stores less likely to face dire existential consequences than small businesses. They also tried to avoid violent conflagrations. In Europe, radical leftists coordinated similar actions.[160]

When the Detroit city government slashed unemployment benefits in 1932, visibly hungry children responded by snatching food from grocery stores, with unemployed "men, usually in twos and threes," entering chain stores and ordering "all the food they could possible carry," and then walking out without paying. Interestingly, "chain-store managers refused to report the incidents to the police lest the practice be encouraged by the resultant publicity."[161] Newspaper chains were reluctant to report such episodes because they hoped to avoid instigating copycat acts. West Virginia coal miners threatened similar actions to feed their families, with one union leader announcing that "no state has a right to call you a criminal if you take what you must have to live."[162] In the state capital, Charleston, a local sheriff managed to get miners to hold off only by convincing county officials to provide emergency food relief.

Excepting only the most doctrinaire defenses of existing property relations, *all* major theories of property "have agreed in affirming the notion that private property must give way in the face of extreme economic necessity," and therefore that the law is obliged to treat those in dire economic straits differently from those acting opportunistically or absent necessity.[163] One hardly needs to turn to Proudhon or Marx to find a defense of this simple intuition. Medieval Christianity's greatest political thinker, Thomas Aquinas, noted, "It is not theft, properly speaking, to take secretly and use another's property in case of extreme need: because that which he takes for the support of life becomes his own property by reason of that need."[164] Hegel, a principled defender of modern *bourgeois* property, nonetheless declared, "Life . . . has a right in opposition to abstract right. If, for example, it can be preserved by stealing a loaf, this certainly constitutes an infringement of someone's property, but it would be wrong to regard such an action as a common theft. If someone whose life is in danger were not allowed to take measures to save himself, he would be destined to forfeit all his rights [and] . . . his entire freedom would be negated."[165] Those forced to steal to survive engage in illegal violations of property rights. Yet their acts are disanalogous to those of ordinary criminals and thus should be treated more charitably.[166]

This venerable tradition has been tapped by recent legal scholars seeking more merciful official responses to subsistence-based looting during natural disasters.[167] Yet others have argued for the legal relevance of *economic necessity* as a mitigating circumstance in cases involving political looting. The law already allows for a necessity defense, in which defendants concede they have committed an offense but justify it by claiming that (1) their act was necessary to avoid a greater harm, (2) there were no reasonable alternatives, and (3) any harm incurred by breaking the law was the lesser evil, that is, greater harms would have resulted from obeying it.[168] Although US courts customarily restrict efforts to employ the necessity defense to advance political causes, it remains relevant to cases concerning "those who are without shelter and illegally obtain shelter, and those who are without food and who illegally obtain food."[169] People squat because their own harsh experiences teach them that homelessness is a substantially greater harm than occupying unused buildings. Similarly, hungry people who illegally seize material necessities know that starvation is the greater evil.

One advocate of an expanded role for economic necessity defenses, the legal scholar R. George Wright, concedes some difficulties: "Not all thefts of food or shelter . . . fall within the proper scope of a necessity defense," in part because some episodes may result not only in disproportionately severe property harms but also endanger business owners.[170] By the same token, "common sense . . . suggests that some cases of economic necessity are not as dangerous or threatening, at least to the shop owner, as others."[171] One possible advantage of an enhanced reliance on an economic necessity defense is that it would allow judges and juries to make suitably fine-tuned distinctions. The nature and extent of the looter's need, character and quantity of goods stolen, and scope of harms to property owners should count when deciding what legal penalties, if any, are appropriate. Where mitigating circumstances are weighty (for example, the emergency is imminent, or offenders take only what is minimally necessary to survive), courts should respond leniently. In contrast, where aggravating circumstances are serious (for example, looters take luxury goods they intend to sell), penalties probably should be more severe.[172] This seems like a legally and politically more sensible approach than, for example, trying to codify laws selectively permitting some types of looting.

Why has the legal system generally failed to take economic necessity seriously as a mitigating circumstance? When facing squatters and looters, Wright claims, prosecutors and judges aim "to stabilize and reaffirm established property institutions" and "existing economic arrangements," rather than treating property disobedients' implicit and explicit criticisms of those arrangements with the seriousness they deserve.[173] They do so at the cost not only of subjecting poor people to unduly harsh penalties but also discounting the vital contributions to political life property disobedients potentially make.

*   *   *

This chapter has analyzed property seizure and suggested some normative and political guidelines for evaluating it. Despite overlap between and among property seizure's three main types, each raises somewhat distinct questions. Seizures of commodity goods are the most difficult to justify since they often rely on and fuse with violence. The relationship between property reclamations and reusages, on the one hand, and violence, on the other, is less clearcut. In principle, they remain consistent with a principled commitment to nonviolence vis-à-vis persons.

Now that we have explored symbolic and disruptive property disobedience, as well as property seizures, we are better positioned to summarize some general lessons.

First, it would be naive and irresponsible to ignore many perfectly understandable considerations against property disobedience. Even when nonviolent, or approximating civil disobedience, it may prove poorly conceived and politically counterproductive. Political authorities and the media often succeed in framing property damage as political violence; social scientific evidence suggests that public opinion generally reacts negatively to violent protest.[174] Nothing I have said can replace political judgment, which demands of all politically serious actors that they pay careful attention to context, history, and other contingencies that unavoidably fall beyond the scope of my analysis. Given the sacrosanct status enjoyed by property in the existing social order, and the fact that state officials have been tasked with upholding existing property relations, political actors would do well to pay careful attention to such matters. Even when justified on the terms outlined here, property disobedience can prove inappropriate and end up generating nothing more than severe legal penalties. In a more rational political universe, authorities would be more accommodating. But that is not the world in which we presently find ourselves. Especially for possible protest participants, pretending otherwise may prove costly.

Second, anyone who pursues property disobedience should expect to meet some demanding tests I have tried to identify. In the most general terms, property disobedience should always be "constrained, proportionate, and discriminating, such that their intended impacts are concentrated as far as possible on wrongdoing," with any damage necessarily appropriate as well as proportionate to the injustice at hand.[175] Excessive and unnecessary property losses, as well as collateral damage to property unrelated to a protested injustice, should be avoided. Property disobedience seems most readily justifiable when targeting imminent or severe injustices, requiring an urgent response. Even then it should usually only be undertaken when a good faith effort has already been made to pursue other political methods (for example, lawful advocacy and protest, more conventional modes of civil disobedience), or such methods can be plausibly viewed as likely to be ineffectual. It also seems most easily justifiable when basically defensive in character, that is, it wards off or minimizes some manifest harm or extreme injustice, and those engaging in it only do the minimum necessary to obstruct it. Other types—for example, ideologically motivated squatting that aims to prefigure an alternative postcapitalist order—will usually require more ambitious justifications.

Third, property disobedients should minimize any possible loss to human life, acting with "respect for other people's interests . . . in life and bodily integrity," always seeking the least harmful course of action.[176] For reasons I have outlined, nonviolence vis-à-vis persons is fundamental in more or less democratic contexts where we are obliged to treat political peers with respect and dignity. Crucially, it is "difficult to envisage any circumstance where . . . campaigns should use, or threaten, either lethal force or vigorous psychological attacks," and "no risk of physical or psychological harm to persons" should be permitted.[177] Beyond the boundaries of basically democratic polities, things get more complicated, but even there we can frequently identify moral and tactical reasons favoring nonviolence.

CHAPTER 6

Revisiting Property

O ur analysis so far has gotten by with only the most rudimentary
ideas about property. In Chapter 1, I recalled standard definitions
and some general traits of public and private property, before
quickly moving to explore property disobedience and its relationship to violence. Although I hope to have now made a plausible case that property disobedience can be congruent with political nonviolence, in the process tough
questions about property were sidelined. Even as our analysis unavoidably
raised them, much more remains to be said.

My reasons for putting off a sustained engagement with property have
been both methodological and analytic. First, rather than starting with a
detailed defense of some preferred view of property, it seemed more fruitful to consider what the phenomenon of property disobedience might tell
us. What could we learn about property from protest participants who, in
some cases, have thought long and hard about it? Might their protests reveal
something significant? When property disobedience is poorly conceived and
executed, are there wider lessons about property to be drawn? Looters who
seize goods from small shops, for example, face universal opprobrium, with
their acts condemned even by leaders of movements under whose shadows
they act. Can we learn from property disobedience's critics?

Second, modern societies are irrepressibly pluralistic. This means that
we commonly encounter a wide spectrum of views about property. Not surprisingly, in previous chapters we observed that property disobedients tap
diverging justifications. Some appeal to ideas of property as based on or
relating to labor, personhood, possession, or use. Lawyers tells us that not
just our ideas but also property law itself is characterized by a remarkable
heterogeneity of values, with many pieces of the extraordinarily complicated
legal puzzle pointing in opposing directions.[1] Historians of recent political

thought sketch a similarly messy portrait.[2] The discussion here has corroborated such claims: legal systems penalize property disobedients, yet they also offer them some tools (for example, adverse possession). Given pluralism, at any rate, it made sense to avoid loading the deck analytically, rather than first digging into the particulars of property disobedience and trying to find out what could be learned.

A third reason for holding off before tackling property's complexities relates to my ideal-typical taxonomy. Its building block, *symbolic* property disobedience, often involves targeting public property (for example, public monuments and statues). Such incidents raise a comparably narrow range of questions about property per se. Activists who damaged Confederate memorials during the recent BLM protests, for example, did not interpret their endeavors primarily as challenges to existing property relations; they thought they were simply making use of basic political rights. That interpretation, revealingly, overlaps to some degree with government officials' view of monuments as justifiable expressions of state speech. Even as some BLM protestors faced criminal damage charges, property was only secondarily of interest to them, many critics, and even some state officials.

In some contrast, *disruptive* property disobedience more immediately poses questions about property. Those engaging in sabotage regularly delineate legitimate targets from property that remains out of bounds. Eco-saboteurs disrupt property allegedly complicit in environmentally destructive activity. Climate activists propose going after luxury carbon emissions by the wealthy but not subsistence emissions by those just getting by. Disruptive property disobedience not only marks both public *and* private property, but participants have formulated a range of claims that rely on delineating between and among property types and corresponding economic activities. Even when those distinctions sometimes seem odd (and protestors occasionally ignore them), disruptive property disobedience suggests that not all forms of property are cut from the same cloth. Only when culpable for extreme harms are they targeted.

Property seizures thematize property most directly. Participants in property reclamations, for instance, reoccupy lands they claim were stolen from them. Squatters repurpose unused, neglected buildings and lands, often owned by public entities or large absentee proprietors, but not private residences or small family farms. Here again, property disobedients make a wide range of claims about these and other distinctions; some infer the necessity of changing and prospectively reforming property relations. Consequently,

148Chapter 6

illegal occupations often prefigure the alternative property order they hope to establish. It seems wrong, at any rate, to interpret their protests as frontal assaults on private property or property qua property. Participants condemn existing property relations while appealing to familiar normative intuitions about it.

As we progressed through property disobedience's ideal-typical variants, questions concerning property took on growing prominence. How might distinctions made, either implicitly or explicitly, by property disobedients be grounded? Can we identify some basis for conceiving of property as a multisided, variegated institution, with its variants potentially posing different normative and political challenges? More generally, how best to make sense of property disobedience, when viewed as a contribution to critical discourse about political activity concerning property? Beyond what we have already stated about its nonviolent credentials, how might it relate to democracy? It is high time we address these questions.

*   *   *

Both scholars and laypersons who discuss property regularly distinguish between its private, public (or collective), and (sometimes) common types, but when it comes to treating them individually, key distinctions between and among various *subtypes* often vanish from view.[3] Unfortunately, this tendency gets in the way of making sense of property disobedience. It also potentially sidelines valuable insights implicit in property disobedience as a political practice.

Protest movements often make fine-grained distinctions even when aiming at private property. Although the distinctions, unavoidably, take contextually specific forms, property disobedients sometimes condone damage to large-scale private businesses (e.g., banks that own foreclosed homes, or multinational energy firms), for example, while rejecting attacks on personal property or small-scale businesses. This demarcation makes sense from the perspective of political nonviolence: when vital personal property (a private residence, for example) or a small individually owned enterprise is severely damaged, owners may face grave, potentially existential consequences.

The boundary also makes sense for other reasons. Personal property in objects that we rely on to pursue our lives, on any reasonable account, deserves strong protections, even as we unavoidably disagree about their scope. The personality theory of property aptly captures the key intuition that control over a potentially significant diversity of objects—an apartment or home, wedding ring, treasured photographs—helps provide an indispensable sense of personal identity, who we are in relation to others and the social universe at large.[4] These are objects we use or potentially tap to get by and pursue the kind of life we hope to lead. Without them, it would be difficult to survive let alone have a place in the world allowing us to gain autonomy or develop our capacities. "To take the most basic need as an example, a person cannot flourish without the ability to occupy some physical space within which she can carry out activities essential to her existence, such as eating and sleeping."[5] Personhood presupposes secure, relatively durable control over certain assets essential to our self-constitution. The fact that millions of impoverished people lack even a bare modicum of personal property should shock us—not only on grounds of material fairness, but also because it debilitates people in far-reaching ways. It quite rightly angered Marx and his closest ally, Friedrich Engels, whose *Communist Manifesto* savaged industrial capitalism for robbing the working classes of personal property.[6]

In temporally accelerated societies subject to incessant change, personal property in some relatively durable set of tangible objects arguably takes on heightened importance. Given empirically ascertainable speed-ups in technology, the pace of social change, and everyday life, a relatively secure place or condition—and set of complementary objects—that we can meaningfully describe as our "own" remains appealing and probably indispensable.[7] Similarly, as property undergoes an intensified *dematerialization* and morphs into increasingly immaterial and intangible forms (e.g., intellectual property, property in "big data"), the traditional association of personal property with concrete material objects potentially gains in attractiveness as well.[8] Overwhelmed by the constant whirl of high-speed digital activities, tangible personal property serves, for some of us, as a haven in an otherwise heartless commodified, high-speed, ever more immaterial social world, even as that haven daily seems to shrink.[9]

Of course, personal property's significance does not render it exempt from critical scrutiny. If my neighbor's luxury yacht contributes to global warming or other societal harms, activists may be right to target it. Interestingly, however, many social movements seem reluctant to go after personal property, even when it takes harmful forms: most of us intuitively appreciate personal property's merits while disagreeing about its rightful parameters. Those whose hearts have not yet been hardened by humanity's capacity for awful violence are disgusted to learn that racist Americans have plundered

not just Black-owned businesses but also their homes and personal possessions, and that the Nazis successfully egged on ordinary Germans to do the
same to Jews.

What then about other types of private property? Small and some
medium-sized businesses are often legally constituted as *sole proprietorships*
or *partnerships*.[10] Crucial to both is that owners carry the burdens of liability
and are therefore responsible for financial gains and losses. They make key
decisions about business operations, benefit from economic gains, but also
are obliged to cover any debts. What this means, stated bluntly, is that protests
resulting in damage to or destruction of their operations are ultimately likely
to be borne by individual owners and partners. Extensive harm, potentially,
will be costly and perhaps devastating, even when not resulting in tangible
physical or severe psychological injuries to or violations of owners. Property
disobedience can expose owners to "sudden changes in the major elements
and crucial determinants of [their] established position in the world, as one
has come reasonably to understand that position."[11] For some, their small
businesses are constitutive of personal identity: severe damage may prove
analogous to, and perhaps worse than, destructive attacks on private homes
or treasured personal possessions. Small enterprises can indeed represent
extensions of persons and their aspirations in many easily recognizable ways.

There may be extraordinary circumstances in which property disobedience targeting personal property or small businesses may prove justifiable.[12]
However, those activists who argue by and large against doing so intuitively
grasp some of personal and small-scale property's special features. One of
looting's many blemishes, as discussed in Chapter 5, is that participants tend
to end up indiscriminately damaging a wide range of small shops and businesses. Of course, not all property harms are equivalent: spray painting a shop
display window is different from plundering the shop's shelves or burning it
to the ground. So here, once again, it is necessary to highlight the importance
of evaluating the messy particulars of property disobedience before passing
judgment. While doing so, however, we should not lose sight of key differences between and among private property's subtypes.

Significantly, most economic activity in contemporary society is conducted by large-scale business firms organized legally as some type of for-
profit *corporation* possessing limited liability, that is, shareholders, managers,
and corporate directors are only financially responsible to a limited degree.
I cannot explore the reasons behind the ascent of one of modernity's major
economic institutions, except to note that it makes sense for large businesses

to incorporate: doing so allows them to raise large sums of capital, for example, since investors are only financially liable to a limited degree. For our purposes, what matters is that the for-profit corporation is legally very different from personal property, sole proprietorships, and partnerships. What the legal scholar and New Dealer Thurman Arnold famously described as the "folklore of capitalism" leads us instinctively to think of corporations as basically akin to personal property or small businesses, despite quantitative differences in scale and significant qualitative differences in legal and organizational structure.[13] The myth of the modern corporation as nothing but a "bigger" private residence or grocery story is partly why it has been able to acquire legal personhood, along with a significant range of associated rights. In the US, "corporations have nearly all the same rights as individuals: freedom of speech, freedom of the press, religious liberty, due process, equal protection, freedom from unreasonable searches and seizures, the right to counsel, the right against double jeopardy, and the right to trial by jury, among others."[14] By allowing massive, hierarchically organized corporations to wrap themselves in "the garments of rugged individuals," we ignore messy institutional realities and encourage the illusion that our individual and personal liberties are tied up with corporate rights.[15] Doing so buttresses the misleading view of property harms resulting from a strike or protest at a large corporation, for example, as violence against the person of the entrepreneur, as though damaging an automobile plant during a sit-down strike were no different from assaulting owners in their private residences.[16] Arnold knew this was a mistake: the traditional image of the individual or familial entrepreneur no longer corresponded to the realities of corporate capitalism, in which ownership takes on complex, surprisingly impersonal forms.

At least since the publication of Adolph A. Berle and Gardiner Means's landmark *The Modern Corporation and Private Property* (1933), lively debates about the contours of corporate property have preoccupied scholars.[17] The orthodox position is that *shareholders* constitute the corporation's *owners*, even as those advancing this view concede that stockholders lack some key rights traditionally associated with private property. Berle and Means noted, for example, that real control over corporate assets lies in the hands of managers, in principle accountable to a body elected by shareholders, but in fact relatively autonomous. Another complication for the conventional portrayal of corporate property are sizable variations between and among corporate organizations and ownership patterns across national settings. Corporate personhood's specifics are not chiefly the result of free market exchanges between economic agents, but instead conscious policy choices and social struggles between and among affected parties.[18]

For now, let me point out that the folkloric conflation of corporate with small-scale property continues to distort social reality. Limited liability helps shield shareholders from potentially devastating economic consequences. Who today are those shareholders? In the US, 70 percent of stock is in the hands of large institutional (pension funds, mutual funds, hedge funds) but not individual investors. In 1960, stock was owned for an average of eight years; by 2010, the average was down to a mere four months, with stockholders expecting rapid-fire gains.[19] Stocks are typically owned for fleeting conjunctures. By the early 2000s, "most shares changed hands at least once a year."[20] Of course, institutional investors are tasked with "looking out" for concrete individuals whose investments or pensions they manage. However, the ties connecting natural persons to corporations seem attenuated and extraordinarily indirect. Those whose pensions or savings are managed by big investment firms occupy a universe remote from corporate leadership. Anyone with retirement savings in a pension fund whose investments were negatively impacted by recent protests would probably find the claim that they suffered "violence" idiosyncratic. Even more telling, the harmful material impact may prove limited: pension managers will simply have shifted investments elsewhere before their clients are even aware of what has transpired.

The point is not that large-scale corporate capitalism makes property disobedience costless. Rather, the mindboggling complexity of corporate ownership means that many protests engender relatively minor economic nuisances for real-life human beings. I do not want to trivialize possible economic perils or invite irresponsible political action. Yet, placing property disobedience in this light allows us to push back against those who categorically label it "violent" or as a frontal assault on private property. Such views tend to rely on the old individualistic "folklore of capitalism." They ignore, at any rate, how political acts impacting large corporations are different creatures from those going after "mom-and-pop" businesses. As the liberal political theorist Judith N. Shklar once correctly pointed out, to consider corporate business enterprises "in the same terms as the local mom and pop store is unworthy of serious social discourse."[21]

In fact, some scholars point out that that the corporation *as a legal entity*— not stockholders or *any* natural persons—is its owner or proprietor. Defenders of this view concede that stockholders select and influence corporate boards of directors but possess few rights of ownership vis-à-vis corporate

assets. The point is not merely that "they do not have all the rights of ownership . . . but then neither does a landlord or mortgager."[22] Rather, stockholders lack private ownership's *core* traits: they cannot use, exclude others from,
lend, borrow on, alienate (or transfer), or profit directly from sales of corporate assets. They own stock, of course, but that does not grant them property
vis-à-vis corporate assets.[23] Investor assets and liabilities are disentangled
from those of the corporation.[24] In corporate capitalism, "more individual
investors of all sorts become *rentiers*," with their property consisting "less of
their ownership of some part of the corporation's physical plant and stock
of materials and products than of their right to a revenue from the ability
of the corporation to maneuver profitably."[25] And even that "right" rests on
payments allocated to shareholders at the discretion of corporate managers.

For the moment we can set aside the question of whether this alternative account of corporate property is empirically accurate. If correct it would
infer an even more attenuated link between economic losses incurred during
property disobedience and possible damages to real or natural persons. At
any rate, there are sound reasons—relating to property law and present-day
economic realities—why some property disobedients delineate large corporations from personal property and small businesses, with property damage
viewed as potentially justifiable in the context of the former but only infre-
quently the latter.

However, these refinements only take us so far: they do not help make
sense of fine-grained property-related distinctions political activists occasionally invoke. Recent antiracist protesters, for example, generally targeted
public but not privately owned monuments and statues. Indigenous militants
reassert rights to lands taken away by European settlers, regardless of who
owns them. Squatters occupy unused private and public properties. Climate
militants disable large climate-killing public and private utilities but not environmentally responsible firms. They demarcate property that exploits and
uses up nonrenewable resources (coal, oil) from ecologically sustainable economic activities. Some of them think it fair game to damage climate-killing
personal property (for example, SUVs or yachts), which they do not consider
equivalent to other personal goods worthy of respect.

One immediate lesson is that it seems misleading to draw a sharp line
between public and private property. Since both prospectively partake in
injustice, both constitute potential targets. Nor should we assume that protests targeting public rather than private property are necessarily more justifiable.[26] A destructive, politically motivated attack on a public school or health

clinic, for example, can prove massively consequential to those impacted, particularly when public funds are scarce and budgetary restraints prevent repair or replacement. When people depend on public property for the satisfaction of basic needs, or their identities are meaningfully linked to it, they may pay a high price for protests that incur damages, even when playing no role in some purported injustice. Imagine, for example, a teacher or school principal who spent decades working at a public school, only one day to learn that it faced the prospect of closure because of severe damages incurred by political extremists. It is hard to see how the consequences for the teacher or principal would be qualitatively different, either economically or in terms of personal identity, from that of a small business owner whose shop has been hard hit by riot-related arson attacks.

How then might we make sense of the complicated distinctions property disobedients draw? The social philosopher Tilo Wesche suggests one promising answer. Wesche argues that we should abandon the traditional view of property as relating to an object or thing, interpreted in strictly formal terms.[27] Quite astutely, he notes that some protest movements hint at the need to disaggregate the abstract "thingness" of modern property into a variety of qualitatively distinct goods.[28]

On the conventional account, property is a legally mediated social relationship in which owners have principally unlimited rights over resources, viewed either in material (e.g., land, manufactured goods) or immaterial (e.g., intellectual) terms. Property's "thingness" is conceived abstractly, without attention to its concrete types, in part because of the complexity of modern economic life and the vast range of objects that potentially become property.[29] Wesche points out that this view implicitly treats the exploitation of natural resources as analogous to countless basically dissimilar activities. Property in and over nature, even when manifestly destructive, becomes no different from property in everyday goods people use (computers, telephones, etc.) or a shopkeeper's small business. Providing a conceptual cover for a wide range of environmentally unsustainable activities, the conventional framework obfuscates qualitative differences between and among different goods. It homogenizes what should be treated as different subsets of property's "thingness": consumer goods we use and which contribute to personal identity and some place in the social world; infrastructural goods (for example, a functioning power grid, or healthcare and school systems) that rely on costly investments and cannot be generated by individuals' own efforts; productive goods (or what Marxists call the means of production) that allow for the production of additional goods; finally, natural goods that may be altered or worked on but cannot be produced (for example, coal or oil) by our efforts.[30] These distinctions, Wesche suggests, are at least as fundamental as familiar differences, for example, between public and private property.

By taking natural goods' distinctive contours seriously, Wesche hopes that we can recognize why we should not treat them as akin or equivalent to other goods. Once we have done so, we can move to formulate a superior view of what property vis-à-vis nature specifically entails. Wesche ultimately defends the idea of nature's own property rights, that is, nature as a legal entity having legitimate property rights. He correctly observes that many legal and constitutional documents already reference nature as a rights-bearing entity: we need to make sense of this trend. Wesche offers an impressive theoretical framework that seeks to do just that.

His is an innovative project that deserves careful attention. For our limited purposes, it suggests how we might understand property disobedients' intuitions about property's variegated contours. Most immediately, it meshes with those green activists who view themselves as standing in and advocating for nature and its "rights." More generally, it offers useful tools for interpreting the sorts of distinctions concerning property that activists periodically make.

However, I worry that this approach risks undermining the formality and generality of modern law in ways that might inadvertently prove troublesome. The abstract "thingness" of property expresses the fact that we encounter both a wide variety of different (possible) types of property and sharply diverging views about how to relate to and evaluate them. Property's abstractness does not necessarily homogenize objects or reduce them to the least common denominator. Instead, it allows real-life social actors to make determinations about property, its innumerable prospective varieties, and their possible merits and demerits. Minus property's abstract contours, we risk building excessively controversial, politically contestable claims about property into its conceptual—and, presumably, core legal—framework.

Of course, some types of property are troublesome and must be restricted. Nineteenth-century abolitionists were justified in opposing ownership in other human beings. Contemporary environmentalists are right to criticize unsustainable extractive practices. By the same token, law's formality remains essential to equal freedom: without it, fundamental questions about property might be inappropriately predetermined, by conceptual (and normative) fiat, something that seems unappealing and unrealistic given social dynamism and modern pluralism. Law's formality always invites political contestation:

if we believe property is serving harmful or destructive purposes, we are obliged to try to convince our peers, hopefully succeeding in bringing about appropriate reforms. Ideally, those changes then become durable. Yet they remain, in principle, matters for contestation and social experimentation, not something to be built from the start, per abstract philosophical reflections (likely to prove time-bound and socially determined), into property's conceptual and legal substructure.

The abstract right to free expression, similarly, allows for people to voice a vast range of competing views, including some we will find unpalatable. That right's formal character means that it is left to us to use as we like, for better or worse. Of course, there are always instances in which the employment of general rights to free expression or property should be regulated or prohibited, for a variety of familiar reasons. But law's formality means that the burden lies with state institutions to justify such restraints, a practice that remains essential to any free society.[31] Such restraints are best arrived at by political action and subsequent legal changes, not by a fundamental reconfiguration of the modern right to property that risks a priori determining how people should properly relate to different types of goods.

Where then does this leave property disobedients? My answer, admittedly, is anticlimactic: they are obliged to publicly defend the various distinctions about property that they make. When push comes to shove, such demarcations will have to be justified politically and thus in the public arena. I have tried to suggest how we might interpret distinctions between personal property and small businesses, on the one hand, and large corporations, on the other. Property disobedients should explain—and via their acts symbolically express—their criticisms of troublesome, allegedly harmful property and its uses. Some of them might build on Wesche's insight that natural goods should be treated differently from other types of property.

Here again, we see why it makes sense for property disobedience to approximate nonviolent civil disobedience, interpreted as a public, generally communicative practice that seeks to persuade political peers. Unless protestors can successfully convince others of their ideas about property, their efforts are unlikely to succeed.

*   *   *

In this volume I have highlighted property disobedience's heterogeneity. It takes a wide array of forms, many only marginally focused on challenging property relations, and some that many people will find unacceptable. Hopefully, I have succeeded in sketching some general pointers for evaluating it. By doing so I hope to have aided both observers and participants in better understanding property disobedience's virtues *and* possible dangers.

Its diversity means that we should hesitate before subjecting it to some overarching interpretative framework. Nonetheless, some general observations seem apposite.

Property disobedients usually aim to criticize some state of affairs, hoping that their protests will build support for movement positions and ignite change. We can describe their efforts as *politically situated social critique*, with participants employing a motley mix of ideas and tactics to advance their claims and corresponding causes.

Philosophers who have reflected on social criticism have usefully delineated its *external, internal,* and *immanent* forms.[32] Typically, they do so to defend one over the other, hoping to formulate the best or most plausible account of social criticism. This is a useful task. However, property disobedience offers a messier picture: it mixes competing modes of social criticism in ways participants deem politically advantageous.

External critique relies on an independent standpoint, that is, some critical yardstick external to and separate from the norms and social practices criticized. The launching pad for critique, stated baldly, is "outside" the norms and practices to be interrogated. Frequently, external critique claims some basis in a purportedly universal moral perspective or truth. One advantage is that it offers the requisite distance from social norms and practices that may be profoundly unjust. One disadvantage is that justifying an independent, external standpoint poses hard questions. Where do these independent standards come from?

Internal and *immanent* criticism try to answer this question. Internal critique compares social actors' self-understanding to actual behavior and practice, with the gaps between them serving as a starting point for criticism. It identifies tensions between social actors' normative self-understanding and real-life practices to criticize the latter. In some distinction, immanent critique evaluates both the self-understanding of social actors and their practices by appealing to normative yardsticks internal to both. Immanent critique does not simply call out social practices for failing to follow widely shared norms. Rather, it seeks transformative changes to existing norms and practices, justifying them nonetheless on internal rather than external grounds.[33]

Property disobedience embodies elements of these competing versions of social critique. For instance, BLM activists who targeted Confederate monuments occasionally tapped *universal* notions of human dignity and basic respect. Appealing to ideals that in principle are grounded independently of and *externally* to contemporary societies, their symbolic protests were able to provide a thoroughgoing critique of racist norms and practices. Simultaneously, participants criticized oversight mechanisms for monuments and statues by highlighting *internal* inconsistencies between expressed democratic norms and less-than-democratic procedures. Obviously, they did not aim simply to call out white supremacy for failing to live up to its unexploited possibilities. They sought instead to *transcend* its long and ugly history, in the US and elsewhere, hoping to trigger the construction of a novel multiracial democracy. That political community would presumably realize not only new social practices but also innovative shared norms and ideals.

We find a similarly messy pattern among property seizures. Squatters sometimes speak the language of universal, context-transcending rights and moral claims to decent housing, a discursive framing that provides distance from and a critical perspective on local conditions. At the same time, they take advantage of widely held normative intuitions about property to criticize real-life economic relations, emphasizing gaps between property's norms and current institutions. Because both popular thinking and laws relating to property rest on a wide range of competing intuitions, doing so offers a launching pad for social criticism and political action. Finally, some activists hope to transform—and perhaps transcend—the status quo in property relations, building a new, more egalitarian property order accompanied by corresponding egalitarian norms and ideas.[34]

Admittedly, similar discursive patterns can surely be found among other protest movements and modes of political disobedience. Without attention to them, however, we cannot make sense of how property disobedience functions.

*   *   *

These general comments still say too little about property disobedience as politically situated social critique specifically directed at existing property relations. How might we view its possible contribution to the theory and practice of property?

The full ideal-typical package of private property rights, in which the owner is viewed as not only controlling but also excluding others from, using, managing, deriving income from, alienating or transferring, and bequeathing some object or resource, all for a potentially unlimited duration, has perhaps never been realized, even during the heydays of nineteenth-century liberalism. Nor should property's "complete" bundle or package be taken as describing some set of necessary or jointly sufficient traits.[35] Real-life property regimes usually compromise some of them. Lawyers point out that even core features tend to get relaxed in legal systems favoring private ownership. In the US, for example, we find tensions between the idea of property as entailing an absolute right to exclude nonowners and existing law, which is "pock-marked . . . with exceptions" when it comes to upholding the owner's exclusionary privileges.[36]

It is also well-known that the twentieth century interventionist and regulatory state drove sharp wedges between and among private property's ideal-typical traits. Berle and Means, as we saw, identified a disconnect between control or management and property's other attributes. Libertarians have long attacked modern governments for taxing and regulating private property so extensively that its foundations have allegedly buckled. Writing in 1985—ironically, just as President Reagan had begun aggressively advancing deregulation policies—legal scholar Richard A. Epstein pilloried the "current relaxed approach to regulation," which he described as working alongside an overly narrow judicial interpretation of eminent domain to invite unwarranted takings of private property. On Epstein's assessment, most twentieth-century US legislation concerning property rights not only threatened to decimate them but was legally unsound.[37]

The same trends lamented by Epstein and other conservatives were celebrated by left liberals and social democrats. Writing in the early 1970s (and thus before the ascent of Margaret Thatcher and Reagan), Macpherson agreed that the regulatory and interventionist state threatened property's key traits, arguing that the welfare state had already begun jettisoning the traditional idea of property as lasting, potentially alienable control over resources in favor of a new universal right to revenue or income. On this view, "The rise of the welfare state has created new forms of property and distributed them widely—all of them being rights to revenue. The old-age pensioner, the unemployed, and the unemployable, may have as his sole property the right to such a revenue as his condition entitles him to receive from the state. Where in addition the state provides such things as family allowances and various free or subsidized services, almost everyone has some property in such rights to a revenue."[38] Social rights to a basic income and work were emerging phoenix-like from the debris of classically liberal private property. Even those proprietors who "still might be counted as independent enterprises—the self-employed, from taxi operators to doctors—find that their property in their enterprises increasingly depends on governmental licenses to ply their trade or exercise their profession."[39] Where traditional ideas about property intuitively made sense, stringent regulations were nonetheless producing major changes.

How might property disobedience relate to these debates? One immediate answer is that it meshes with the common observation that property's "bundle" is typically incomplete. Disruptive property disobedience by those targeting environmentally irresponsible activities, for example, does not challenge the property owner's rights in toto, but instead chiefly the public utility's or private company's right to use property in destructive ways. Property seizures that involve reclaiming or reusing property violate the owner's right to exclude and potentially other rights as well. However, property's exclusionary privileges are *already* limited. Nor do squatters necessarily attack private property qua property. They seize resources to enact their own ideas of legitimate ownership, many of which reproduce familiar defenses of private property. While doing so they mimic components of its multisided bundle: they control, use, and oversee their (squatted) possessions, and sometimes hope to exclude others from impeding their endeavors.

This observation provides no normative or political defense for property disobedience. However, it illuminatingly recalls both the complexities of property as a real-life practice and property disobedience's analogous nuances. Private property's messy bundle is always unpacked and realized in different ways and to greater or lesser degrees. When viewed through this lens, property disobedience represents less a frontal attack on property rights than another attempt to disaggregate its components, in the process realizing some but not others. Some of its varieties directly parallel the interventionist and regulatory state's complicated property remix: contemporary climate eco-saboteurs strip owners of those "sticks" in property's bundle they deem harmful and inconsistent with the public good. Not surprisingly, those instinctively hostile to their and related efforts often presuppose some view of real-life property regimes as resting on absolute, "despotic" rights and perfect instantiations of its different elements. But that view is both historically misleading and normatively problematic.

Of course, what sets property disobedience's real-world modifications to property's complete package apart from others are their *illegal* contours, that is, participants break the law. In contrast, in democracy economic regulations are in principle supposed to emerge from normal legislative and judicial channels.

I have tried to attend to the various reasons property disobedients provide when justifying illegal protest. They regularly assert that the political process has been unfairly blocked or stacked against them, and that the targeted injustice or wrongdoing is sufficiently egregious to warrant immediate political action. Whether or not their claims hold water cannot be predetermined as a general matter; evaluating them calls for political judgment and attention to context and history. Significantly, property disobedients often claim, in the spirit of King and other illustrious practitioners of civil disobedience, to be expressing respect for or fidelity to law more generally. They tap a wide assortment of legal sources. Nonetheless, their acts remain illegal, and this is obviously why they remain controversial, especially in democratic societies in which a reasonable expectation of legal fidelity obtains.

Debates among property theorists are pertinent here as well. To put it crudely: social democrats like Macpherson were soon marginalized, while libertarians like Epstein won major battles. To put it in less personalized terms, major political and legal transformations since the 1980s have refurbished private property rights, pushing back against the welfare state's efforts at disaggregating and weakening some of property's traditional features. In the United States, organized business and its political allies played decisive roles in this largely successful counteroffensive.[40] Both national governments and powerful postnational global organizations (the European Union, IMF, WTO, etc.) have buttressed investor and other property rights, throwing up new roadblocks to legislatively based economic regulation and possible expropriations.[41] In the United States ours is a legal era aptly characterized as "property resurgent," as courts have made it difficult to regulate or take property without government being forced to provide costly compensation.[42]

Democratic regimes are still tasked with tackling economic challenges, and some do so with a measure of success. There is also at present a sizable pushback afoot, from both the left and right, against neoliberal ideology and policy. Nonetheless, we should hesitate before overstating its impact: large banks and corporations remain extraordinarily well positioned to ward off interventionist measures.[43] Despite the ways in which technological innovations and especially digitalization potentially challenge the old idea of property as exclusive control over some object or "thing," we continue to witness a remarkable proprietization of creative activity, data, information, and knowledge, disproportionately benefiting companies able to secure copyrights, patents, and trademarks to a massive range of intangible but highly profitable goods and services (data, biotech, personal information, etc.). Even as recent technologies have opened the door to common or public access (e.g., the new "sharing economy"), corporations have beaten back efforts to do so.[44] Not surprisingly, property disobedience now often fuses with hacktivism, that is, politically inspired hacking, with hacktivists advancing their causes by damaging computers or stealing intangible property and valuable public and private data.[45]

In Chapter 1, I cautiously suggested that this broad political shift is important *empirically* for understanding property disobedience's apparent proliferation. Now let me suggest that it is *normatively* important for evaluating its possible legitimacy. As both nation-states and postnational political orders have loaded the dice against efforts by ordinary people and their elected representatives to regulate property, people have taken things into their own hands, that is, pursued illegal protests targeting property. This should come as no surprise: when peaceful legal change becomes difficult or effectively impossible, militant extra-legal protest frequently ensues.

Protests targeting property can always prove poorly conceived or executed. But when participants act nonviolently and with some sense of proportion, while making identifiably public appeals, their acts become in principle justifiable even when illegal. Given the urgency of the identified problems, in conjunction with sizable roadblocks to challenging property rights via ordinary political channels, we should appreciate why property disobedients take to the streets. That hardly means giving them a free hand, or endorsing everything they do or stand for. Nor does it entail legalizing acts that should remain, on general grounds, illegal. Quite understandably, people should not have to worry about squatters occupying their living rooms, or small businesses distress over opportunistic shoplifting. But it does suggest that we need to recognize property disobedience's potential legitimacy, and that state actors—including judges and prosecutors—should respond respectfully and sometimes with magnanimity, when appropriate. The rule of law is a complicated ideal, but it is conceptually wrong and politically irresponsible to reduce its multipronged quest for legal generality, publicity, and stability to nothing more than "law and order."[46]

It would also be a mistake to equate the rule of law with stringent protections for existing property rights: on the most defensible interpretations of the rule of law, it remains analytically separate from any defense of private property. To be sure, the rule of law's preference for constancy and predictability in the law militates against abrupt shifts in property relations. Property disobedience can obviously produce such shifts. Even so, "it by no means follows that the law has to preserve the value of any given item of property, in order to facilitate market transactions" and provide a general measure of legal security to most proprietors.[47] Property disobedience does not, in other words, typically pose a fundamental threat to market relations. The rule of law's various elements often protect existing property owners, but their realization can also be achieved by carefully crafted legislation that legitimately reins them in when their endeavors generate harm.[48] In a similar vein, property disobedients sometimes plausibly claim that they, in fact, are respectful of legality or the constitution, and that existing proprietors are the ones who have in fact neglected their legal obligations.

Especially when protest participants—for example, unhoused squatters—face dire material circumstances, it is terribly unfair to categorically condemn their efforts. Yes, they *take* property owned by others, but arguably in part because *legal* takings by government, when justified on redistributive grounds, are now too often out of bounds. Before the ascent of neoliberalism, one might have realistically expected their and parallel concerns to get a fair hearing in the halls of government, with a real possibility for constructive policy responses. Not that long ago, even relatively middle-of-the-road politicians might have called for new public housing, for example, in response to dire housing shortages. Today, many governments are afraid of raising taxes to foot the bill, let alone infringing on sacred property rights when asserted by the privileged and powerful. They find it easier to pass draconian statutes that criminalize and demonize poor and sometimes desperate people.

* * *

But doesn't this defense of property disobedience invite irresponsible attacks on property? Even if it makes sense to delineate it from political violence, might not the justification I have sketched downgrade the virtues of a consistently enforced system of general rights and legality, even in less than ideal political and social circumstances? The rule of law is not everything, yet it is still more than nothing.[49]

These are serious reservations. Throughout this volume I have tried to respond to them. When responsibly conducted, property disobedience implicitly acknowledges them by, for example, drawing on the law to ground its acts and practicing strict nonviolence vis-à-vis persons. Political nonviolence, I have argued, is essential to democracy and the ideal of political equality. To the extent that the rule of law can also be interpreted as relating to basic ideas of human dignity, nonviolence is essential to it as well.

To respond in a somewhat different vein to these worries, let me conclude by identifying another link between property disobedience and democratic politics.

If the (apparent) proliferation of property disobedience is indeed related to heightened property protections and dramatic proprietarization of social existence, then the way to reduce its frequency would be to counter them. That is, if we could revitalize our democracies, giving electorates and their representatives enhanced oversight of property, then ordinary people would not have to take to the streets to act illegally.[50] Since property disobedients often face harsh legal sanctions, the vast majority would likely prefer following more conventional political paths. If the unhoused could count on respectful responses from public authorities, they would not have to squat. Green militants could return their copies of *How to Blow Up a Pipeline* to the library and focus on lobbying legislators for stricter restrictions on climate-killing economic activities.

Of course, no political or social order is ever likely to be perfect; even superior democratic and more egalitarian polities will provide grounds for principled nonviolent lawbreaking. But some of property disobedience's sources would then have dissipated.

Pertinent here is that a great deal of property disobedience involves efforts to guarantee the basic fundaments of equal political membership. Recent symbolic protests, for example, push back against monuments and statues that systematically degrade and humiliate political peers, communicating to them on behalf of the community at large fundamental disrespect. This is why racist public statues and monuments have no place in democracy. Some disruptive protests target activities (for example, climate-killing emissions) that threaten the natural premises of human existence, without which no political community—and certainly no successful *democratic* polity—can realistically flourish. Property seizures by Native peoples can be interpreted as efforts to gain respect and reassert basic rights to self-determination. In the US, they are often calls to renegotiate the badly frayed ties between Native sovereignty, on the one hand, and federal and state governments, on the other. Squatters insist that people deserve land from which they can earn a living or a home granting them some place in the world without which autonomy is unrealizable.

Let me reiterate that any generalizing analysis of property disobedience risks ignoring its complexity and heterogeneity. Still, viewed from a wider lens many variants constitute endeavors to reestablish necessary preconditions for effective democratic citizenship. They highlight the necessity of mutual respect, meaningful access to basic material goods, and protections for the natural presuppositions of a decent social existence.

This author appreciates the reasons so many flinch at the suggestion that such goods can only be acquired by illegal means. There is, indeed, a preferable *legal* alternative. Macpherson pointed to its features many decades ago: property needs to be reconceived primarily as a right "to the means of a fully human life," without which the "right to share in political power" is necessarily impaired.[51] Contemporary property theorists endorse the same general point: property and laws supporting it should better "promote the ability of each person to obtain the material resources necessary for full and equal participation" in a shared democratic community, which means that property serving exploitative and humiliating purposes has to be out bounds.[52] More generally, property relations will need to be better organized to "establish the framework for a kind of social life appropriate to a free and democratic society."[53] Doing so requires experiments with novel forms and mixes of public and private property. This is not the place to speculate about their ideal contours. However, we can be sure that bringing about significant changes will prove extraordinarily difficulty: those benefiting from the present-day property status quo have "enormous resources at their disposal," many of which can be quickly translated into political advantages, whereas "those who have very little to lose fear losing what they have."[54] For this reason as well, we should acknowledge property disobedience's possible merits: it offers a valuable tool to challenge existing property relations and help level the political playing field.

In an eloquent intellectual eulogy for Supreme Court Justice William Brennan, legal theorist Frank Michelman argued for reconceiving property as the "material foundation for political competence," and thus an "indispensable ingredient in the constitution of the individual as a participant in the life of society, including not least the society's processes for collectively regulating" social affairs.[55] If property is to complement democratic ideals of equal concern and mutual respect, it needs to be reinvented as a legal guarantee for material security, broadly conceived.[56] Property rights should morph, in part, into robust welfare and social rights, without which a thriving democracy cannot be constructed.

Those vexed by the prospect of lawless attacks on property should sympathize with this project. Property disobedients pursue illegal routes to gain necessary goods because the existing political order too often denies them legal access. Until we have forged a more egalitarian and just property order, we cannot in good faith categorically condemn their efforts.

CHAPTER 7

Goodbye to Nonviolence?

T his volume has sought to carve out political space for property disobedience. Even as it remains illegal and participants should generally expect to face legal repercussions, property disobedience can
serve constructive purposes. Both citizens and state officials should treat it
with a measure of respect denied run-of-the-mill criminality. Property disobedience's justifiability, however, says nothing about its efficacy. Even variants most akin to nonviolent civil disobedience often prove controversial and
ignite fierce backlashes. Determining whether property disobedience in any
context makes political sense demands nuanced judgments depending on
complicated contingencies. Political theorists can provide only limited advice
about such matters.

Pragmatic political grounds militate against normalizing types of property disobedience that ideally would remain exceptional, and thus only to be
pursued in the face of pressing injustice after other political and legal channels
have been exhausted. Property disobedience breaks taboos: because of property's privileged status even relatively innocuous renditions prove contentious. For its practitioners, of course, that is precisely the point: they want to
bring attention to some inequity. Their reasons for doing so may be laudable,
yet breaking taboos is a double-edged sword. Those who have conscientiously
targeted property with their nonviolent protests "constrained, proportionate,
and discriminating, such that their intended impacts are concentrated as far
as possible on wrongdoing" inadvertently invite copycat acts that ignore similar restrictions.[1] Taboo breaking tends to pave the way for "moral holidays"
like those characterizing riot-related looting. Protestors who violated taboos
against property damage may have done so carefully and discriminately, but
once the genie is out of the bottle things sometimes get messier.

Part of a widespread right-wing narrative of the January 6, 2021 attack on the US Capitol, for example, is that the prior summer 2020 BLM protests were at least as—and probably more—destructive. Participants in the January 6 upheavals like to pose a rhetorical question: if "they" (that is, political progressives) get away with political violence, why are "we" (i.e., "real" Americans supporting President Trump) being prosecuted for less violent acts?

Despite the Trump Administration's pardon of January 6 militants, that question remains tone-deaf. The BLM protests were predominantly nonviolent. In contrast, physical intimidation and violence were essential to the Capitol attacks. This strategic misappropriation nonetheless highlights a danger. Property disobedients may conduct themselves responsibly, yet their acts can still serve as precedents to be exploited by the irresponsible. In the heat of political battle, as basic a distinction as nonviolence vis-à-vis persons but not property can get lost. That prospect should not deter protest movements targeting injustice: they cannot be held fully responsible for how others down the road interpret their acts. But it must remain central to their political calculations. Political responsibility always demands that we reflect on likely consequences and minimize foreseeable dangers.

My effort to provide limited room for property disobedience has relied heavily on demonstrating its congruence with political nonviolence vis-à-vis persons, interpreted as resting on the basic democratic ideal of equal respect. When property disobedience instead is complicit in—or turns out to be intimately related to—violence against persons, it undermines democracy's normative bases. Although commonly viewed as intrinsically violent, property disobedience turns out to be significantly more complex. Our examination has not only challenged broad-brushed condemnations but also corroborated common intuitions. Many people, for instance, instinctively reject looting or other acts substantially damaging to private residences or small businesses; they rightly view them as less defensible than knocking down a public memorial or spray-painting the office front of a globally operating corporation. That difference partly stems from an intuitive sense that the former but not the latter entail violence to persons. It also derives from an implicit grasp that not all property is cut from the same cloth, and that differences between and among property's varieties matter.

Nonetheless, my approach remains out of sync with those who reject principled political nonviolence. For a growing number of activists and intellectuals, nonviolent movement politics is at best quaint and at worst naive and perhaps dangerous.[2] Within recent decades, the tide seems to have turned against what had previously been a broad consensus that nonviolent protest was not only morally superior but also more likely to be politically effective than its violent cousin.[3] Those now riding that tide are likely to view my efforts as a rearguard action. With the continued rise of authoritarian populism, their voices may come to dominate the debate.

I cannot fully respond to the many criticisms now being levelled against political nonviolence; doing so would take us beyond the scope of the present study. But I will try to sketch provisional responses to the most pertinent criticisms.

*   *   *

Many writers endorsing violent protest operate with broad and frequently open-ended notions of violence along the lines criticized in Chapter 2, with some going so far as to suggest that its indefinability implies omnipresence.[4] Whenever a vast array of activities gets viewed as intrinsically or prospectively violent, it indeed becomes hard to escape its logic. To put it bluntly: if we consider violence ubiquitous, even at first glance nonviolent protests are likely to appear latently violent. Political actors may naively claim they can jettison violent for nonviolent protest, but in fact they simply face "a question of choosing between two different forms of violence."[5] Accordingly, some writers not only discount clear boundaries between violence and nonviolence but also describe seemingly harmless activities as potentially dangerous.

The philosopher Kimberley Brownlee sketches a sophisticated version of this position. As she points out, "catapulting stuffed animals at the police or shooting into the sky" might be seen as violent because such acts contain a "considerable risk of harm."[6] Initially innocent protests can prove destructive. Therefore, it is no longer useful to insist on civil disobedience taking strictly nonviolent forms. Like many others, Brownlee thinks violence a confused concept likely to get in the way of clear thinking about civil disobedience.[7] The real issues up for debate should be "harm, abuse, and neglect of person's needs," and when and how they should be minimized.[8]

Brownlee is right that violence is an irrepressibly contestable concept. Yet so are harm, abuse, and neglect. Moreover, they and other similar terms are neither equivalent to violence nor fully capture what we commonly associate with it.[9] She is also right that even apparently innocuous acts can prove injurious: that is why political judgment is essential to their evaluation. Nonetheless, it is illusory to think that we can sideline messy debates about violence by simply shifting conceptual terrains: the dilemmas we face when trying to understand violence inevitably resurface elsewhere. For reasons already explored we should be skeptical of overly inclusive definitions reminiscent of what Hegel described as a night in which all cows are black. Even if the boundaries between force, coercion, and violence sometimes blur, predominantly nonviolent protests can still be distinguished from violent ones.[10] Violence's conceptual contestability does not require that we abandon the quest to identify more rather than less sound renditions.

I recognize that many will be reluctant to accept tightly circumscribed definitions of violence. Yet such skeptics should still appreciate my attempt in this volume to take on board one of their intuitions, namely: stringent nonviolence vis-à-vis objects (and property) is normatively expendable. Crucially, those writers allowing more room for political violence rarely endorse it in respect to *persons* or as *organized collective violence*; on those rare occasions when doing so, they often have *nondemocratic* contexts in mind.[11] When discussing protest-related violence they tend in fact to reference property damage.[12] Of course, I have rejected categorizing property disobedience as essentially violent. Like such writers, however, I endorse the claim that property damage plays a potentially fruitful role in protest politics. Overstated criticisms of political nonviolence notwithstanding, critics in fact are often merely defending acts of property damage potentially congruent with it.[13]

Similar confusion surfaces in another context. According to the perspective defended in this book, political nonviolence and democracy go together. Democratic commitments to equal respect do not ordinarily permit violence between and among political peers. This claim is consistent with a wide variety of democratic theories, so long as they pay more than lip service to the crucial idea of political equality.[14] Unfortunately, some writers today rejecting nonviolence suggest that permissible political lawbreaking in a democracy is structurally analogous to that in dictatorship, a view that discounts democracy's real—but increasingly fragile—virtues.[15] There are reasons why violent protest is permissible in authoritarian states. In contrast, since democracy presumably guarantees basic rights and provides meaningful possibilities to shape lawmaking, anyone who opts to pursue extra-legal protest (including property disobedience) should be expected to pass more demanding tests—for instance, practicing nonviolence vis-à-vis other members of the political community.

In a related vein, some writers condone violent protest because of critical assessments of existing democracy.[16] Delmas, for example, characterizes societies like our own as plagued by deep structural inequalities and "all-too-often-unjust conditions."[17] Existing liberal polities "fall somewhere between the two extremes" of basically legitimate and illegitimate regimes.[18] There is much to be said on behalf of this assessment. But it still rests on complex *political* diagnoses and judgments about messy empirical matters, rather than more general theoretical or philosophical theses. While raising pressing questions about the nexus between democracy's real-life instantiations and its normative contours, this view leaves unchallenged the core idea of a fundamental elective affinity between democracy and political nonviolence.

To be clear: I agree that present-day democracies often fail to pass muster. Authoritarian populism and democratic backsliding, as we will see, exacerbate this enigma.[19] Even so, such diagnoses do not necessarily offer a principled critique of democracy, conceived as a relatively demanding political project, premised on a commitment to nonviolence between and among political peers. Democratic ideals relate in complicated ways to empirical realities: without implicit appeals to demanding normative counterfactuals, we cannot make sense of real-world democratic practice. In pluralistic communities, we are likely to encounter reasonable disagreements, resting on a wide range of empirical assessments and judgments, concerning the extent to which any real-existing democracy satisfies some democratic normative minimum. Those legitimately worried about existing democracy's blemishes should remain in principle committed to nonviolence, even when assessments of conditions sometimes lead them to relax some of its strictures.

Among some political thinkers, hard-headed empirical diagnoses occasionally fuse with a more far-reaching skepticism and principled denial of democracy's superiority vis-à-vis its authoritarian rivals. For example, the libertarian philosopher Jason Brennan insists that potentially violent uncivil lawbreaking is permissible even in "reasonably just democratic states."[20] Why? In part because they apparently are *not* just in any minimal sense. Brennan's skeptical views about democracy lead him to blur any divides vis-à-vis dictatorship: "If you may kill a Gestapo agent to stop him from murdering innocent people, may you do the same to a police officer [in the contemporary USA] who uses excessive violence?"[21] Brennan's answer seems to be "yes," in part because there is supposedly little separating the Gestapo from police officers in existing democratic states. Brennan has few qualms, unsurprisingly, about abandoning universal suffrage.

I cannot fully address such principled theoretical assaults on democracy. But their most relevant prongs involve sidelining nonviolence by building on congenitally *anti-statist* intuitions. For anarchists and some libertarians, the most egregious problem with principled nonviolence is that it ignores and thereby trivializes the horrors of state violence and its many pathologies—for example, racialized, excessively violent policing.[22] On this view, supposedly "moralistic" nonviolence aficionados deny the weakest and most vulnerable members of society the right to defend themselves against state actors who—sometimes working at the behest of the economically privileged—repressively wield state power. The state's monopoly on legitimate violence means that "systemic violence is prevalent throughout liberal democratic societies."[23] Given that reality, it seems misguided to discount the possibility of "protest violence that seeks to reject this wider violence."[24] Especially when protest-related violence invigorates debate or unlocks previously closed political doors, it contributes constructively to self-government. Nonviolence's defenders not only hypocritically deny the democratic state's own congenitally violent contours but also naively ignore violent protest's constructive role.

This view directly counters the idea of an elective affinity between democracy and nonviolence, in part with empirical claims about the political utility of protest-related violence targeting persons. Yet that claim requires scrutiny; it marginalizes substantial empirical research.[25] More fundamentally, it downplays that even when violent protest prospectively generates political benefits it does so at the cost of attacking the idea of equal respect on which democracy depends. Violence disables and disempowers political peers, something hard to sync with efforts to preserve democracy. Since Niccolo Machiavelli we have known that political means and ends do not always neatly mesh: immoral means can serve moral ends, whereas strictly moral means may generate immoral consequences. Yet, political violence in a democracy is not simply another morally ambivalent tool, akin to a sordid political deal or shady legislative compromise. Politicians who unleash military force against peaceful protestors, for example, attack the foundations of shared democratic politics. Violence violates other persons in profoundly injurious ways, threatening to remove them from the political playing field altogether. In a democratic community, political violence does not simply remind us of the familiar tensions between morality and politics: it entails an assault on fundamental commitments to political equality.

It also seems ungenerous to assert that practitioners and theorists of nonviolence have trivialized the harsh realities of modern state power. That political tradition's most famous representatives (Gandhi, King) can hardly be accused of having done so. If anything, they were preoccupied with the modern Leviathan's violent capacities. That is precisely why they sought to transform it into a decidedly less dangerous creature, an admirable political goal they thought realistically achievable, for a variety of reasons, only via nonviolent political paths.

More to the point, nothing in my defense of an elective affinity between democracy and nonviolence denies the ugly realities of state violence. Rather, it provides a springboard for criticizing state practices that degrade and injure citizens and other community members. Legal enforcement is a sine qua non of any institutional framework we might plausibly call a "state." But in *democratic* states, where violence vis-à-vis political peers is always normatively suspect, we are obliged to seek enforcement mechanisms that do not harm or violate them. When police officers brutalize prisoners or shoot unarmed suspects, or customs officials brutalize migrants or refugees, they engage in violence inconsistent with basic commitments to mutual respect and political equality. The fact that they are state officials and wear uniforms hardly renders their acts less violent or a priori legitimate. Of course, there are difficult questions about state officials' political and legal obligations, which potentially vary from those of ordinary citizens.[26] But in democratic settings, officials are expected to abide the general rules of law. In principle, they are empowered to deploy violence only under exceptional circumstances, after having cleared the highest legal and normative hurdles.

Those who condemn racialized policing or draconian criminal sanctions correctly intuit that those hurdles are now too low. In the US, police officers possess extraordinary discretion in managing political protests to a degree inconsistent with any view of the rule of law as requiring generality and regularity in state action.[27] Militarized law enforcement means that even peaceful protestors now often face disproportionate state violence. During the 2020 BLM protests, for example, police in at least 100 US cities fired tear gas at overwhelmingly nonviolent protestors.[28] They also launched "flash grenades, assaulted demonstrators and members of the press, made mass arrests, targeted journalists, and used force in many situations where negotiations or de-escalation were clear options."[29] It is hard to envisage how such acts cohere with democracy's core commitment to political equality.

State-backed violence targeting the political community's constituents always threatens to damage democracy's egalitarian core. The fact that such violence remains widespread suggests that democracy's essential presuppositions have been neglected. Democracy remains an ongoing, incomplete political project. Yet its evident failings hardly demonstrate that the democratic state is a priori hypocritical and its quest for nonviolence between and among its members vacuous.

*   *   *

Another challenge to principled nonviolence is posed by militants and sympathetic intellectuals who endorse violent self-defense, usually in response precisely to the harsh police and security crackdowns that many governments now endorse. Because my focus has been property disobedience, I have ignored this part of the story. Nonetheless, it complicates the idea of democratic nonviolence.

Violent self-defense can be linked to a variety of political and ideological causes. Its justifications can take right- as well as left-wing forms, and sometimes a confused medley of both. Recent BLM protestors occasionally responded to police violence by fighting back; those who opposed stringent coronavirus restrictions did so as well. On January 23, 2022, for example, Belgian COVID-19 anti-lockdown protestors hurled metal fences and burning dustbins at police officers, with both police officers and protestors requiring hospitalization.[30] The sources of this now seemingly global trend are complicated, yet there is no question that some militants are rejecting nonviolence when interpreted as categorically prohibiting *any* physical violence against other persons. Nonviolence as requiring, as King insisted, that protestors "accept blows from the opponent without striking back" and thus refrain from acts of violent self-defense, now seems naive to many protestors and their sympathizers.[31] Some engaging in self-defense are doing so as part of collective, politically coordinated efforts. In Hong Kong, for example, pro-democracy activists countered repressive attacks on their initially peaceful protests by employing heat-resistant gloves to toss tear gas canisters back at security officials. Like many others elsewhere, they had apparently lost faith in King's Gandhian hope that accepting violence possesses "tremendous educational and transformational possibilities."[32]

Correspondingly, theorists of civil disobedience are providing space for "some measure of self-defense in the face of assault by others, such as the police or security personnel."[33] Delmas and others defend politically motivated, collective vigilantism, when justifiable as self-defense and meeting basic normative standards.[34] Anarchists and libertarians give yet wider berth to violent self-defense.[35] The radical French philosopher Elsa Dorlin has recently penned a celebratory defense of it.[36]

These developments raise difficult questions. Some modest observations will have to suffice for now.

Self-defense has always represented a borderline case for largely nonviolent movements. Why condemn predominantly peaceful protestors who fight back against militarized police and security forces? If acts of self-defense ward off avoidable harms and remain strictly proportionate to the threats at hand, why not allow them? Every legal system provides room for self-defense in the face of imminent threats to persons and property. Why deny that right to otherwise peaceful protestors? For pacifists and those, like Gandhi, who reject violence on spiritual grounds, the answers are clear enough. But for many others, when defensive violence is strictly limited and usefully circumvents unnecessary injuries it represents an unavoidable but morally defensible compromise with an imperfect political world.

Recent writers providing normative leeway for violent self-defense have even tapped King to do so.[37] King, after all, publicly declared that the individual's right to defend "one's home and person against lawless assaults" was respected in moral and legal codes around the world.[38] Such a right to self-defense, he observed, had long been "guaranteed by the Constitution and respected even in the worst areas of the South."[39]

In fact, King helps us avoid some politically perilous confusion, though not in the manner suggested by those sympathetic to calls for violent self-defense.

Although recognizing the individual's right to self-defense, King refused to defend such a right in the context of *organized political movements*. He condemned "the advocacy of violence as a tool of advancement, organized as in warfare, deliberately and consciously," as part of collective political efforts for self-defense.[40] Amid political protests, "self-defense must be approached from quite another perspective" than in conventional moral codes or existing legal systems.[41] He never embraced calls for armed self-defense emanating from Robert F. Williams, Stokely Carmichael, Malcolm X, and others whose hostility to his nonviolent choices gained political traction in the mid-1960s. For King their mistake was to move too quickly from endorsing an individual moral and legal to a collective political right to self-defense.

The individual's right to ward off assaults to their person and property was qualitatively different from protest movements that arm and train their followers, "as in warfare, deliberately and consciously," for violent self-defense.[42]

For King, violence as part of a "collective struggle" for social change had to be distinguished from individual violence aimed at protecting one's person or home.[43] The former was a political intervention; the latter an individual's effort to preserve bodily integrity and personal possessions. They followed different logics, usually pursued different goals, and generated different consequences. Conflating them was a mistake.

Why the widespread tendency to do so? Calls for individual self-defense are easily transformed into demands to defend some broader collectivity. Butler has nicely captured the dilemma: "Who is this 'self' defended in the name of self-defense? How is that self delineated from other selves, from history, land, or other defining relations" and identities?[44] Given the ways in which the "self" is always dependent on and intermeshed with others, what impedes calls for individual self-defense from quickly encompassing a defense of one's family, political allies, or "own" people or nation? "If one will kill for this or that person who is proximate and affiliated, what finally distinguishes the proximate from the non-proximate, and under what conditions could that distinction be regarded as ethically justifiable?"[45] Especially when political conflicts become explosive, the boundaries between individual and collective self-defense become porous. Self-defense risks getting "defined so loosely as to allow all sorts of aggressive actions."[46]

King sketched many reasons for insisting on preserving the distinction. But there is no question that he took it seriously. He repeatedly praised militants who refused to respond to violence with self-defensive counterviolence. Nonviolent activists, he argued, should know that "suffering becomes a powerful social force when you willingly accept that violence on yourself."[47] Doing so sometimes meant incurring real dangers; in such instances, identifiably nonviolent protective measures were a proper response. Describing the violent reprisals faced by peaceful activists on August 5, 1966 in Chicago's Marquette Park, King commented: "These marchers endured not only the filthiest kind of verbal abuse, but also barrages of rocks and sticks and eggs and cherry bombs. They did not reply in words or violent deeds. . . . [T]heir only weapon was their own bodies. I saw boys like Goat leap into the air to catch with their bare hands the bricks and bottles that were sailed toward us."[48] Such acts were acceptable since bricks and bottles posed immediate, life-threatening perils. Snatching them out of the air generated no such perils. Measures of this type remained nonviolent because they did not involve harmful retaliation against violent wrongdoers. Catching a brick or bottle before it smashes your skull is different from aggressively throwing them back at counterdemonstrators.

Admittedly, King's view relied on Christian and Gandhian foundations that many will reject.[49] Nonetheless, it still poses difficult questions for contemporary writers who defend violent self-defense as a potentially legitimate contribution to protest politics.

In contrast to King's careful reflections, some now justify self-defense as little more than an afterthought.[50] Others make precisely the quick leap from individual to collective self-defense King rejected: "The individual case for self-defensive violence can extend to the collective."[51] Like King, writers now doing so reject retaliatory and aggressive violence: any harm inflicted by self-defensive political vigilantes "must be a proportional (necessary and fitting) response to an immediate threat."[52] Yet their expositions still remain insufficiently attuned to the dynamics of *collective political* violence. Movements that embrace violent self-defense tend to take on martial contours and treat their acts as contributions to organized warfare, something that meshes poorly with democracy and the idea of political equality. Militaristic calls for organized self-defense distort and frequently poison political discourse. When political groups opt for paramilitary tactics, the cause at hand—along with the exploitation and oppression that motivated protestors—frequently gets submerged in overheated, emotional debates about violence and its tactics. Calls for violence personalize political issues that are properly viewed in structural or systemic terms: "For through violence you may murder a murderer but you can't murder murder."[53] Violence humiliates political opponents, making it impossible to win them over. In deeply unjust societies in which dominant groups are always ready and eager to clamp down on dissent, organized, collective self-defense invites repression: "The minute a program of violence is enunciated, even for self-defense, the atmosphere is filled with talk of violence, and the words falling on unsophisticated ears" open the door to an authoritarian backlash.[54]

Contemporary writers now busily outlining abstract conditions (usually derived from just war theory) for the justifiable deployment of self-defensive violence risk ignoring hard-won political lessons. They downplay, for instance, the very real prospect that even tightly circumscribed calls for self-defense invite privileged groups angered by protest violence to pursue supposedly self-defensive vigilante action *against* protestors, with sometimes disastrous ramifications.[55] One particularly ominous contemporary trend, as encouraged by the US Supreme Court's expansive interpretation of the Second Amendment, is the growing prominence of openly armed protestors and counter-protestors at public rallies.[56] Whatever its constitutional merits, the failure to restrict firearms at public demonstrations appears to have had a "significant negative impact on individuals' willingness to attend public protests, vocalize their opinions at protest events, carry signs, and bring children to public protests."[57] As King predicted, a martial mindset—including what increasingly appears to take the form of an arms race between protestors and their opponents—impairs the difficult work of democratic politics and movement building.

I cannot in good faith categorically deny *any* place for political self-defense, especially under increasingly undemocratic and unjust conditions. Like King, however, I worry that movements that embrace it risk succumbing to a martial mindset inconsonant with democratic politics. In the violent societies in which many of us reside, King's vision of an alternative universe in which it has been reduced to a minimum remains attractive. Anyone practicing or endorsing violent self-defense needs to be sure that their acts will minimize and not contribute to more terrible violence. In more or less democratic contexts, they should be expected to jump some extraordinarily high hurdles. Only in the most extreme circumstances will they probably be able to clear them.

* * *

There is now a rough scholarly consensus "that some time in the late 1990s the bloom started to go off the democratizing rose," with a growing number of observers "introducing notes of worry and sometimes alarm about the global health of democracy," a trend that accelerated in the aftermath of the 2008 global financial crisis.[58] Evidence of democratic decay, in conjunction with the ascent of political leaders such as Narendra Modi, Viktor Orban, and Donald Trump, vividly highlight the dangers at hand. These worrisome tendencies do not undermine the idea of an elective affinity between democracy and political nonviolence. However, as existing democracies become *decreasingly* democratic, that elective affinity risks becoming politically less relevant. Nonviolence follows from our commitments to mutual respect and political equality. When authoritarian populists establish regimes that systematically violate them, nonviolence's foundations become precarious. If state repression becomes regularized, an ongoing "irruption of violence" into the lives of ordinary people results, releasing "citizens from their democratic duty of nonviolence."[59]

Moral, prudential, and tactical reasons will understandably lead many to reject violent protest. Smart political actors might still decide that nonviolence provides the best path to counter authoritarianism. Yet they cannot exclude it categorically based on appeals to fundamental political principle.

Populism relies on a political imaginary in which "the people," interpreted in exclusionary terms, is sharply juxtaposed to a corrupt "elite."[60] In principle, it can take either left- or right-wing forms. Populists devalue constitutionalism and the rule of law, as conventionally viewed from various liberal and democratic perspectives. They exploit tensions internal to democracy itself while disfiguring it. Populism parasitically taps gaps between the principle of popular sovereignty and the institutions of representative democracy to discredit the latter.[61] At present, populism's right-wing authoritarian variants—some of which have already taken sizable steps toward disabling core democratic institutions and norms—pose the greatest threats in the Global North. In extreme cases, authoritarian populist regimes will successfully institutionalize what political scientist Andreas Schedler calls "electoral authoritarianism." They maintain "institutions of liberal democracy on paper, yet subvert them in practice through severe, widespread, and systematic manipulation."[62] Hungary, for example, formally remains a multiparty system that holds regular elections for key officeholders, while subjecting them "to manifold forms of authoritarian manipulation" that are "severe and systematic enough to fracture the [democratic] *minima moralia*," or democracy's minimal core elements.[63] The regime mimics democracy while robbing it of essential features.[64] Elections take place and remain modestly competitive. Yet opposition parties and candidates are subjected to harassment and intimidation. Electoral results may be manipulated. Civil society is eviscerated, either by direct or indirect means. The media are rendered compliant and subservient. Staged forms of manipulated deliberation and participation manufacture popular consent. Although populist leaders there and elsewhere prefer to avoid deploying violence against critics, they still revert to it when convenient. They use the power and prestige of their official positions to legitimize novel modes of conspiracy thinking that function to degrade democracy and its pillars.[65] Doing so is part of an updated authoritarian playbook having some new instruments of "smart repression" designed to prevent politically destabilizing popular backlashes.[66]

In less extreme scenarios, populist leaders and their followers aspire to disable democracy's *minima moralia* and may have begun doing so. Some democratic decay notwithstanding they have failed to bring about major institutional shifts. Yet other scenarios represent even messier, more fully hybrid cases, with elements of authoritarianism and liberal democracy confusingly overlapping and crisscrossing.

Such variations matter: whether a particular regime has only incompletely but not severely or systematically fractured democracy's basic core or minimum is crucial.[67] Democracy's friends need to distinguish between and among different political contexts, for example, Xi Jinping's China, Orban's Hungary, Trump's United States, or contemporary Australia or Norway. The political obligations normally owed "extensively" or "mostly" democratic states are surely greater than those owed "barely" democratic ones. Only a sufficiently nuanced understanding of the relevant political particulars allows us to delineate more fully authoritarian (e.g., China) from basically liberal and democratic (Germany or Sweden) states, or cases like Modi's India, where authoritarian populists have successfully maintained power and chalked up substantial antidemocratic victories. We also need similarly fine-grained political assessments of *specific* types of politically oriented lawbreaking and their preconditions. Some but not all potentially violent acts may be acceptable and perhaps appropriate under mostly or extensively authoritarian conditions that should remain basically unacceptable elsewhere.[68]

Where authoritarian populists have taken office and made inroads yet failed to bring about extensive backsliding, we encounter updated versions of an otherwise familiar phenomenon: political systems that in key respects remain identifiably democratic yet include significant democratic lacunae and injustices. Since passage of the Voting Rights Act (1965), the United States, for example, has guaranteed a measure of political competition and basic rights, even as it has suffered from anachronistic and arguably undemocratic institutions and practices (for example, the electoral college, gerrymandering) and many social ills, including high levels of material inequality. The idea that nonviolence should only obtain under some (perhaps unrealizable) ideal democratic condition would render it politically meaningless. Since democracy is an ongoing, perhaps necessarily imperfect project, even the existence of some defects should not impede the embrace of nonviolence. In political affairs, as in other areas of social existence, shortcomings are unavoidable. Even as many of us recognize that political equality has only been realized incompletely, we remain committed to it as a foundational norm. If we agree that political equality demands nonviolence vis-à-vis our political peers, then it should also remain generally applicable.

This remains a defense of principled *yet imperfect* democratic nonviolence vis-à-vis persons. Recall that even Rawls left room for militant, potentially violent protest in existing democracies, while arguing that violence against persons should generally be avoided.[69] He correctly recognized that under more or less democratic conditions people would disagree about controversial political matters, with some activists likely pursuing more militant resistance when nonviolent protest and civil disobedience failed to block extreme injustice.[70]

If existing democracies descend into unambiguously authoritarian territory, more of our political peers are likely to do just that. As President Trump and his associates successfully degrade America's increasingly embattled constitutional democracy, some citizens may end up kissing goodbye to nonviolence, at least as a principled commitment grounded in political equality.

In some contrast, the left-liberal Rawls hoped that as existing democracies underwent successful reforms, any grounds for violent uncivil protest would dissipate. For his part, King—Rawls's political contemporary and inspiration for his reflections on civil disobedience—had no illusions about American democracy's myriad failings and terrible injustices. Yet he adamantly rejected political violence: he doubted its capacity to contribute constructively to some more just, superior democratic future. On King's view, only principled nonviolence could help build a future political and social world worth inhabiting. As Andrew Sabl has nicely put it, for King and his associates it was a matter of "looking forward rather than backward," acknowledging that even when violence seems permissible it would make future cooperation between the oppressed and oppressors impossible.[71]

Admittedly, the possibility of such cooperation presupposes a shared commitment to living together in a basically democratic polity. Authoritarian populists who demonize rivals and treat them like existential "enemies" directly undermine that possibility. Political systems that come to occupy a sort of halfway house between dictatorship and democracy do so as well.

Given the severe challenges many democracies presently face, these and similar calls for political nonviolence are likely to seem quaint and perhaps obsolete. Nonetheless, there is no reason to assume that violent political resistance is better suited to resisting authoritarian tendencies rather than simply reproducing their logic, particularly when democracy is under attack but remains part of the real-world equation. This should not surprise us: both political violence and authoritarian populism negate the principle of political equality on which democracy depends.

In her illuminating study of the frequently ugly history of violent, uncivil political disobedience in the US, the political theorist Jennet Kirkpatrick has demonstrated how its practitioners frequently presupposed a troublesome anti-pluralistic idea of "the people," outfitted with unchecked authority to act beyond and against law, and thus as rightfully equipped with power to override ordinary legal mechanisms blocking its will. Frontier vigilantes, lynch mobs, and homegrown terrorists who engaged in violent political acts ignored productive tensions between law-based constitutional government and popular sovereignty, crudely collapsing the former into the latter, with the people conceived as a homogeneous (and racially exclusionary) collectivity.[72] They interpreted their acts as a type of direct action necessary to realize morally "good' law by a people viewed as virtuous, in sharp contrast to the "corrupt" legal system that allegedly had betrayed them. Even when promising to target only individuals complicit in specific injustices, their acts generated indiscriminate violence: "Some lynch mobs in the post-Reconstruction South killed innocent relatives when they could not locate the ostensibly guilty party."[73] Participants refused to accept any legal consequences since they saw no reason to endorse checks on the "authentic" popular will they allegedly embodied.

Kirkpatrick's analysis suggests some disturbing parallels to contemporary authoritarian populism and its anti-pluralistic vision of a (mythical) homogeneous "people," empowered to pursue basically unchecked, potentially violent political action. Authoritarian populists and their disciples practice incivility by engaging in offensive attacks against opponents and showing disdain for any notion of politics as a common project among equals. The idea of open exchange based on mutual respect gets push to the wayside. Populists break the law when convenient and aggressively evade legal consequences. They discard the rule of law and constitutionalism when limiting strongman plebiscitary leaders who allegedly stand in for the popular will. They tolerate and sometimes celebrate violence against "enemies."

In sum, we should not ignore affinities between authoritarian populism and violent protest, or the danger that the latter might aggravate democratic decay. Such protests seem susceptible, for example, to being labeled "terrorist" and/or "foreign-funded" by populists and their media lackeys.[74] In previous chapters I distinguished *prefigurative* from *retaliatory* protests: property disobedience falling under the former category generally seems better suited to achieving movement goals and communicating an effective message. Although it would be misplaced to deny the potential legitimacy of violent resistance under increasingly authoritarian conditions, it remains hard to see how it anticipates a political future premised on equality and mutual respect. Violent self-defense directed against the police, for example, potentially prevents injuries protestors otherwise might suffer. But it hardly gives expression to some sought-for political scenario where officials are strictly bound to the rule of law. Assassination potentially eliminates a wannabe despot while leaving the broader political and social conditions buttressing despotism in place. Even when tragically necessary, violence can play only a limited role in building a more equitable democratic future. It may be necessary to help clear the deck on a ship that has been commandeered by tyrants, but it contributes little to the requisite constructive tasks at hand.[75]

By favoring nonviolence whenever at all possible we support an egalitarian political community premised on mutual respect. When conducted responsibly and avoiding injuries to persons, with targets carefully selected to impart a clear symbolic message, property disobedience coheres with political nonviolence. Participants then demonstrate the requisite respect for their peers and potentially play a constructive role in democratic politics. It is wrong, at any rate, to brand politically based property harms a priori violent or view them as a frontal assault on property rights. To be sure, property disobedience poses political dangers; those pursuing it need to take them seriously and minimize possible damage to other persons. But as King correctly commented, no decent political order can legitimately treat "machines and computers, profit motives and property rights" as equivalent to or perhaps even "more important than people."[76] For democracy to flourish, property disobedience can sometimes prove both justifiable and politically smart. As we struggle to hold onto and reform our beleaguered democracies, we would do well to grant property disobedience the normative and political recognition it deserves.

NOTES

Introduction

1. "Remarks by President Biden on Recent Events on College Campuses," White House, May 2, 2024, https://www.whitehouse.gov/briefing-room/speeches-remarks/2024/05/02/remarks-by-president-biden-on-recent-events-on-college-campuses/, accessed June 4, 2024.

2. Quoted in Chris Cameron, "Trump Again Compares Violent White Supremacist March in Charlottesville to Campus Protests," *New York Times*, April 24, 2024, https://www.nytimes.com/2024/04/24/us/politics/trump-charlottesville-campus-protests.html?searchResultPosition=4, accessed June 4, 2024.

3. Lois Beckett, "Nearly All Gaza Campus Protests in the US Have Been Peaceful, Study Says," *Guardian*, May 10, 2024, https://www.theguardian.com/us-news/article/2024/may/10/peaceful-pro-palestinian-campus-protests, accessed June 4, 2024.

4. For pertinent empirical findings: Erica Chenoweth, *Civil Resistance: What Everyone Needs to Know* (New York: Oxford University Press, 2021).

5. Adam Swift and Stuart White, "Political Science, Social Science, and Real Politics," in *Political Theory: Methods and Approaches*, ed. David Leopold and Marc Stears (New York: Oxford University Press, 2008), 49–69; Peter Niesen, "Politsche Theorie als Demokratiewissenschaft," in *Politische Theorie und Politikwissenschaft*, ed. Hubertus Buchstein and Gerhard Göhler (Wiesbaden: VS Verlag, 2007), 126–55; William E. Scheuerman, "Political Theory as Democratic Underlaboring: The Case of Property Disobedience," *Journal of International Political Theory* 21, no. 2 (2025).

6. William E. Scheuerman, *Civil Disobedience* (Cambridge: Polity Press, 2018).

7. Clayton Sinyai, *Schools of Democracy: A Political History of the American Labor Movement* (Ithaca: Cornell University Press, 2006), 93.

8. For the US case: Timothy Zick, *Managed Dissent: The Law of Public Protest* (New York: Cambridge University Press, 2023).

9. The Trump Administration has acted aggressively to suppress campus protests, for example, and to deny basic rights to US legal residents who participate in them. It also appears to believe that the 1807 Insurrection Act allows the president to deploy federal troops against political protestors.

10. For example, on recent climate activism: Nina Lakhani, Damien Gale, Matthew Taylor, "How Criminalization Is Being Used to Silence Climate Activists Around the World," *Guardian*, October 12, 2023, https://www.theguardian.com/environment/2023/oct/12/how-criminalisation-is-being-used-to-silence-climate-activists-across-the-world, accessed June 8, 2024.

Chapter 1

1. Their worries proved prescient: Aileen Brown, "Five Spills, Six Months in Operation: Dakota Access Track Record Highlights Unavoidable Reality–Pipelines Leak," *Intercept*, January 9, 2018, https://theintercept.com/2018/01/09/dakota-access-pipeline-leak-energy-transfer-partners/, accessed January 5, 2024. For a timeline of the Dakota Access protests: see "Dakota Access Pipeline Protests," Wikipedia, https://en.wikipedia.org/wiki/Dakota_Access_Pipeline_protests, accessed June 20, 2024.

2. Pacifist Catholic Worker activists Berrigan and the Plowshares Eight broke into and vandalized a nuclear missile site at King of Prussia, PA on September 9, 1980. Their action garnered global attention.

3. Jessica Reznicek and Ruby Montoya, "Why We Acted," *Via Pacis: The Voice of the Des Moines Catholic Worker Community*, October 2017, 1, 3.

4. Philip Joens, "Iowa Climate Activist Sentenced to Eight Years in Federal Prison for Dakota Access Pipeline Sabotage," *Des Moines Register*, June 30, 2021, https://www.desmoinesregister.com/story/news/crime-and-courts/2021/06/30/iowa-activist-jessica-reznicek-sentenced-dakota-access-pipeline-sabotage-catholic-workers/7808907002/, accessed July 30, 2023; David Pitt, "Woman Gets 6 Years in Prison for Damaging Pipeline," September 22, 2022, https://apnews.com/article/fires-crime-iowa-dakota-access-pipeline-11f0b30fc86fa2326d8e09fe526d9157, accessed July 30, 2023.

5. Joens, "Iowa Climate Activist Sentenced."

6. Andreas Malm, *How to Blow Up a Pipeline* (New York: Verso, 2021), 97–8.

7. For the details, Antony Dapiron, *City on Fire: The Fight for Hong Kong* (London: Scribe, 2020).

8. Zick, *Managed Dissent*, xi.

9. See the report from the September 2, 2020 Armed Conflict Location and Event Data (ACLED) report *Demonstrations and Political Violence in America: New Data for Summer 2020*, https://acleddata.com/2020/09/03/demonstrations-political-violence-in-america-new-data-for-summer-2020/, accessed July 30, 2023; see also the October 2020 *Report on the 2020 Protests & Civil Unrest* compiled by the Major Cities Chiefs Association (MCAA) Intelligence Commanders Group, https://majorcitieschiefs.com/wp-content/uploads/2021/01/MCCA-Report-on-the-2020-Protest-and-Civil-Unrest.pdf, accessed July 30, 2023.

10. Geoffrey Skelley, "How Americans Feel About George Floyd's Death and the Protests," *FiveThirtyEight*, June 5, 2020, https://fivethirtyeight.com/features/how-americans-feel-about-george-floyds-death-and-the-protests/, accessed July 28, 2023.

11. See "List of Monuments and Memorials Removed During George Floyd's Protests," Wikipedia, https://en.wikipedia.org/wiki/List_of_monuments_and_memorials_removed_during_the_George_Floyd_protests, accessed July 29, 2023.

12. By some estimates it has exceeded $2 billion: Thomas Johansmeyer, "How 2020 Protests Changed Insurance Forver," World Economic Forum, February 22, 2021, https://www.weforum.org/agenda/2021/02/2020-protests-changed-insurance-forever/, accessed July 28, 2023.

13. Maya Lau, Alejandro Reyes-Velarde, Matt Hamilton, "Looters Who Hit L.A. Stores Explain Why They Did It," *Los Angeles Times*, June 5, 2020, https://www.latimes.com/california/story/2020-06-05/looting-protests-george-floyd, accessed July 28, 2023.

14. For a list of Anonymous activities: see Wikipedia, "Anonymous (Hacker Group)," https://en.wikipedia.org/wiki/Anonymous_(hacker_group), accessed March 8, 2024.

15. For competing views: Gabiella Coleman, *Hacker, Hoaxer, Whistleblower, Spy: The Many Faces of Anonymous* (New York: Verso, 2014); Adrian Chen, "The Truth About Anonymous's Activism," *Nation*, November 11, 2014, https://www.thenation.com/article/archive/truth-about -anonymouss-activism/, accessed March 8, 2024.

16. On the damage, see "8 January Brasilia Attacks," Wikipedia, https://en.wikipedia.org /wiki/2023_Brazilian_Congress_attack, accessed March 17, 2025. For an analysis, see Bianca Tavolari and Jonas Medeiros, "The Patriots' Repossession," *Verfassungsblog* (blog), February 13, 2023, https://verfassungsblog.de/the-patriots-repossession/), accessed July 30, 2023. On Bolsonaro's political ascent, see Marcos Nobre, *Limits of Democracy: From the June 2013 Uprisings to the Bolsonaro Government* (New York: Springer, 2022).

17. Some incidents of flag-burning, for example, may enjoy First Amendment protections (Zink, *Managed Dissent*, 42–43). But property disobedience is usually viewed as non-peaceable and beyond the boundaries of legally protected protest.

18. Damien Gayle, "BLM Protesters Cleared over Toppling of Edward Colston Statue," *Guardian*, January 5, 2022, https://www.theguardian.com/uk-news/2022/jan/05/four-cleared-of -toppling-edward-colston-statute#:~:text=After%20just%20under%20three%20hours,crown %20court%20on%20Wednesday%20afternoon, accessed August 4, 2023.

19. Natalie Zemon Davis, "The Rites of Violence: Religious Riot in Sixteenth-Century France," *Past and Present* 59 (1973): 51–91. On religious iconoclasm, see Dario Gamboni, *The Destruction of Art: Iconoclasm Since the French Revolution* (New Haven: Yale University Press, 1997).

20. The young Karl Marx defended the traditional customary right of peasants in the Rhineland to collect wood from lands they did not own: Daniel Bensaïd, *The Dispossessed: Karl Marx's Debates on Wood Theft and the Right of the Poor*, trans. Robert Nichols (Minneapolis: University of Minnesota Press, 2021). On the nineteenth-century British "plug riots" targeting steam engines, see Andreas Malm, *Fossil Capital: The Rise of Steam Power and the Roots of Global Warming* (New York: Verso, 2016), 226–37.

21. William Beik, *Urban Protest in Seventeenth-Century France: The Culture of Retribution* (Cambridge: Cambridge University Press, 1997).

22. Charles Tilly, *Contentious Performances* (New York: Cambridge University Press, 2008), 67. Some of these acts fall under the rubric of what James C. Scott calls "hidden resistance" in his *Domination and the Arts of Resistance: Hidden Transcripts* (New Haven: Yale University Press, 1990).

23. Richard Bessel, *Violence: A Modern Obsession* (New York: Simon & Schuster, 2015), 128–32.

24. Johansmeyer, "How 2020 Protests Changed Insurance Forever"; see also the February 2023 report from the insurance giant Allianz: *Strikes, Riots and Civil Commotion–A Test of Business Resilience*, https://commercial.allianz.com/news-and-insights/reports/strikes-riots-civil -commotion-outlook-2023.html, accessed July 31, 2023.

25. One survey suggests a 50 percent increase in worldwide violent protests since 2008: *Global Peace Index 2023* (Sydney: Institute for Economics and Peace, 2023), 27. Others diagnose a large increase overall in protest activity since 2006, with 20 percent of them categorized as violent, with violent protests having undergone a "steady increase" (Isabel Ortiz, *World Protests: A Study of the Key Protest Issues in the 21st Century* [New York: Springer, 2022], 72–74, 11–17).

26. Neoliberalism is a contested term: see Damien Cahill and Martijn Konings, *Neoliberalism* (Cambridge: Polity Press, 2017).

27. Stuart Banner, *American Property: A History of How, Why, and What We Own* (Cambridge: Harvard University press, 2011), 257–75.

28. Among others, see Richard A. Epstein, *Takings: Private Property and the Power of Eminent Domain* (Cambridge: Harvard University Press, 1985); Charles Murray, *By the People: Rebuilding Liberty Without Permission* (New York: Crown, 2015).

29. David Schneiderman, *Constitutionalizing Economic Globalization: Investment Rules and Democracy's Promise* (New York: Cambridge University Press, 2008). Nor is it clear that the ongoing populist backlash has dismantled all elements of neoliberalism: see Nicolas Perrone, "The International Investment Regime After the Global Crisis of Neoliberalism: Rupture or Continuity?," *Indiana Journal of Global Legal Studies* 23, no. 2 (2016): 603–27.

30. Jeremy Rifkin, *The Age of Access: The New Culture of Hypercapitalism* (New York: Penguin, 2000).

31. Rifkin, *The Age of Access*, 98.

32. Michel Foucault observed that increased peasant illegality in eighteenth-century France may simply have reflected enhanced protections for private property, which rendered previously widespread acts (e.g., confiscation of hoarded goods, forced sales of goods at "fair" prices) unambiguously illegal and more effectively controlled (Foucault, *Discipline und Punish*, trans. Alan Sheridan [New York: Pantheon, 1977], 273–75). There may be parallels to recent developments.

33. See, for example, Adrienne LaFrance, "The New Anarchy," *Atlantic*, April 2023, 22–37. Also, Rachel Kleinfeld, "The Rise of Political Violence in the United States," *Journal of Democracy* 32, no. 4 (2021): 160–76. More generally, see Vincent Bevins, *If We Burn: The Mass Protest Decade and the Missing Revolution* (New York: Public Affairs, 2023).

34. John Rawls, *A Theory of Justice* (Cambridge: Harvard University Press, 1971), 364.

35. For an analysis: David Lefkowitz, "On a Moral Right to Civil Disobedience," *Ethics* 117, no. 2 (2007): 202–33. Legal fidelity can be demonstrated in ways others than appearances before a tribunal or the acceptance of penalties: see William E. Scheuerman, "Whistleblowing as Civil Disobedience: The Case of Edward Snowden," *Philosophy & Social Criticism* 40, no. 7 (2014): 609–28.

36. Candice Delmas, "(In)Civility," in *Cambridge Companion to Civil Disobedience*, ed. William E. Scheuerman (New York: Cambridge University Press, 2021), 210–14.

37. Hugo Bedau, "Civil Disobedience and Personal Responsibility for Injustice," in *Civil Disobedience in Focus*, ed. Hugo Bedau (New York: Routledge, 1991), 51.

38. Tilly, *Contentious Performances*, 14–15.

39. Selina R. Gallo-Cruz, *Have Repertoire, Will Travel: Nonviolence as Global Contentious Performance* (New York: Cambridge University Press, 2024).

40. See, however, the special issue of the Brazilian journal *Revista Direito et Praxis* 15, no. 2 (2024), curated by Bianca Tavolari.

41. Gamboni, *Destruction of Art*, 18.

42. Vicky Osterweil, *In Defense of Looting: A Riotous History of Uncivil Action* (New York: Bold Type Books, 2020), 3.

43. Before it took on the recognizably modern meaning of a violent attack or disturbance, usually by a crowd or "mob," the *Oxford English Dictionary* records that "riot" meant "debauchery," as in a "wanton, dissolute, or extravagant lifestyle."

44. As suggested by Elizabeth Hinton, *America on Fire: The Untold History of Police Violence and Black Rebellion Since the 1960s* (New York: Liveright, 2021), 3–7.

45. Erica Chenoweth and Maria Stephan, *Why Civil Resistance Works: The Strategic Logic of Nonviolent Conflict* (New York: Columbia University Press, 2011), 10.

46. Chenoweth and Stephan, *Why Civil Resistance Works*, 10.

47. Chenoweth and Stephan, *Why Civil Resistance Works*, 13, emphasis mine.

48. Mohammad Al Kadivar and Neil Ketchley, "Sticks, Stones, and Molotov Cocktails: Unarmed Collective Violence and Democratization," *Socius: Sociological Research for a Dynamic World* 4 (2018): 3; Frabrice Lehoucq, "Does Nonviolence Work?," *Comparative Politics* 48, no. 2 (2016): 269–87.

49. A point conceded by Chenoweth's recent update, in which she defines violence more strictly as "an action or practice that physically harms or threatens to harm another person," conceding that some political activities widely described in everyday language as "violent" (e.g., property damage, self-harm, even some rioting) should not always be characterized as such (Chenoweth, *Civil Resistance*, 145); Erica Chenoweth, "The Role of Violence in Nonviolent Resistance," *Annual Review of Political Science* 26 (2023): 55–77.

50. Charles Tilly, *The Politics of Collective Violence* (New York: Cambridge University Press, 2003), 3.

51. Dieter Rucht, "Violence and the New Social Movements," in *International Handbook of Violence Research*, ed. Wilhelm Heitmeyer and J. Hagan (Dordrecht: Kluwer Academic Publishers, 2003), 369.

52. Lorenzo Boso and Stefan Mathanen, "Political Violence," in *Oxford Handbook of Social Movements*, ed. Donatella Della Porta and Mario Dani (Oxford: Oxford University Press, 2015), 439. Clumping property damage with protest-related violence also makes it difficult to determine its gendered contours, something that deserves scrutiny: see Gabrielle Bardell, Elin Bjarenegard, and Jennifer M. Piscopo, "How Is Political Violence Gendered? Disentangling Motives, Forms, and Impacts," *Political Studies* 69, no. 4 (2020): 916–35.

53. Scheuerman, *Civil Disobedience*.

54. Rawls, *A Theory of Justice*, 363–68.

55. Andreas Marcou, "Violence, Communication, and Civil Disobedience," *Jurisprudence* 12, no. 4 (2021): 491–511. See also William E. Scheuerman, "Goodbye to Nonviolence?," *Political Research Quarterly* 75, no. 4 (2021): 1284–96.

56. See, among others, Jason Brennan, *When All Else Fails: The Ethics of Resistance to State Injustice* (Princeton: Princeton University Press, 2019); Stephan D'Archy, *Languages of the Unheard: Why Miltant Protest Is Good for Democracy* (London: Zed, 2014); Costas Douzinas, *Philosophy and Resistance in the Crisis* (Cambridge: Polity Books, 2013); Derek Edyvane and Enes Kulenovic, "Disruptive Disobedience," *Journal of Politics* 79, no. 4 (2017): 1359–71; James Greenwood-Reeves, *Justifying Violent Protest: Law and Morality in Democratic States* (New York: Routledge, 2023); William Smith, "Disruptive Democracy: The Ethics of Direct Action," *Raisons Politiques* 69, no. 1 (2018): 13–27.

57. Candice Delmas, "Civil Disobedience," *Philosophy Compass* 11 (2016): 685; Candice Delmas, *A Duty to Resist: When Disobedience Should Be Uncivil* (New York: Oxford University Press, 2018). While Delmas rejects Rawls, Gabriele Badana and Alasia Nuti tap Rawls to justify uncivil, potentially violent protest: "Must the Subaltern Speak Publicly? Public Reason Liberalism and the Ethics of Fighting Severe Injustice," *Journal of Politics* (forthcoming).

58. Rob Jubb, "Disaggregating Political Authority: What's Wrong with Rawlsian Civil Disobedience?," *Political Studies* 67 (2019): 955–71; William E. Scheuerman, "Why Not Uncivil Disobedience?," *Critical Review of International Social and Political Philosophy* 25, no. 7 (2022):

980–99. For Delmas's rejoinder: "From Resistance to Protest: The Paradigm Shift in Theories of Civil Disobedience," *Contemporary Political Theory* 19, no. 3 (2020): 522–28.

59. David Waddington, "Riots" in *Oxford Handbook of Social Movements*, ed. Donatella Della Porta and Mario Dani (Oxford: Oxford University Press, 2015), 423.

60. Avia Pasternak, "Political Rioting: A Moral Assessment," *Philosophy and Public Affairs* 46, no. 4 (2019): 388–89.

61. Jonathan Havercroft, "Why Is There No Just Riot Theory?," *British Journal of Political Science* 51 (2021): 915.

62. This is why I have decided to neglect discussing property self-harm, e.g., the burning of a flag owned by those who burn it, because in such cases typically no other owners are negatively affected.

63. Rawls, *A Theory of Justice*, 365.

64. Rawls, *A Theory of Justice*, 365.

65. Legal charges can vary from relatively minor misdemeanors to more serious felonies. In the United States, police possess extraordinary discretion to respond to protests; protestors can be charged with a variety of public order-related offenses ("breach of peace," "conspiracy to riot," "trespassing," "unlawful assembly") as well as others relating directly to property harms (Zick, *Managed Dissent*, 55–58).

66. "Everyday," usually anonymous, vandalism, expressing dissatisfaction with the status quo, is a commonplace phenomenon: Maren Lorenz, *Vandalismus als Alltagsphänomen* (Hamburg: Hamburger Edition, 2009), 119.

67. Freedom House's annual survey of democracy's global status offers a bird's-eye view: "Global Freedom Status," Freedom House, https://freedomhouse.org/explore-the-map?type=fiw&year=2024, accessed April 19, 2024.

68. Paul A. Gilje, *Rioting in America* (Bloomington: Indiana University Press, 1999), 87–115.

69. Eduardo Moises Peñalver and Sonia K. Katyal, *Property Outlaws: How Squatters, Pirates, and Protestors Improve the Law of Ownership* (New Haven: Yale University Press, 2010), 9.

70. C. Edwin Baker, "Property and Its Relation to Constitutionally Protected Liberty," *University of Pennsylvania Law Review* 134, no. 4 (1986): 741–816.

71. Baker, "Property and Its Relation to Constitutionally Protected Liberty," 752.

72. Jeremy Waldron, *The Right to Private Property* (Oxford: Oxford University Press, 1990), 41–2.

73. For a classic statement, see A. M. Honore, "Ownership," *Oxford Essays in Jurisprudence* (Oxford: Oxford University Press, 1961), 107–47.

74. Epstein, *Takings*, p. 65.

75. On public property, see Shmuel Nils, "The Idea of Public Property," *Ethics* 129 (2019): 347–48.

76. David Ewing, quoted in Victoria Smith Holden, "Effective Voice Rights in the Workplace," in *Freeing the First Amendment: Critical Perspectives on Freedom of Expression*, ed. David S. Allen and Robert Jensen (New York: New York University Press, 1995), 114. Also, Elizabeth Anderson, *Private Government: How Employers Rule Our Lives (and Why We Don't Talk About It)* (Princeton: Princeton University Press, 2017).

77. Holden, "Effective Voice Rights in the Workplace," 114. "The Supreme Court has held there is no First Amendment right to protest on *private* property" (Zick, *Managed Dissent*, 49).

78. Zick, *Managed Dissent*, 1.

79. Zick, *Managed Dissent*, 66.

80. Zick, *Managed Dissent*, 117–42.

81. Tabatha Abu El-Haj, "Defining Peaceably: Policing the Line Between Constitutionally Protected Protest and Unlawful Speech," *Missouri Law Review* 80, no. 4 (2015): 961.

82. Abu El-Haj, "Defining Peaceably," 965.

83. Herbert Marcuse, "The Problem of Violence and the Radical Opposition," in *Five Lectures*, by Herbert Marcuse (Boston: Beacon Press, 1970), 89.

84. Zick, *Managed Dissent*, 61.

85. Margaret Kohn, "Privatization and Protest: Occupy Wall Street, Occupy Toronto, and the Occupation of Public Space in a Democracy," *Perspectives* 11, no. 1 (2013): 99–110. Cigdem Cidam, *In the Street: Democratic Action, Theatricality, and Political Friendship* (New York: Oxford University Press, 2021), argues that those occupying public squares enacted a radical democratic "politics of friendship."

86. During the 1960s, New York City zoning authorities created the POPS category to encourage the creation of public spaces by private developers. Though a form of private property, POPS owners are required to provide public access, in exchange for permission for new development projects. They can issue extensive rules concerning the property's use, including many designed to prohibit political activity.

87. I rely loosely on Max Weber's notion of ideal types. For a discussion, see Fritz Ringer, *Max Weber: An Intellectual Biography* (Chicago: University of Chicago Press, 2004), 101–4.

88. I do not share the view that prefiguration constitutes an "ethical practice" sharply distinguished from political action (Karuna Mantena, "Competing Theories of Nonviolent Politics," in *Nomos LXII: Protest and Dissent*, ed. Melissa Schwartzberg [New York: New York University Press, 2020], 87–88). More generally, see Paul Raekstad and Sofa Saio Gradin, *Prefigurative Politics: Building Tomorrow Today* (Cambridge: Polity Press, 2020).

Chapter 2

1. Thomas Platt, "The Concept of Violence as Descriptive and Polemic," *International Social Science Journal* 44 (1992): 186.

2. On the German *Gewalt*, for example, see Peter Imbusch, "The Concept of Violence," in *International Handbook of Violence Research* (Amsterdam: Kluwer, 2003), 13–39.

3. Martin Luther King Jr., *The Trumpet of Conscience* (Boston: Beacon Press, 2010 [1968]), 59.

4. Vittorio Bufacchi, "Two Concepts of Violence," *Political Studies Review* 3 (2005): 193.

5. C. A. J. Coady, "The Idea of Violence," in *Violence: A Philosophical Anthology*, ed. Vittorio Bufacchi (New York: Palgrave, 2009), 244–45. Coady also describes a third conservative or "legitimist" view, according to which violence is never used to describe acts by legally constituted police and security forces. This view obfuscates the harsh realities of state action that may result in severe injuries and harms.

6. Johan Galtung, "Violence, Peace and Peace Research," in *Violence: A Philosophical Anthology*, ed. Vittorio Bufacchi (New York: Palgrave, 2009), 80. Slavoj Zizek, in *Violence* (New York: Picador, 2008), has formulated a similarly comprehensive view, with violence interpreted as having subjective (or interpersonal), symbolic, and systemic components. I focus on Galtung because his original rendition is more rigorous. Some criticisms of Galtung likely apply to Zizek.

7. Galtung, "Violence, Peace and Peace Research," 83.

8. Galtung, "Violence, Peace and Peace Research," 83.

9. On the latter, see Deane Curtin and Robert Litke, eds., *Institutional Violence* (Amsterdam: Rodopi, 1999).

10. Galtung, "Violence, Peace and Peace Research," 84.

11. Platt, "The Concept of Violence as Descriptive and Polemic," 188; see also, Sergio Cotta, *Why Violence? A Philosophical Interpretation* (Gainesville: University of Florida Press, 1985), 50.

12. Coady, "The Idea of Violence," 255.

13. Coady, "The Idea of Violence," 255.

14. For example: Hannah Arendt, *On Violence* (New York: Harcourt, Brace & Jovanovich, 1970).

15. Robert Paul Wolff, "On Violence," in *Violence: A Philosophical Anthology*, ed. Vittorio Bufacchi (New York: Palgrave, 2009), 59.

16. Joan V. Bondurant, *Conquest of Violence: The Gandhian Philosophy of Conflict* (Berkeley: University of California Press, 1958), 9.

17. Martin Luther King, "Letter from Birmingham City Jail," in *Civil Disobedience in Focus*, ed. Hugo Bedau (New York: Routledge, 1991), 71, emphasis mine.

18. Guy Aitchison, "Coercion, Resistance, and the Radical Side of Non-Violent Action," *Raisons Politiques* 69, no. 1 (2018): 45–61; Alexander Livingston, "Nonviolence and the Coercive Turn," in *Cambridge Companion to Civil Disobedience*, ed. William E. Scheuerman (New York: Cambridge University Press, 2021), 254–79.

19. Coady, "The Idea of Violence," 259–62.

20. Ted Honderich, *Political Violence* (Ithaca: Cornell University Press, 1976), 9.

21. Wolff, "On Violence," 59; see also Joseph Raz, *The Authority of Law* (Oxford: Clarendon, 1979), 267.

22. Chenoweth, *Civil Resistance*, 142–81.

23. Robin Celikates, "Democratizing Civil Disobedience," *Philosophy & Social Criticism* 42, no. 10 (2016): 986.

24. See also Kimberley Brownlee, *Conscience and Conviction: The Case for Civil Disobedience* (Oxford: Oxford University Press, 2012), 21–22. Brownlee relies on an example from Joseph Raz, i.e., of an ostensibly nonviolent, legal strike by ambulance workers that inadvertently produces harmful consequences for those denied medical aid (Brownlee, *Conscience and Conviction*, 22). The example is odd, however, since (1) if the strike is legal, it does not constitute an example of civil disobedience; (2) if immediately or directly injurious to persons, not only Gandhi and King, but perhaps also many liberals might plausibly deny that the protest should be viewed as "nonviolent" in the first place.

25. Scheuerman, "Goodbye to Nonviolence?"

26. John Keane, *Reflections on Violence* (New York: Verso, 1996), 66–67.

27. Vittorio Bufacchi, *Violence and Social Justice* (New York: Palgrave, 2007), 96.

28. Bufacchi, *Violence and Social Justice*, 42.

29. C. Edwin Baker, "Property and Its Connection to Constitutionally Protected Liberty," *University of Pennsylvania Law Review* 134, no. 4 (1986), 747.

30. Margaret Jane Radin, *Reinterpreting Property* (Chicago: University of Chicago Press, 1993).

31. Newton Garvey, "What Violence Is," in *Violence: A Philosophical Anthology*, ed. Vittorio Bufacchi (New York: Palgrave, 2009), 173; also: Gerald C. MacCallum, "What Is Wrong with Violence," in *Violence: A Philosophical Anthology*, ed. Vittorio Bufacchi (New York: Palgrave, 2009), 128.

32. Richard Lowry, "Of Course Destruction of Property Is Violence," *Politico*, June 3, 2020, https://www.politico.com/news/magazine/2020/06/03/of-course-destruction-of-property-is-violence-299759#:~:text=Harming%20a%20person%20is%20much,aren%27t%20acts%20of%20violence.&text=Rich%20Lowry%20is%20editor%20of,contributing%20editor%20with%20Politico%20Magazine, accessed August 23, 2023. For a defense of BLM, see Nathan J. Robinson, "Why Damaging Property Isn't the Same As 'Violence,'" *Current Affairs*, June 1, 2020, https://www.currentaffairs.org/2020/06/why-property-destruction-isnt-violence, accessed August 15, 2023.

33. Waldron, *The Right to Private Property*, 137–252.

34. Tellingly, the modern corporation vanishes from Robert Nozick's neo-Lockean defense of property rights, as though the basketball star Wilt Chamberlain and not General Motors or Apple were an appropriate representative of contemporary capitalism (*Anarchy, State, and Utopia* [New York: Basic Books, 1974]).

35. A point made, for example, by defenders at the sitdown strikes at US auto plants in the 1930s: see Joel Seidman, *"Sit-Down"* (Chicago: Socialist Party/League for Industrial Democracy, 1937)

36. As noted by, among others, Thomas Grey, "The Disintegration of Property," in *Ethics, Economics, and the Law of Property*, ed. J. Roland O. Pennock and John Chapman (New York: NYU Press, 1980), 69–85.

37. Tony Milligan, *Civil Disobedience: Protest, Justification, and the Law* (London: Bloomsbury, 2013), 16.

38. Radin, *Reinterpreting Property*, 56.

39. Waldron, *The Right to Private Property*, 374.

40. John Morreall, "The Justifiability of Violent Civil Disobedience," in *Civil Disobedience in Focus*, ed. Hugo Bedau (New York: Routledge, 1991), 133.

41. Among others, see Robert L. Holmes, "Violence and the Perspective of Morality," in *Violence: A Philosophical Anthology*, ed. Vittorio Bufacchi (New York: Palgrave, 2009), 275.

42. Kai Nielsen, "On Justifying Violence," in *Violence: A Philosophical Anthology*, ed. Vittorio Bufacchi (New York: Palgrave, 2009), 221.

43. For example, see Malm, *How to Blow Up a Pipeline*, 97–132.

44. For example, see Brownlee, *Conscience and Conviction*, 199.

45. Holmes, "Violence and the Perspective of Morality," 291n12, emphasis mine.

46. Mark Vorobej, *The Concept of Violence* (New York: Routledge, 2016), 55n15, emphasis mine.

47. Robert Audi, "On the Meaning and Justification of Violence," in *Violence: A Philosophical Anthology*, ed. Vittorio Bufacchi (New York: Palgrave, 2009), 143.

48. Audi, "On the Meaning and Justification of Violence," 145.

49. Keane, *Reflections on Violence*, 67.

50. Elaine Scarry, *The Body in Pain: The Making and Unmaking of the World* (New York: Oxford University, Press, 1985).

51. Karl Marx, *Capital*, vol. 1 (Moscow: Progress Publishers, 1954), 78.

52. Ludvig Beckman has helped me think more clearly about this point.

53. See, for example, the Model Penal Code, on which many US states have modeled criminal law sanctions. Punitive policies have blurred crucial distinctions between bodily and property-related harms (Alice Ristroph, "Criminal Law in the Shadow of Violence," *University of Alabama Law Review* 62, no. 3 [2011]): 571–622; David Alan Sklansky, *A Pattern of Violence:*

How the Law Classifies Crimes and What It Means for Justice [Cambridge: Harvard University Press, 2021]). In UK criminal law, violence "always involves the intention to endanger life or recklessness as to whether life would be endangered" (Marcou, "Violence, Communication, and Civil Disobedience," 502.) I am indebted to Samira Akbarian for bringing some of the legal complexities of these matters to my attention.

54. Keane, *Reflections on Violence*, 67.

55. Ristroph, "Criminal Law in the Shadow of Violence," 587.

56. Adriana Cavarero, *Horrorism: Naming Contemporary Violence* (New York: Columbia University Press, 2009), 31. I am hesitant to attribute any transhistorical, anthropological status to this claim: doing so risks obscuring the historicity and socially constructed contours of violence, and the ways in which it is conceived—and perhaps experienced—in different contexts. See Gesa Lindemann, Jonas Barth, and Johanna Fröhlich, "The Methodological Relevance of a Theory-of-Society Perspective for the Empirical Analysis of Violence," *Historical Social Research* 47, no. 1 (2022): 266–88.

57. Judith Butler, *Precarious Life: The Powers of Mourning and Violence* (New York: Verso, 2004), 28–29.

58. Ristroph, "Criminal Law in the Shadow of Violence," 587.

59. In a related vein, see N. P. Adams, "Uncivil Disobedience: Political Commitment and Violence," *Res Publica* 24, no. 4 (2018): 483; see also Marcou, "Violence, Communication, and Civil Disobedience," 503.

60. Steven Lee, "Poverty and Violence," *Social Theory and Practice* 22, no. 1 (1996): 67–82.

61. Piero Moraro, *Civil Disobedience: A Philosophical Overview* (London: Rowman & Littlefield, 2019), 92–93.

62. Bufacchi, *Violence and Social Justice*, 96.

63. Todd May, *Nonviolent Resistance: A Philosophical Introduction* (Cambridge: Polity Press, 2015), 67.

64. May, *Nonviolent Resistance*, 68.

65. King, *The Trumpet of Conscience*, 58.

66. King, *The Trumpet of Conscience*, 57.

67. King, *The Trumpet of Conscience*, 58.

68. King, *The Trumpet of Conscience*, 58.

69. King, *The Trumpet of Conscience*, 58.

70. King, *The Trumpet of Conscience*, 59.

71. Clayborne Carson, ed., *The Autobiography of Martin Luther King, Jr.* (New York: Warner Books, 1998), 293.

72. King, *The Trumpet of Conscience*, 59.

73. King, *The Trumpet of Conscience*, 57.

74. Martin Luther King Jr., "The Violence of Poverty," *New York Amsterdam News*, January 1, 1966, 2.

75. King, *The Trumpet of Conscience*, 59–60.

76. Martin Luther King Jr., *Where Do We Go from Here?* (Boston: Beacon Press, 2010 [1968]), 22.

77. This is something not sufficiently acknowledged in the literature on King's nonviolence. For important treatments, see Alexander Livingston, "Power for the Powerless: Martin Luther King, Jr.'s Late Theory of Civil Disobedience," *Journal of Politics* 82, no. 2 (2020): 700–713;

Tommie Shelby and Brandon M. Terry, eds., *To Shape a New World: Essays on the Political Philosophy of Martin Luther King, Jr.* (Cambridge: Harvard University Press, 2018).

78. King, *The Trumpet of Conscience*, 8.

79. Warren E. Steinkraus, "Martin Luther King's Contributions to Personalism," *Idealistic Studies* 6, no. 12 (1976): 26.

80. Martin Luther King Jr., *Stride Toward freedom: The Montgomery Story* (Boston: Beacon Press, 2010 [1958]), 88.

81. Steinkraus, "Martin Luther King's Contributions to Personalism," 25-27.

82. Rachel Neumann, "A Place for Rage," *Dissent*, Spring 2000, https://www.dissentmagazine.org/article/a-place-for-rage/, accessed April 24, 2024. Many have commented on protest-related political violence's gendered contours.

83. Secularizing King's exposition, admittedly, may come at a price: see Maeve Cooke, "The Ethical Dimension of Civil Disobedience," in *Cambridge Companion to Civil Disobedience*, ed. William E. Scheuerman (New York: Cambridge University Press, 2021), 231-53.

84. Keane, *Reflections on Violence*, 67.

85. Adams, "Uncivil Disobedience," 486.

86. Simone Chambers, *Contemporary Democratic Theory* (Cambridge: Polity, 2023), 36. All defensible ideas about democracy require some more or less robust idea of political equality; by implication, my exposition is congruent with a wide range of democratic theories. Unfortunately, the literature on democracy and equality tends to marginalize discussions of nonviolence. See, however, Thomas Christiano, *The Constitution of Equality: Democratic Authority and Its Limits* (New York: Oxford University Press, 2018), 270; Daniel Viehoff, "Democratic Equality and Political Authority," *Philosophy & Public Affairs* 42, no. 4 (2014): 372.

87. John Keane, *Violence and Democracy* (Cambridge: Cambridge University Press, 2004), 1.

88. Gallo-Cruz, *Have Repertoire, Will Travel*, 2.

89. John Rawls, *Lectures on the History of Political Philosophy* (Cambridge: Harvard University Press, 2007), 135.

90. Rawls, *A Theory of Justice*, 366.

91. Rawls, *A Theory of Justice*, 364n19.

92. Rawls, *A Theory of Justice*, 366.

93. Neera Chandhoke, in *Democracy and Revolutionary Politics* (London: Bloomsbury, 2015), 12, comments in this vein that political violence is only potentially legitimate amid "overlapping forms of [extreme] injustice that betray the basic presuppositions of democracy." Even then, however, it may be politically unwise and counterproductive.

94. Adams, "Uncivil Disobedience," 488.

95. Ian Attack, *Nonviolence in Political Theory* (Edinburgh: Edinburgh University Press, 2012); May, *Nonviolent Resistance*; Stellan Vinthagen, *A Theory of Nonviolent Action: How Civil Resistance Works* (London: Zed, 2015).

96. King, "Letter from Birmingham City Jail," 69.

97. Judith Butler, *The Force of Nonviolence* (New York: Verso, 2020), 25.

98. Gene Sharp, *The Politics of Nonviolent Action, Parts I-III* (Boston: Sargent Publishers, 1973). Sharp rejects sabotage (pp. 608-11) and has little to say about property disobedience, yet much of his account still could be adapted to cover my defense of strict nonviolence vis-à-vis persons.

99. Among others, see Chenoweth and Stephan, *Why Civil Resistance Works*; Kurt Schock, *Unarmed Insurrections: People Power Movements in Nondemocracies* (Minneapolis: University of Minnesota Press, 2005).

100. Vinthagen, *A Theory of Nonviolent Action*, 209.

101. Barbara Deming, "On Revolution and Equilibrium," in *Nonviolence in America*, ed. Staughton Lynd and Alice Lynd (Maryknoll, NY: Orbis, 1995), 418–19.

102. Mantena, "Competing Theories of Nonviolent Politics," 94–100.

103. Alan Ryan, *Property and Political Theory* (Oxford: Blackwell's, 1984); see also C. B. Macpherson, "Property as Means or End," in *The Rise and Fall of Economic Justice and Other Papers*, by C. B. Macpherson (Oxford: Oxford University Press, 1985), 86–91.

104. Ryan, *Property and Political Theory*, 11.

105. Steinkraus, "Martin Luther King's Contributions to Personalism."

106. Thomas F. Jackson, *From Civil Rights to Human Rights: Martin Luther King Jr. and the Struggle for Economic Justice* (Philadelphia: University of Pennsylvania Press, 2007).

107. King, *Where Do We Go from Here?*, 196–97.

108. Martin Luther King Jr., *All Labor Has Dignity* (Boston: Beacon Press, 2011), 27.

109. Martin Luther King Jr., "Pilgrimage to Nonviolence" [1960], in *The Radical King*, ed. Cornell West (Boston: Beacon Press, 2015), 43.

110. C. B. Macpherson, *Democratic Theory: Essays in Retrieval* (Oxford: Clarendon Press, 1973), 136.

111. Baker, "Property and Its Connection to Constitutionally Protected Liberty," 745.

112. Macpherson, *Democratic Theory*, 138.

113. In a similar vein, King defended the idea of a (generous) guaranteed minimum income: King, *All Labor Has Dignity*, 133.

114. Morreall, "The Justifiability of Violent Civil Disobedience," 133.

115. Radin, *Reinterpreting Property*, 56.

116. Waldron, *The Right to Private Property*, 4.

117. Waldron, *The Right to Private Property*, 5.

Chapter 3

1. Michael S. Foley, *Confronting the War Machine: Draft Resistance During the Vietnam War* (Chapel Hill: University of North Carolina Press, 2003).

2. On political symbolism, see Thomas Meyer, *Die Inszenierung des Scheins: Essay-Montage* (Frankfurt: Suhrkamp, 1992).

3. Sanford Levinson, *Written in Stone: Public Monuments in a Changing Society* (Durham: Duke University Press, 2018), 130.

4. Alison Brysk, "'Hearts and Minds': Bringing Symbolic Politics Back In," *Polity* 27, no. 4 (1995): 561.

5. Benjamin Abrams and Peter Gardner, "Contentious Politics and Symbolic Objects," in *Symbolic Politics in Contentious Politics*, ed. Benjamin Abrams and Peter Gardner (Ann Arbor: University of Michigan Press, 2023), 17.

6. BLM eschews traditional organizational forms; there is no single BLM "line" on public memorials. My attributions here are based on a variety of comments by activists and also the burgeoning scholarly literature: Juliet Hooker, "Black Lives Matter and the Paradoxes of US Black Politics: From Democratic Sacrifice to Democratic Repair," *Political Theory* 44, no. 4 (2016): 448–69; Charles Olney, "Black Lives Matter and the Politics of Redemption," *Philosophy*

& *Social Criticism* 48, no. 7 (2021): 956–76; Barbara Ransby, *Making All Black Lives Matter: Reimagining Freedom in the 21st Century* (Berkeley: University of California Press, 2018); Keeanga-Yamahtta Taylor, *From #BLACKLIVESMATTER to Black Liberation* (Chicago: Haymarket, 2016). On the movement's origins, see Christopher Lebron, *The Making of Black Lives Matter* (New York: Oxford University Press, 2023).

7. Similar damage to and topplings of monuments transpired globally in the wake of the summer 2020 BLM protests. I focus on the US case, in part simply because others elsewhere often took inspiration from events there.

8. Benjamin Abrams and Peter Gardner, "Conclusion," in *Symbolic Politics in Contentious Politics*, ed. Benjamin Abrams and Peter Gardner (Ann Arbor: University of Michigan Press, 2023), 295.

9. Sidney Tarrow, *Power in Movement: Social Movements and Contentious Politics*, 2nd ed. (New York: Cambridge University Press, 1998), 106–22.

10. David E. Snow and Robert Benford, "Master Frames and Cycles of Protest," in *Frontiers in Social Movement Theory*, ed. Aldon Morris and Carol McClurg Mueller (New Haven: Yale University Press, 1992), 137.

11. Robert Benford and David E. Snow, "Framing Processes and Social Movements," *Annual Review of Sociology* 26 (2000): 611–39.

12. James M. Jasper, *The Art of Moral Protest: Culture, Biography, and Creativity in Social Movements* (Chicago: University of Chicago Press, 1997), 159.

13. Jasper, *The Art of Moral Protest*, 160.

14. Jasper, *The Art of Moral Protest*, 107.

15. Jasper, *The Art of Moral Protest*, 161.

16. Jasper, *The Art of Moral Protest*, 326.

17. Vittoria Benzine, "Here Is Every Artwork Attacked by Climate Activists This Year," *Artnet News*, October 31, 2022, https://news.artnet.com/art-world/here-is-every-artwork-attacked-by-climate-activists-this-year-from-the-mona-lisa-to-girl-with-a-pearl-earring-2200804, accessed October 1, 2023.

18. Maximilian Pichl, *Law statt Order: Der Kampf um den Rechtsstaat* (Berlin: Suhrkamp, 2024), 109.

19. Carlie Porterfield, "Climate Activists, Protesting Against Federal Charges Against Their Colleagues, Rally at Metropolitan Museum," *Art Newspaper*, June 27, 2023, https://www.theartnewspaper.com/2023/06/27/climate-activists-protest-federal-charges-degas-metropolitan-museum, accessed October 1, 2023; Zachary Small, "After a Year of Climate Protests, the Toll Rises for Museums and Activists," *New York Times*, July 11, 2023, https://www.nytimes.com/2023/07/11/arts/design/climate-protests-museums-sentences-art.html, accessed October 1, 2023.

20. Quoted in Haleema Shah, "Can Art Destruction Save Us from Climate Destruction?," *Vox*, December 22, 2022, https://www.vox.com/podcasts/2022/12/22/23522831/just-stop-oil-uk-climate-protests-sunflowers-van-gogh, accessed March 18, 2025.

21. Peter Singer, "In Defense of the Art-Targeting Climate Activists," *The New Times*, October 10, 2023, https://www.newtimes.co.rw/article/4053/opinions/in-defense-of-the-art-targeting-climate-activists, accessed October 11, 2023.

22. Kathleen Massara, "Environmental Activists Focus on Museums That Take Oil," *New York Times*, October 9, 2018, https://www.nytimes.com/2018/10/09/business/environmental-activists-take-on-oil-money.html, accessed October 1, 2023.

23. Just Stop Oil press release, "Young Supporters of Just Stop Oil Glue Themselves to a Van Gogh Painting," June 30, 2022, https://juststopoil.org/2022/06/30/young-supporters-of-just-stop-oil-glue-themselves-to-a-van-gogh-painting/, accessed October 1, 2023.

24. David Boyd, *The Rights of Nature: A Legal Revolution That Could Save the World* (London: Ingram, 2017).

25. Editorial Board, "Attacking Art Isn't Climate 'Protest.' It's Vandalism," *Washington Post*, May 8, 2023, https://www.washingtonpost.com/opinions/2023/05/08/climate-protest-degas-national-gallery/, accessed October 1, 2023; Jerry Saltz, "Mashed Potatoes Meet Monet: Climate Activists Have Been Celebrated for Defacing Great Paintings? Why?," *New York*, December 6, 2022, https://www.curbed.com/2022/12/climate-change-activists-fine-art-vandalism.html#new_tab, accessed October 1, 2023; Robinson Meyer, "The Climate Art Vandals Are Embarrassing," *Atlantic*, October 27, 2022, https://www.theatlantic.com/science/archive/2022/10/vermeer-glue-soup-climate-protest-outrage/671904/, accessed October 1, 2023.

26. Quoted in Shah, "Can Art Destruction Save Us from Climate Destruction?"

27. William E. Scheuerman, "Busyness and Citizenship," *Social Research* 72, no. 2 (2005): 447–70.

28. Andreas Malm, "History May Absolve the Soup Throwers," *New York Times*, October 20, 2022, https://www.nytimes.com/2022/10/20/opinion/just-stop-oil-soup-sunflowers-climate.html, accessed October 1, 2023.

29. The memorials include many colleges, parks, schools, bridges, and highways named after Confederate worthies or honoring its veterans.

30. Andrew Valls, "What Should Become of Confederate War Monuments? A Normative Framework," *Public Affairs Quarterly* 33, no. 3 (2019): 172–93.

31. Between 1996 and 2018, for example, the State of Virginia distributed $1.6 million in funding for the upkeep of Confederate cemeteries. Clint Smith, *How the Word Is Passed: A Reckoning with the History of Slavery Across America* (New York: Back Bay, 2021), 133.

32. Southern Poverty Law Center, *Whose Heritage? Public Symbols of the Confederacy*, 3rd ed., 2022, https://www.splcenter.org/sites/default/files/whose-heritage-report-third-edition.pdf, accessed October 10, 2023; see also Karen L. Cox, *No Common Ground: Confederate Monuments and the Ongoing Fight for Racial Justice* (Chapel Hill: University of North Carolina Press, 2021), 1–11.

33. "How Statues Are Falling Around the World," *New York Times*, September 12, 2020, https://www.nytimes.com/2020/06/24/us/confederate-statues-photos.html.

34. Jeffrey C. Isaac, "When Protest Crosses the Line: Why the Toppling of U.S. Grant Is Idiocy Run Amok," *Democracy in Dark Times* (Blog), June 21, 2020, https://jeffreycisaacdesign.wordpress.com/2020/06/21/when-protest-crosses-the-line-why-the-toppling-of-u-s-grant-is-idiocy-run-amok/, accessed October 1, 2023.

35. Wisconsin Democratic State Senator Tim Carpenter was assaulted by protestors toppling Madison's Heg statue.

36. I am interested in the latter here, though the distinction between the two types sometimes blurs.

37. Gamboni, *The Destruction of Art*, 67.

38. Gamboni, *The Destruction of Art*, 27.

39. Cox, *No Common Ground*, 6–7.

40. Erin L. Thompson, *Smashing Statues: The Rise and Fall of America's Public Monuments* (New York: Oxford University Press, 2022), 168–70.

41. Jessica Owley, Jess Phelps, and Sean W, Hughes, "Private Confederate Monuments," *Lewis and Clark Law Review* 25, no. 1 (2021): 254-302.

42. See "List of Monuments and Memorials Removed During the George Floyd Protests," Wikipedia, https://en.wikipedia.org/List_of_monuments_and_memorials_removed_during _the_George_Floyd_protests, accessed October 1, 2023.

43. Cox, *No Common Ground*; Thompson, *Smashing Statues*.

44. J. Michael Martinez, "Traditionalist Perspectives on Confederate Symbols," in *Confederate Symbols in the Contemporary South*, ed. J. Michael Martinez, William D. Richardson, and Ron McNinch-Su (Gainesville: University Press of Florida, 2000), 243-80.

45. Roger C. Hartley, *Monumental Harm: Reckoning with Jim Crow Era Confederate Monuments* (Columbia: University of South Carolina Press, 2020), xii.

46. Key contributions include: Macalester Bell, "Against Simple Removal: A Defence of Defacement as a Response to Racist Monuments," *Journal of Applied Philosophy* 39, no. 5 (2022): 778-92; Joanna Burch-Brown, "Is It Wrong to Topple Statues and Rename Schools?," *Journal of Political Theory & Philosophy* 1 (2017): 59-87; Helen Frowe, "The Duty to Remove Statues of Wrongdoers," *Journal of Practical Ethics* 7, no. 3 (2019): 1-31; Ten-Herng Lai, "Political Vandalism as Counter-Speech: A Defense of Defacing and Destroying Tainted Monuments," *European Journal of Philosophy* 28 (2020): 602-16; Travis Timmerman, "Removing Historical Monuments," in *Ethics, Left and Right: The Moral Issues That Divide Us*, ed. Bob Fisher (New York: Oxford University Press, 2020), 513-22.

47. Summarizing preservationist arguments, see Chong-Ming Lim, "Vandalizing Tainted Commemorations," *Philosophy and Public Affairs* 48, no. 2 (2020): 192-97.

48. Robert Bevan, *Monumental Lies: Culture Wars and the Truth About the Past* (New York: Verso, 2022), 266.

49. Michele Moody-Adams, *Making Space for Justice: Social Movements, Collective Imagination, and Political Hope* (New York: Columbia University Press, 2022), 118-19.

50. Lim, "Vandalizing Tainted Commemorations," 187.

51. Thompson, *Smashing Statues*, xviii.

52. Hartley, *Monumental Harm*, 163-80; J. Michael Martinez, "Confederate Symbols, the Courts, and the Political Question Doctrine," in *Confederate Symbols in the Contemporary South*, ed. J. Michael Martinez, William D. Richardson, and Ron McNinch-Su (Gainesville: University Press of Florida, 2000), 224-39. For criticism of the judiciary's refusal to limit racist commemorations, see James Forman Jr., "Driving Dixie Down: Removing the Confederate Flags from Southern State Capitols," *Yale Law Journal* 101, no. 2 (1991): 195-223.

53. Johannes Schulz, "Must Rhodes Fall? The Significance of Commemoration in the Struggle for Relations of Respect," *Journal of Political Philosophy* 27, no. 2 (2019): 173.

54. Quoted in Levinson, *Written in Stone*, 151.

55. Lim, "Vandalizing Tainted Commemorations," 185-216.

56. Thompson, *Smashing Statues*, xviii.

57. Moody-Adams speaks, for example, of "expressive harms" (*Making Space for Justice*, 141-42); see also Timmerman, who associates the monuments with harm and suffering ("Removing Historical Monuments," 516). In a related vein, Arianne Shahvisi views colonialist monuments as a type of harmful "slurring speech" (Arianne Shahvisi, "Colonial Monuments as Slurring Speech," *Journal of Philosophy of Education* 55 [2021], 453-68).

58. Chelsey R. Carter, "Racist Monuments Are Killing Us," *Museum Anthropology* 43, no. 2 (2018): 140.

59. There are echoes here of what Pierre Bourdieu has called "symbolic violence" (Pierre Bourdieu et al., *The Weight of the World: Social Suffering in Contemporary Society*, trans. Priscilla Parkhurst Ferguson [Palo Alto, CA: Stanford University Press, 1999], 126). Yet, revealingly, even Bourdieu's more sympathetic readers (e.g., David L. Swartz, *Symbolic Power, Politics and Intellectuals: The Political Sociology of Pierre Bourdieu* [Chicago: University of Chicago University Press, 2013], 98–101) concede that his notion of symbolic violence blurs into what others have described as ideology, hegemony, or power. In short, violence's distinctive contours disappear from view.

60. Exec. Order 13933, 85 FR 40081 (July 2, 2020).

61. Alexander Adams, *Iconoclasm, Identity Politics, and the Erasure of History* (Exeter: Imprint Academic, 2020), 19.

62. Anne Nassauer, *Situational Breakdowns: Understanding Protest Violence and Other Surprising Outcomes* (New York: Oxford University Press, 2019), 78. Thus, it makes sense to train police and other security officials to recognize that property damage can occur absent violence against persons.

63. Lai, "Political Vandalism as Counter-Speech," 613.

64. Alexander Demandt, *Vadalismus: Gewalt gegen Kultur* (Berlin: Siedler, 1997), 262–70.

65. Quoted in Levinson, *Written in Stone*, 145.

66. Levinson, *Written in Stone*, 145.

67. Kate Wagner, "The Secret History of America's Worthless Confederate Monuments," *New Republic*, August 6, 2020, https://newrepublic.com/article/158715/secret-history-americas -worthless-confederate-monuments, accessed October 1, 2023.

68. For the legal particulars: John Henry Merryman and Albert E. Elsen, *Law, Ethics, and the Visual Arts*, 3rd ed. (London: Kluwer, 1998), 231–94.

69. Schulz, "Must Rhodes Fall?," 183.

70. Thompson, *Smashing Statues*, 181–82.

71. Dan Demetriou and Ajume Wingo, "The Ethics of Racist Monuments," in *Palgrave Handbook of Philosophy and Public Policy*, ed. David Boonin (New York: Palgrave, 2018), 349.

72. On this problem, see Thompson, *Smashing Statues*. Similar byzantine rules exist elsewhere, e.g., in London (Bevan, *Monumental Lies*, 306–7).

73. Jessica Owley and Jess Phelps, "The Life and Death of Confederate Monuments," *Buffalo Law Review* 68, no. 5 (2020): 1443–54; for a list of relevant statutes, see "Removal of Confederate Monuments and Memorials," Wikipedia, https://en.wikipedia.org/wiki/Removal_of _Confederate_monuments_and_memorials, accessed October 1, 2023.

74. Abhinav S. Krishnan, "How GOP Lawmakers Are Pushing for Confederate Monuments to be (Legally) Set in Stone," *USA Today*, August 17, 2023, https://www.usatoday.com/story /news/investigations/2023/08/17/confederate-monuments-protected-new-laws/70576502007/, accessed October 1, 2023.

75. Cited in Thompson, *Smashing Statues*, 140, emphasis mine.

76. Stone Mountain, part of a George state park, includes massive mountain reliefs of Confederate leaders Jefferson Davis, Robert E. Lee, and Stonewall Jackson. They were completed in 1972 (!).

77. Cox, *No Common Ground*, 27–56; Hartley, *Monumental Harm*, 24–52; Owley and Phelps, "Life and Death of Confederate Monuments," 1401–8.

78. Carl Fox, "Down with This Sort of Thing: Why No Public Statue Should Stand Favor," *Critical Review of International Social and Political Philosophy* (forthcoming).

79. Owley and Phelps, "Life and Death of Confederate Monuments," 1468.

80. Quoted in Owley and Phelps, "Life and Death of Confederate Monuments," 1456.

81. Owley and Phelps, "Life and Death of Confederate Monuments," 1456–57. The Lee statue was removed.

82. Owley and Phelps, "Life and Death of Confederate Monuments," 1429.

83. Owley and Phelps, "Life and Death of Confederate Monuments," 1477.

84. Owley, Phelps, and Hughes, "Private Confederate Monuments."

85. On efforts to remove and/or contextualize confederate monuments, see Cox, *No Common Ground*, 57–167.

86. Scheuerman, *Civil Disobedience*.

87. King, "Letter from Birmingham City Jail," 74.

88. Marshall Cohen, "Civil Disobedience in a Constitutional Democracy," *Massachusetts Review* 10 (1969): 211–26.

89. Lim, "Vandalizing Tainted Commemorations," 209.

90. Paul Gowder, *The Rule of Law in the United States: An Unfinished Project of Black Liberation* (Oxford: Hart, 2021), 117.

91. For one influential statement of this position, see Rawls, *A Theory of Justice*, 363–91.

92. Thompson, *Smashing Statues*, 108.

93. Thompson, *Smashing Statues*, 117–18.

94. Moody-Adams, *Making Space for Justice*, 145.

95. Thompson, *Smashing Statues*, 101.

96. Peter Singer, *Democracy and Civil Disobedience* (Oxford: Oxford University Press, 1973), 83–4.

97. There have been many such incidents—for example, on July 6, 2021, in Long Beach, California, when racists painted swastikas on a statue of Martin Luther King Jr.

98. Rawls, *Theory of Justice*, 376.

99. Zick, *Managed Dissent*, 41–44.

100. Ristroph, "Criminal Law in the Shadow of Violence," 587.

Chapter 4

1. On disruptive disobedience, see Oscar Berglund, "Disruptive Protest, Civil Disobedience, and Direct Action," *Politics* (forthcoming); Stephen D'Arcy, *Languages of the Unheard: Why Militant Protest Is Good for Democracy* (London: Zed, 2013), 89–118; Smith, "Disruptive Democracy."

2. On sabotage as "hidden resistance," see James C. Scott, *Weapons of the Week: Everyday Forms of Resistance* (New Haven: Yale University Press, 1985), 29–31.

3. Eric Hobsbawm, "The Machine Breakers," *Past & Present* 1, no. 1 (1952): 52–70. The Luddites remain an inspiration for recent defenders of sabotage: Gavin Mueller, *Breaking Things at Work: The Luddites Were Right About Why You Hate Your Job* (New York: Verso, 2021); David F. Noble, *Progress Without People: In Defense of Luddism* (Chicago: Charles Kerr, 1993); Kirkpatrick Sale, *Rebels Against the Future: The Luddites and Their War on the Industrial Revolution* (Reading, MA: Addison-Wesley, 1995).

4. On sabotage in workers' movements, see Pierre Dubois, *Sabotage in Industry*, trans. Rosemary Sheed (New York: Penguin, 1979); Gerald Mars, ed., *Work Place Sabotage* (Aldershot, UK: Ashgate, 2001).

5. Philip S. Foner, *History of the Labor Movement in The United States: The Industrial Workers of the World, 1905–1917* (New York: International Publishers, 1973), 161.

6. T. K. Wilson, *Killing Strangers: How Political Violence Became Modern* (New York: Oxford University Press, 2020), 169–205.

7. *Simple Sabotage Field Manual: Strategic Services (Provisional)* (Washington, DC: Office of Strategic Services, 1944).

8. For recent theoretical defenses of sabotage, see Brennan, *When All Else Fails*, 46–48, 155–86; Delmas, *A Duty to Resist*, 37–38. On ecotage, see Joseph M. Brown, "Civil Disobedience, Sabotage, and Violence in Environmental Activism," in *Oxford Handbook of Comparative Environmental Politics*, ed. Jeannie Sowers, Stacy D. VanDeVeer, and Erika Weinthal (New York: Oxford University Press, 2021), 356–74; Matthew Humphrey, "Democratic Legitimacy, Public Justification and Environmental Direct Action," *Political Studies* 54, no. 2 (2006): 310–27; Michael Martin, "Ecosabotage and Civil Disobedience," *Environmental Ethics* 12 (1990): 291–310; Jennifer Welchman, "Is Ecosabotage Civil Disobedience?," *Philosophy & Geography* 4, no. 1 (2001): 97–107.

9. King, *Where Do We Go from Here?*, 196–97.

10. For example, see Mathew Humphrey and Marc Stears, "Animal Rights Protest and the Challenge to Deliberative Democracy," *Economy and Society* 35, no. 3 (2006): 400–422; John Medearis, *Why Democracy Is Oppositional* (Cambridge: Harvard University Press, 2015), 29. For a smart discussion, see William Smith, "Deliberative Democratic Disobedience," in *Cambridge Companion to Civil Disobedience*, ed. William E. Scheuerman (New York: Cambridge University Press, 2021), 105–27.

11. Dina Gilio-Whitaker, *As Long as Grass Grows: The Indigenous Fight for Environmental Justice. From Colonization to Standing Rock* (Boston: Beacon, 2019), 6.

12. Ronald Dworkin, *A Matter of Principle* (Cambridge: Harvard University Press, 1985), 111–13.

13. Bondurant, *Conquest of Violence*, 9.

14. In an affluent Stockholm neighborhood, activists in July 2007 vandalized SUVs to temporarily disable one source of "luxury" carbon emissions (Malm, *How to Blow Up a Pipeline*, 79–84).

15. Steve Vanderheiden, "Ecoterrorism or Justified Resistance? Radical Environmentalism and the 'War on Terror,'" *Politics & Society* 33, no. 3 (2005): 436.

16. Barbara Epstein, *Political Protest & Cultural Revolution: Nonviolent Direct Action in the 1970s and 1980s* (Berkeley: University of California Press, 1991).

17. For the details, see "1998 Vail Arson Attacks," Wikipedia, https://en.wikipedia.org/wiki/1998_Vail_arson_attacks, accessed April 20, 2025.

18. Martin Oppenheimer, *The Sit-In Movement of 1960* (Brooklyn: Carlson, 1989); Christopher W. Schmidt, *The Sit-Ins: Protest and Legal Challenge in the Civil Rights Era* (Chicago: University of Chicago Press, 2018).

19. Peñalver and Katyal, *Property Outlaws*, 7.

20. William E. Scheuerman, "From Labor Sit-downs to Civil Rights Sit-ins: A Genealogy of Liberal Civil Disobedience," *Review of Politics* 86, no. 3 (2024): 356–79.

21. Some civil rights sit-ins morphed into temporally longer protests. In Chicago in 1965, King "improvised a sit-in," helping to take over a badly neglected apartment building, with tenants refusing to pay rent until the owner addressed its shameful state. See Jonathan Eig, *The Life of Dr. Martin Luther King* (New York: Simon & Schuster, 2023), 478.

22. Katrina Forrester, *In the Shadow of Justice: Postwar Liberalism and the Remaking of Political Philosophy* (Princeton: Princeton University Press, 2019), 40–71; Erin Pineda, *Seeing*

Like an Activist: Civil Disobedience and the Civil Rights Movement (New York: Oxford University Press, 2021).

23. In this vein, see Marcou, "Violence, Communication, and Civil Disobedience"; Milligan, *Civil Disobedience*, 103–36.

24. Jordan Simmons, "'Overt Bastardization of the Truth': Valve Turner Listed as 'Extremist' by US Government Faces Upcoming Trial," *Ecowatch*, February 7, 2020, https://www.ecowatch .com/valve-turners-climate-direct-action-2645054934.html, accessed November 10, 2023.

25. Cited in Malm, *How to Blow Up a Pipeline*, 98.

26. Scheuerman, *Civil Disobedience*, 122–39; see also Molly Sauter, *The Coming Swarm: DDOS Actions, Hacktivism, and Civil Disobedience on the Internet* (London: Bloomsbury, 2014).

27. S.3880 (109th), Animal Enterprise Terrorism Act (2006).

28. Kevin Johnson, "I Released 2,000 Minks from a Fur Farm. Now I'm a Convicted Terrorist," *Guardian*, November 15, 2017, https://www.theguardian.com/commentisfree/2017/nov /15/i-released-2000-minks-fur-farm-convicted-terrorist, accessed November 10, 2023. Civil libertarians worry about its chilling impact on protest and public contestation: see "Rights Group Challenges Law that Punishes Animal Rights Activists as 'Terrorists,'" Center Constitutional Rights, May 9, 2016, https://ccrjustice.org/home/press-center/press-releases/rights-group -challenges-law-punishes-animal-rights-activists, accessed November 10, 2023. US Attorney General Pam Bondi has announced that she will treat politically motivated damage to Tesla vehicles as terrorist acts (Minho Kim and Glenn Thrush, "Pam Bondi Calls Tesla Vandalism 'Domestic Terrorism,' Promising Steep Consequences," *New York Times*, March 18, 2025, https://www.nytimes.com/2025/03/18/us/politics/tesla-vandalism-domestic-terrorism.html? searchResultPosition=1, accessed March 19, 2025.

29. Since the Capitol attacks were egged on by then–President Trump, and the Brazilian copycat protests by Jair Bolsonaro, they represent cases combining "top-down" and "bottom-up" features. My interest in this volume lies predominantly with the latter.

30. Stathis N. Kalyvas, *The Logic of Violence in Civil War* (New York: Cambridge University Press, 2006).

31. United States Attorney's Office, District of Columbia, "30 Months Since the Jan. 6 Attack on the Capitol," July 6, 2023, https://www.justice.gov/usao-dc/30-months-jan-6-attack -capitol, accessed November 5, 2023. The US Supreme Court, however, ruled against the Justice Department's reading of statutes prohibiting obstruction of official proceedings (Fischer v. United States, No. 23–5572 [2024]). President Trump subsequently pardoned even those January 6 participants who participated in violent acts against police officers. Political violence and property damage, it seems, is acceptable, even when committed by white supremacists and other far-right fringe groups, as long as it meshes with Trump's political preferences. There is a long and ugly history in the United States of tolerating such acts when committed by racists and other defenders of white supremacy, while aggressively cracking down when committed by marginal groups or social critics.

32. From the perspective of those prosecuting crimes, of course, the difference remains legally significant.

33. Lax restrictions of the Second Amendment mean that the appearance of armed protestors and counter-protestors is increasingly commonplace at US demonstrations (Zick, *Managed Dissent*, 143–62).

34. Melvyn Dubofsky, *We Shall Be All: A History of the Industrial Workers of the World* (Chicago: Quadrangle, 1969).

35. Foner, *History of The Labor Movement in The United States*, 161; see also Rebecca H. Lossin, "The Point of Destruction: Sabotage, Speech, and Progressive-Era Politics" (PhD diss., Columbia University, 2020).

36. Emile Pouget, *Sabotage*, trans. and introduced by Arturo M. Giovannitti (Chicago: Charles H. Kerr, 1913). Key IWW pamphlets on sabotage are collected in Salvatore Salerno, ed., *Direct Action & Sabotage* (Oakland: PM Press, 2014).

37. Arturo M. Giovannitti, "Introduction," in *Sabotage*, by Emile Pouget (Chicago: Charles H. Kerr, 1913), 13–14; Pouget, *Sabotage*, 78, 97.

38. Foner, *History of The Labor Movement in The United States*, 162.

39. Walker C. Smith, "Sabotage: Its History, Philosophy & Function" [1913], in *Direct Action & Sabotage*, ed. Salvatore Salerno (Oakland: PM Press, 2014), 60; Pouget, *Sabotage*, 104; see also Elizabeth Gurley Flynn, "Sabotage" [1916], in *Direct Action & Sabotage*, ed. Salvatore Salerno (Oakland: PM Press, 2014), 94.

40. Smith, "Sabotage: Its History," 86.

41. Gurley Flynn, "Sabotage," 114.

42. Salvatore Salerno, "Introduction," in *Direct Action & Sabotage*, ed. Salvatore Salerno (Oakland: PM Press, 2014), 1–33.

43. Pouget, *Sabotage*, 105–7.

44. Ahmed White, *Under the Iron Heel: The Wobblies and the Capitalist War on Radical Workers* (Berkeley: University of California Press, 2024), 14.

45. William E. Trautmann, "Direct Action and Sabotage" [1912], in *Direct Action & Sabotage*, ed. Salvatore Salerno (Oakland: PM Press, 2014), 42; Smith, "Sabotage: Its History," 65–67. Thorsten Veblen built on the Wobbly juxtaposition of worker to capitalist sabotage in a rare discussion of the topic by a major social thinker: see "On the Nature and Uses of Sabotage" [1919], in *Work Place Sabotage*, ed., Gerald Mars (Aldershot, UK: Ashgate, 2001), 3–18.

46. Smith, "Sabotage: Its History," 85–86.

47. Smith, "Sabotage: Its History," 80.

48. Trautmann, "Direct Action and Sabotage," 34–35.

49. Ahmed A. White, "The Crime of Economic Radicalism: Criminal Syndicalism Laws and the Industrial Workers of the World, 1917–1927," *Oregon Law Review* 85, no. 3 (2006): 692.

50. White, "Crime of Economic Radicalism," 710–47.

51. Adam Hochschild, *American Midnight: The Great War, A Violent Peace, and Democracy's Forgotten Crisis* (New York: Mariner, 2022), 85–86.

52. Hochschild, *American Midnight*, 160.

53. King, *Where Do We Go From Here?*, 196–97.

54. Revealingly, Dubofsky barely mentions incidents of IWW sabotage; see also Foner, *History of The Labor Movement in The United States*, 163–64.

55. Foner, *History of The Labor Movement in The United States*, 163.

56. Foner, *History of The Labor Movement in The United States*, 163–64.

57. Gurley Flynn, "Sabotage," 113; Smith, "Sabotage: Its History," 71.

58. Pouget, *Sabotage*, 64.

59. Foner, *History of The Labor Movement in The United States*, 159.

60. For the sordid details, see Smith, "Crime of Economic Radicalism," 710–69.

61. Edward Abbey, *The Monkey Wrench Gang* (New York: Harper, 1985 [1975]).

62. Keith Makoto Woodhouse, *The Ecocentrists: A History of Radical Environmentalism* (New York: Columbia University Press, 2018), 94–142.

63. David Foreman, *Ecodefense: A Field Guide to Monkeywrenching* (Tucson, AZ: A Ned Ludd Book, 1985). Abbey wrote what he dubbed a "Forward!" to the handbook.

64. Abbey, *The Monkey Wrench Gang*, 170, 189.

65. Abbey, *The Monkey Wrench Gang*, 170.

66. Foreman, *Ecodefense*, 10.

67. On debates among radical US-based greens on violence, see Woodhouse, *The Ecocentrics*.

68. Eugene Hargrove, "Ecological Sabotage: Pranks or Terrorism?," *Environmental Ethics* 4, no. 4 (1982): 292.

69. Hargrove, "Ecological Sabotage: Pranks or Terrorism?," 292.

70. The libertarian writer Ron Arnold, who has appeared before Congress, may have first introduced the term and helped popularize it: Ron Arnold, "Eco-Terrorism," *Reason*, February 1983, https://reason.com/1983/02/01/eco-terrorism/, accessed November 14, 2023.

71. For legal details, see Rebecca K. Smith, "'Ecoterrorism'? A Critical Analysis of the Vilification of Radical Environmentalists as Terrorists," *Environmental Law* 38, no. 2 (2008): 537-76.

72. Testimony of James F. Jarboe, FBI Domestic Terrorism Section Chief, US House Resources Committee, February 12, 2002, https://archives.fbi.gov/archives/news/testimony/the-threat-of-eco-terrorism, accessed November 14, 2023.

73. Jerry Markon, "FBI Probes Were Improper, Justice Says," *Washington Post*, September 20, 2010, https://www.washingtonpost.com/wp-dyn/content/article/2010/09/20/AR2010092003100_pf.html, accessed November 5, 2023.

74. Madeline Johl, "Activism or Domestic Terrorism? How the Terrorism Enhancement Is Used to Punish Acts of Political Protest," *Fordham Urban Law Journal* 50, nos. 3/4 (2023): 465-503.

75. Michael Loadenthal examined over 27,100 "violent" incidents: 98 percent targeted property, and 99.7 percent resulted in no harm or injury to persons; see Michael Loadenthal, "'Eco-Terrorism': An Incident-Driven History of Attack (1973-2010)," *Journal for the Study of Radicalism* 11, no. 2 (2017): 1-34.

76. Sea Shepherd's leading figure Paul Watson in 2017 suspended its disruption of whalers' activities in part because of anti-terrorism legislation. Prominent Earthfirst! activists also previously pushed back against some of the group's more militant tactics (Woodhouse, *The Ecocentrics*, 183-234).

77. April Carter, *Direct Action and Liberal Democracy* (New York: Harper, 1973), 20.

78. Carter, *Direct Action and Liberal Democracy*, 21.

79. William E. Scheuerman, "Political Disobedience and the Climate Emergency," *Philosophy & Social Criticism* 48, no. 6 (2022): 791-812. For an effort to deploy King to defend nonviolent protest in response to the climate crisis, see Darrel Moellendorf, *Mobilizing Hope: Climate Change and Global Poverty* (New York: Oxford University Press, 2022).

80. Naomi Klein, *This Changes Everything: Capitalism vs. The Climate* (New York: Simon & Schuster, 2014), 293-336.

81. Malm, *How to Blow Up a Pipeline*, 67.

82. Malm, *How to Blow Up a Pipeline*, 69.

83. Kaylana Mueller-Hsia, "Anti-Protest Laws Threaten Indigenous and Climate Movements," Brennan Center, March 17, 2021, https://www.brennancenter.org/our-work/analysis-opinion/anti-protest-laws-threaten-indigenous-and-climate-movements, accessed November 10, 2023. Hilary Beaumont and Nina Lakhani, "Revealed: How the Fossil Fuel Industry Helps Spread Anti-Protest

Laws Across the US," *Guardian*, September 26, 2024, https://www.theguardian.com/us-news/2024/sep/26/anti-protest-laws-fossil-fuel-lobby, accessed October 24, 2024.

84. Lette Yayler and Cara Schulte, "Targeting Environmental Activists With Counterterrorism Measures Is an Abuse of the Law," Human Rights Watch, November 29, 2019, https://www.hrw.org/news/2019/11/29/targeting-environmental-activists-counterterrorism-measures-abuse-law, accessed November 10, 2023.

85. Pichl, *Law statt Order*, 109–19.

86. Jessie Kindig, "Preface," in *Property Will Cost Us the Earth: Direct Action and the Future of the Global Climate Movement*, ed. Jessie Kindig (New York: Verso, 2022). It is surely Verso's first book to have been adapted into a film for popular audiences. Directed by Daniel Goldhaber, the film *How to Blow Up a Pipeline*, a fictionalization based on Malm's book, was released in April 2023.

87. Malm, *How to Blow Up a Pipeline*, 100.

88. Malm, *How to Blow Up a Pipeline*, 102.

89. Malm, *How to Blow Up a Pipeline*, 161.

90. See Ende Gelände's description of its tactics: https://www.ende-gelaende.org/en/, accessed November 5, 2023.

91. Scheuerman, "Political Disobedience and the Climate Emergency," 803–5. On the climate crisis as an existential risk, see Alex McLaughlin, "Existential Risk, Climate Change, and Nonideal Justice," *Monist* 107, no. 2 (2024): 190–206.

92. See, among others, Chenoweth and Stephan, *Why Civil Resistance Works*.

93. Malm, *How to Blow Up a Pipeline*, 31–34, 241.

94. Malm, *How to Blow Up a Pipeline*, 107, 119.

95. Malm, *How to Blow Up a Pipeline*, 119.

96. Malm, *How to Blow Up a Pipeline*, 104.

97. Malm, *How to Blow Up a Pipeline*, 13.

98. Malm, *How to Blow Up a Pipeline*, 84–93; Henry Shue, "Subsistence Emissions and Luxury Emissions," *Law & Policy* 15 (1993): 39–60.

99. For Malm's updated Leninism, see Andreas Malm, *Corona, Climate, and Chronic Emergency: War Communism in the Twenty-First Century* (New York: Verso, 2020), 109–74.

100. For example, the young Nelson Mandela, a defender of sabotage while leading the African National Congress' military wing, struggled with the issue of how disruptive property disobedience could avoid possible losses of human life. See Jonathan Hyslop, "Mandela on War," in *Cambridge Companion to Nelson Mandela*, ed. R. Barnard (New York: Cambridge University Press, 2014), 162–81.

101. Vanderheiden, "Ecoterrorism or Justified Resistance?," 432–44.

102. Smith, "Disruptive Democracy," 22.

103. Singer, *Democracy and Civil Disobedience*, 83–84.

104. Hochschild, *American Midnight*, 160.

105. Hochschild, *American Midnight*, 162. Germans were targeted because of World War I and their association with recent immigrants who had imported left-wing ideas; Jews because of antisemitism and their assumed links to radicalism.

106. Hochschild, *American Midnight*, 170.

107. For example, in authoritarian Nigeria, MEND (Movement for the Emancipation of the Nigerian Delta) has engaged in acts of violence not only against the fossil fuels infrastructure but also against petroleum industry personnel.

Chapter 5

1. Peñalver and Katyal, *Property Outlaws*, 23–35.

2. Cited in Open Society Justice Initiative, *Strategic Litigation Impacts: Indigenous Peoples' Land Rights* (New York: Open Society Foundations, 2017); Fred Pearce, *The Land Grabbers: The New Fight over Who Owns the Earth* (Boston: Beacon Press, 2012).

3. For a survey, see John-Andrew McNeish, "Indigenous Peoples: Extraction and Extractivism," in *Routledge Handbook of Indigenous Development*, ed. Katharina Ruckstuhl, Irma A. Velasquez Nimatuj, John-Andrew McNeish, and Nancy Postero (New York: Routledge, 2022), 237–45.

4. Joanne Barker, *Red Scare: The State's Indigenous Terrorist* (Oakland: University of California Press, 2021).

5. Nick Estes, *Our History Is the Future: Standing Rock Versus the Dakota Access Pipeline, and the Long Tradition of Indigenous Protest* (New York: Verso, 2019).

6. Estes, *Our History Is Our Future*, 26–27; Gilio-Whitaker, *As Long as Grass Grows*, 130–32. Indigenous activists reference the so-called Sioux Treaties, and especially the Fort Laramie Treaty (1868), to justify property reclamations. The treaties are complicated, yet even the US National Archives website notes that Native peoples forced to give up territory in the Great Plains states reserved some rights to use and benefit from land and resources falling outside of designated reservations. See "Treaty of Fort Laramie (1868)," National Archives, https://www .archives.gov/milestone-documents/fort-laramie-treaty, accessed January 13, 2024.

7. For the jurisprudence, see Carla F. Fredericks and Jesse D. Heibel, "Standing Rock, the Sioux Treaties, and the Limits of the Supremacy Clause," *University of Colorado Law Review* 89 (2018): 477–532.

8. Estes, *Our History Is Our Future*, 43; Gilio-Whitaker, *As Long as the Grass Grows*, 131. The National Historical Preservation Act (1966) established procedural mechanisms so that Native American tribes could protect historical sites.

9. Sue Skalicky and Monica Davey, "Tensions Between Police and Standing Rock Protestors Reach Boiling Point," *New York Times*, October 29, 2016, A10; Gilio-Whitaker, *As Long as Grass Grows*, 7–8.

10. On the history of dispossession in North America, see Allan Greer, *Property and Dispossession: Natives, Empires and Land in Early Modern North America* (New York: Cambridge University Press, 2018). For a critical-theoretical analysis, see Robert Nichols, *Theft Is Property: Dispossession and Critical Theory* (Durham: Duke University Press, 2020).

11. Epstein, *Takings*, 349.

12. Joseph William Singer, "Original Acquisition of Property: From Conquest & Possession to Democracy & Equal Opportunity," *Indiana Law Journal* 86, no. 3 (2011): 773. The problem is old: John Stuart Mill observed in 1871 that contemporary property in Europe was principally a consequence of "conquest and violence." John Stuart Mill, *Principles of Political Economy* (New York: Oxford University Press, 1994 [1871]), 15.

13. Pierre-Joseph Proudhon, *What Is Property?*, trans. Donald R. Kelley and Bonnie G. Smith (New York: Cambridge University Press, 1994).

14. Jeremy Waldron, "Indigeneity? First Peoples and Last Occupancy," *New Zealand Journal of Public and International Law* 55, no. 1 (2003): 55–82.

15. Jeremy Waldron, "Superseding Historical Injustice," *Ethics* 103, no. 1 (1992): 26.

16. Waldron, *The Right to Private Property*, 284–87.

17. For critiques, see Burke A. Hendrix, *Ownership, Authority, and Self-Determination* (University Park: Penn State Press, 2008); Kerstein Reibold, "Why Indigenous Land Rights Have Not Been Superseded—A Critical Application of Waldron's Theory of Supersession," *Critical Review of International Social and Political Philosophy* 25, no. 4 (2022): 480–95; Janna Thompson, "Historical Obligations," *Australasian Journal of Philosophy* 78, no. 3 (2000): 334–45.

18. For a skeptical take on appeals to the Fort Laramie Treaty, see Vine Deloria Jr., "Alcatraz, Activism, and Accommodation," in *American Indian Activism: Alcatraz to the Longest Walk*, ed. Troy Johnson, Joane Nagel, and Duane Champagne (Urbana: University of Illinois Press, 1997), 46–47.

19. On Alcatraz as a positive "catalyst for change," see Troy R. Johnson, *The Occupation of Alcatraz Island: Indian Self-Determination and the Rise of Indian Activism* (Urbana: University of Illinois Press, 1996), 217–21. Under President Richard M. Nixon, the US Congress enacted reforms to enhance tribal self-government, support Indigenous cultural rights, and facilitate economic development. On Alcatraz as an inspiration, see Kent Blansett, *A Journey to Freedom: Richard Oakes, Alcatraz, and the Red Power Movement* (New Haven: Yale University Press, 2018), 166–270.

20. Johnson, *The Occupation of Alcatraz Island*, 40.

21. Cited in Johnson, *The Occupation of Alcatraz Island*, 67–8 (68); Blansett, *A Journey to Freedom*, 154–55.

22. Cited in Johnson, *The Occupation of Alcatraz Island*, 70.

23. Cited in Johnson, *The Occupation of Alcatraz Island*, 58.

24. Johnson, *The Occupation of Alcatraz Island*, 54.

25. Cited in Blansett, *A Journey to Freedom*, 128.

26. Johnson, *The Occupation of Alcatraz Island*, 65.

27. The spiral of violence that contributed to the Alcatraz reoccupation's demise is recounted in Johnson, *The Occupation of Alcatraz Island*, 151–71.

28. Burke A. Hendrix, *Strategies of Justice: Aboriginal Peoples, Persistent Injustice, and the Ethics of Political Action* (New York: Oxford University Press, 2018). Hendrix's argument parallels Tommie Shelby's analysis of political obligation among African Americans subjected to extreme injustice in *Dark Ghettos: Injustice, Dissent, and Reform* (Cambridge: Harvard University Press, 2018).

29. Hendrix, *Strategies of Justice*, 118.

30. Taiaiake Alfred, *Wasase: Indigenous Pathways of Action and Freedom* (Orchard Park, NY: Broadview, 2005).

31. Hendrix, *Strategies of Justice*, 142–45.

32. Martin Luther King Jr., "Nonviolence: The Only Road to Freedom," in *A Testament of Hope: The Essential Writings and Speeches of Martin Luther King, Jr.*, ed. James M. Washington (New York: HarperCollins, 1986), 55.

33. Martin Luther King Jr., "The Social Organization of Nonviolence," in *A Testament of Hope: The Essential Writings and Speeches of Martin Luther King, Jr.*, ed. James M. Washington (New York: HarperCollins, 1986), 32–3. See my additional remarks on this distinction in Chapter 7.

34. A major finding of Chenoweth and Stephan, *Why Civil Resistance Works*.

35. Martin Luther King Jr., "Love, Law, and Civil Disobedience," in *A Testament of Hope: The Essential Writings and Speeches of Martin Luther King, Jr.*, ed. James M. Washington (New York: HarperCollins, 1986), 44–45.

36. Hendrix, *Ownership, Authority, and Self-Determination*, 49.

37. For overviews, see Lorna Fox O'Mahoney and Marc L. Roark, *Squatting and the State: Resilient Property in an Age of Crisis* (New York: Cambridge University Press, 2022); Jo Guldi, *The Long Land War: The Global Struggle for Occupancy Rights* (New Haven: Yale University, 2022); Miguel A. Martinez, ed., *The Urban Politics of Squatter Movements* (New York: Palgrave, 2018); Alexander Vasudevan, *The Autonomous City: A History of Urban Squatting*, 2nd ed. (New York: Verso, 2023).

38. For an exception: Daniel Loick, *The Abuse of Property* (Cambridge: MIT Press, 2023). On the occupation of public buildings, see Gustova A. Beade, "Who Can Blame Whom? Moral Standing to Blame and Punish Deprived Citizens," *Criminal Law & Philosophy* 13 (2019): 271–81.

39. See, for example, the typology developed by Hans Pruijt, "The Logic of Urban Squatting," *International Journal of Urban and Regional Research* 37, no. 1 (2013): 22–45.

40. Jonathan Turley, "'Fairly Big Problem': Squatters Invade Homes and Refuse to Leave; How Is This Legal?," *USA Today*, July 3, 2023, https://www.usatoday.com/story/opinion/2023/07/03/squatters-rights-leave-homeowners-forgotten/70364321007/, accessed January 28, 2024.

41. Hannah Dobbz, *Nine-Tenths of the Law: Property and Resistance in the United States* (Oakland: AK Press, 2012), 33–61; John Suval, *Dangerous Ground: Squatters, Statesmen, and the Antebellum Rupture of American Democracy* (New York: Oxford University Press, 2022).

42. Colin Ward, *Cotters and Squatters: Housing's Hidden History* (Nottingham: Five Leaves, 2002).

43. Scott, *Domination and the Arts of Resistance*, 202–27.

44. A leading UK-based advocate for homeless squatters, Ron Bailey, condemned occupations of temporarily vacant private homes and called for "speeding up procedures to enable wronged private owners to regain possession" in his *Homelessness: What Can Be Done* (Oxford: John Carpenter, 1994), 103.

45. A view shared by those who see *any* challenge to existing property relations as a fundamental attack on private property, as well as anarchist theorists who misleadingly project their own principled hostility to property onto many squatters (Loick, *The Abuse of Property*, ix–xiii).

46. See especially Anders Corr, *No Trespassing: Squatting, Rent Strikes, and Land Struggles Worldwide* (Cambridge: South End Press, 1999).

47. Squatters frequently target vacant, abandoned buildings. On New York City squatters, see Eric Hirsch and Peter Wood, "Squatting in New York City: Justification and Strategy," *New York University Review of Law and Social Change* 16, no. 4 (1987–88): 605–18; Vasudevan, *The Autonomous City*, 211–34. For the postwar UK, see Ron Bailey, *The Squatters* (London: Penguin, 1973). For the Brazilian case, see Lucy Earle, "From Insurgent to Transgressive Citizenship: Housing, Social Movements and the Politics of Rights in São Paulo," *Journal of Latin American Studies* 44 (2012): 98.

48. Valerie Schneider, "Property Rebels: Reclaiming Abandoned, Bank-Owned Homes for Community Uses," *American University Law Review* 65, no. 2 (2015): 405. Those who cannot keep up with payment of rents or mortgages but remain in their homes may fall under the rubric of politically motivated squatting. During the 1930s, for example, political activists worked with poor and working class people to block efforts to evict them, organizing so-called "gas squads to turn the gas back on in people's houses and electric squads to string wires around the meter after it was shut off by the local utility" (Francis Fox Piven and Richard Cloward, *Poor People's Movements: How They Succeed, How They Fail* [New York: Vintage, 1979], 55).

49. Priujt, "The Logic of Urban Squatting," 32–36.

50. Article 185 of the 1989 Brazilian Constitution allows for the expropriation of so-called unproductive lands, unless they are owner-operated small and medium-sized farms. MST is the Portuguese abbreviation for *Movimento dos Trabalhadores Rurais Sem Terra*. See Gabriel Ondetti, *Land, Protest, and Politics; The Landless Movement and the Struggle for Agrarian Reform in Brazil* (University College: Penn State Press, 2008), 106–7, 137–38; Wendy Wolford, *This Land Is Ours Now: Social Mobilization and the Meaning of Land in Brazil* (Durham: Duke University Press, 2010).

51. Anthony Pahnke, *Brazil's Long Revolution: Radical Achievements of the Landless Workers Movement* (Tucson: University of Arizona Press, 2018), 54–55.

52. John L. Hammond, "Land Occupations, Violence, and the Politics of Agrarian Reform in Brazil," *Latin American Perspectives* 36, no. 4 (2000): 156–77.

53. Varun Patil and Martin Fuchs, "Ownership Rights in Practice: Property Dynamics in an Urban Poor Settlement in Mumbai," *Berliner Journal für Soziologie* 34 (2025): 611–45.

54. Corr, *No Trespassing*, 20.

55. "Generally, the law is not accommodating of even the most innocent, conscientious, and desperately necessitous squatter" (R. George Wright, *Does the Law Morally Bind the Poor? Or What Good's the Constitution When You Can't Afford a Loaf of Bread?* [New York: New York University Press, 1996], 142).

56. The Brazilian Alliance of Housing Movements, for example, tries to take advantage of constitutionally based provisions for a right to housing (Earle, "From Insurgent to Transgressive Citizenship").

57. Peñalver and Katyal, *Property Outlaws*, 152–56. I say more about this strategy in the section to follow.

58. Sally Brown Richardson, "Abandonment and Adverse Possession," *Houston Law Review* 5, no. 5 (2015): 1395. Jessica A. Clarke points out that adverse possession ratifies the (proper) performance of property ("Adverse Possession of Identity: Radical Theory, Conventional Practice," *Oregon Law Review* 84 [2005]: 563–654). Adverse possession builds on older practices that condoned residential and land squatting (Ward, *Cotters and Squatters*, 5–11).

59. Although unclear how many squatters have successfully tapped adverse possession (and viewed by some as a double-edged sword given its strict conditions), some advocates see it as a potential weapon (Corr, *No Trespassing*, 68).

60. Minayo Nasiali, "Citizens, Squatters, and Asocials: The Right to Housing and the Politics of Difference in Post-Liberation France," *American Historical Review* 119, no. 2 (2014): 434–59; Ward, *Cotters and Squatters*, 159–60; Vasudevan, *The Autonomous City*, 44–47.

61. David Madden and Peter Marcuse, *In Defense of Housing* (New York: Verso, 2016).

62. Albert O. Hirschman, *Journeys Toward Progress: Studies of Economic Policy-Making in Latin America* (New York: Twentieth Century Fund, 1963), 259.

63. Hirschman, *Journeys Toward Progress*, 260–61.

64. Gregory S. Alexander and Eduardo M. Peñalver, *An Introduction to Property Theory* (Cambridge: Cambridge University Press, 2012), 130–55.

65. Anatole France, *The Red Lily*, trans. Winifred Stephans (New York: John Lane, 1921 [1894]), 95.

66. Jeremy Waldron, "Homelessness and the Issue of Freedom," in *Liberal Rights: Collected Papers 1981-1991*, by Jeremy Waldron (New York: Cambridge University Press, 1993), 309–38.

Homeless people's rights remain vulnerable: Laura Riley, "Do Not Make Survival Even More Difficult for People on the Streets," *New York Times*, April 22, 2024, A23. Judy Failer hits the nail on the head: "When laws make it illegal to sleep, eat, and eliminate in public spaces . . . the law seems to assume that people are free to engage in those activities, as long as they do not do so in public places. But this assumption only makes sense for people who are domiciled. . . . [I]t does not hold true for the homeless. . . . When they face these laws, they must choose between engaging in these essential life activities and thereby disobeying the law, and refraining from them and dying." Judy Failer, *Who Qualifies for Rights? Homelessness, Mental Illness, and Civil Commitment* (Ithaca: Cornell University Press, 2002), 143.

67. This, of course, has transpired under some far-sighted government, including some right-leaning ones, but only rarely.

68. See the discussion to follow in Chapter 6.

69. Lee J. Alston, Gary D. Liebecap, and Bernardo Mueller, *Titles, Conflicts, and Land Use: The Development of Property Rights and Land Reform on the Brazilian Amazon Frontier* (Ann Arbor: University of Michigan Press, 1999), 81–97, 153–91, 201.

70. Peter Weber, "Scenes from the Squatting Life," *National Review* 39, no. 3 (1987): 32.

71. Corr, *No Trespassing*, 53–57.

72. Waldron, *The Right to Private Property*, 329.

73. For references to squatters' own remarks and reflections, see Corr, *No Trespassing*, 52, 59, 65; Nasiali, "Citizens, Squatters, and Asocials," 443; Pahnke, *Brazil's Long Revolution*, 91. On sweat equity, see Corr, *No Trespassing*, 21–2, 71.

74. In the Lockean theory, property "rights are established contingently and historically as the upshot of what individuals have done" (Waldron, *The Right to Private Property*, 137–252; also, 443–44).

75. John Locke, *Second Treatise of Government*, in *Two Treatises of Government*, by John Locke, ed. Peter Laslett (New York: Cambridge University Press, 1988), para. 333, 291. For a Lockean defense of squatting, see Eloise Harding, "Spoilage and Squatting: A Lockean Argument," *Res Publica* 26 (2020): 299–317.

76. Corr, *No Trespassing*, 51–76.

77. Waldron, "Homelessness and the Issue of Freedom," 309–38.

78. Radin, *Reinterpreting Property*, 197.

79. Corr, *No Trespassing*, 57–58. E. P. Thompson made a similar point about poachers who illegally hunted on royal property in early eighteenth-century England: "What was often at issue was not property, supported by law, against no-property; it was alternative definitions of property-rights: for the landowner, enclosure—for the cottager, common rights. . . . For as long as it remained possible, the ruled—if they could find a purse and a lawyer—would actually fight for their rights by means of law." E. P. Thompson, *Whigs and Hunters: The Origin of the Black Act* (New York: Pantheon, 1975), 261.

80. Hannah Arendt, *The Human Condition*, 2nd ed. (Chicago: University of Chicago Press, 1998 [1958]), 61.

81. A view found, for example, in no less a defender of property rights than Hegel: see Waldron, *The Right to Private Property*, 366.

82. This is a key claim of Radin's *Reinterpreting Property*.

83. See Pruijt, "Logic of Urban Squatting," 36–39; Vasudevan, *The Autonomous City*.

84. Wolford, *This Land Is Ours Now*, 55.

85. Loick, *The Abuse of Property*, 73–84.

86. John Stuart Mill, *On Liberty* (Indianapolis: Hackett, 1978), 73–92.

87. Homes Not Jails, for example, is explicitly nonviolent in orientation (Corr, *No Trespassing*, 20), as are many other movements of urban squatters.

88. Lynn Owens, *Cracking Under Pressure: Narrating the Decline of the Amsterdam Squatters' Movement* (University Park: Penn State press, 2009), 63–86, 94–124, 178–79; Vasudevan, *The Autonomous City*, 90.

89. Angus Wright and Wendy Wolford, *To Inherit the Earth: The Landless Movement and the Struggle for a New Brazil* (Oakland: Food First Books, 2003), 311.

90. Gene Sharp, *The Politics of Nonviolent Action*, part 1, *The Methods of Nonviolent Action* (Boston: Porter Sargent, 1973), 405–8; see also Gerrit Huizer, "Land Invasion as a Non-Violent Strategy of Peasant Rebellion," *Journal of Peace Research* 9, no. 2 (1972): 121–32; Kurt Schock, "Rightful Radical Resistance: Mass Mobilization and Land Struggles in India and Brazil," *Mobilization: An International Quarterly* 20, no. 4 (2015): 493–515.

91. Jarbas Passarinho, quoted in Hammond, "Land Occupations, Violence, and the Politics of Agrarian Reform," 171.

92. Rawls, *A Theory of Justice*, 372.

93. Scheuerman, *Civil Disobedience*, 101–21.

94. José Eduardo Bernardes, "Parliamentary Investigation Against MST Is an Opportunity to Dispute Ideas, Says MST Leader," *Brasil de Fato São Paulo*, March 9, 2023, https://www.brasildefato.com.br/2023/05/09/parliamentary-investigation-against-mst-is-an-opportunity-to-dispute-ideas-says-mst-leader, accessed February 2, 2024.

95. Vasudevan, *The Autonomous City*, 6.

96. Vasudevan, *The Autonomous City*, 7; Fox O'Mahoney and Roark, *Squatting and the State*, 90–142.

97. Recent urban squatters have tapped Henri Lefebvre's idea of a "right to the city." Miguel A. Martinez, "European Squatters' Movements and the Right to a City," in *Routledge Handbook of Contemporary European Social Movements*, ed. Ramon Feenstra and Cristina Flesher Fominaya (New York: Routledge, 2020), 155–67.

98. King, *Where Do We Go from Here?*, 196–97.

99. To avoid these dangers, squatter movements often require participants to abide demanding moral codes of conduct, e.g., prohibitions on illegal drug usage, etc. Local BLM activists soon distanced themselves from the "Chaz" occupation.

100. See "Capitol Hill Occupied Protest," Wikipedia, https://en.wikipedia.org/wiki/Capitol_Hill_Occupied_Protest, accessed February 2, 2024.

101. Michael C. Blumm and Olivier Jamin, "The Property Clause and Its Discontents: Lessons from the Malheur Occupation," *Ecology Law Quarterly* 43 (2016): 812.

102. William G. Robbins, "The Malheur Occupation and the Problem with History," *Oregon Historical Quarterly* 117, no. 4 (2016): 574–603.

103. Courtney Irons, "The Patriarch and the Sovereign: The Malheur Occupations and the Hyper-Masculine Drive for Control," *Columbia Journal of Law and Social Problems* 51, no. 3 (2018): 484.

104. Irons, "The Patriarch and the Sovereign," 484.

105. Blumm and Jamin, "The Property Clause and Its Discontents," 824–86. In 2018, the federal government's case against Cliven Bundy resulted in a mistrial. In 2020, a federal court denied an appeal by federal prosecutors who sought to reinstate criminal charges against Ammon Bundy.

106. Ammon Bundy ran as an Independent candidate for governor of Idaho in 2022, gaining 17 percent of the vote.

107. Ray Bush, "Food Riots: Poverty, Power, and Protest," *Journal of Agrarian Change* 10, no. 1 (2010): 119–29.

108. Shoplifting appears to be on the rise, in part because of high inflation and a declining faith in the legitimacy of the economic status quo. Charlie Teasdale, "Did You Pay for That? What Is Driving the Massive Rise in Shoplifting?," *Guardian*, June 2, 2024, https://www.theguardian.com/uk-news/article/2024/jun/02/did-you-pay-for-that-what-is-driving-the-massive-rise-in-shoplifting?, accessed on June 2, 2024.

109. Mark William Jones, *1923: The Crisis of German Democracy in the Year of Hitler's Putsch* (New York: Basic Books, 2023), 287–97; Stephanie Seul, "Transnational Press Discourses on German Antisemitism During the Weimar Republic: The Riots in Berlin's Scheunenviertel, 1923," *Leo Baeck Institute Year Book* 59 (2014): 91–120.

110. Martin Dean, *Robbing the Jews: The Confiscation of Jewish Property in the Holocaust, 1933–1945* (New York: Cambridge University Press, 2008), esp. 84–131.

111. Gilje, *Rioting in America*, 87–115.

112. I draw on Tim Newburn, Kerris Cooper, Rachel Deacon, and Rebekah Diski, "Shopping for Free: Looting, Consumerism and the 2011 Riots," *British Journal of Criminology* 55 (2015): 988.

113. Randall Collins, *Violence: A Micro-Sociological Theory* (Princeton: Princeton University Press, 2008), 247.

114. Ferdinand Sutterlüty, "The Hidden Morale of the 2005 French and 2011 English Riots," *Thesis Eleven* 121, no. 1 (2014): 38–56.

115. Tilly emphasized looting's opportunistic traits (Tilly, *Politics of Collective Violence*, 143–49).

116. Tommie Shelby, "Justice, Deviance, and the Dark Ghetto," *Philosophy & Public Affairs* 35, no. 2 (2007): 156.

117. Roger D. Scott, "Looting: A Proposal to Enhance the Sanction for Aggravated Property Crime," *Journal of Law & Politics* 11 (1995): 133.

118. See *The Kerner Report: The 1968 Advisory Report of the National Advisory Commission on Civil Disorders* (New York: Pantheon, 1988 [1968]); Robert M. Fogelson, *Violence as Protest: A Study of Riots and Ghettos* (Garden City: Doubleday, 1971). For a discussion, see Hinton, *America on Fire*.

119. Lois Beckett, "'Boogoloi Boy' Charged in Fire of Minneapolis Precinct Station During George Floyd Protest," *Guardian*, October 23, 2020, https://www.theguardian.com/world/2020/oct/23/texas-boogaloo-boi-minneapolis-police-building-george-floyd, accessed February 13, 2024.

120. Among others, see Fogelson, *Violence as Protest*, 86–94.

121. Janet L. Abu-Lughod, *Race, Space, and Riots in Chicago, New York, and Los Angeles* (New York: Oxford University Press, 2007), 245–48.

122. Newburn et al., "Shopping for Free," 991.

123. Roger MacGinty, "Looting in the Context of Violent Conflict: A Conceptualization and Typology," *Third World Quarterly* 25, no. 5 (2004): 867.

124. MacGinty, "Looting in the Context of Violent Conflict."

125. Collins, *Violence*, 243–45.

126. Fogelson, *Violence as Protest*, 117.

127. Arendt, *The Human Condition*, 124. I neglect the "looting" of artwork and other cultural artifacts for two reasons. First, they are durable and thus differ from ordinary consumer goods. Second, it usually occurs during violent conflicts and/or when democratic political authority has collapsed, and thus falls beyond the boundaries of my discussion.

128. Russell Dynes and E. L. Quarantelli, "What Looting in Civil Disturbance Really Means," *Trans-Action* (May 1968): 14.

129. King, *Where Do We Go from Here?*, 119.

130. King, *Where Do We Go from Here?*, 119.

131. Newburn et al., "Shopping for Free," 994.

132. Maya Lau, Alejandra Reyes-Velarde, and Matt Hamilton, "Looters Who Hit LA Stores Explain What They Did," *Los Angeles Times*, June 5, 2020, https://www.latimes.com/california/story/2020-06-05/looting-protests-george-floyd, accessed February 15, 2024.

133. King, *The Trumpet of Conscience*, 58.

134. Lau, Reyes-Velarde, and Hamilton, "Looters Who Hit LA Stores Explain What They Did."

135. King, *Where Do We Go from Here?*, 119–20.

136. Martin Luther King Jr., "The Role of the Behavioral Scientist in the Civil Rights Movement" [1968], American Psychological Association, https://www.apa.org/topics/equity-diversity-inclusion/martin-luther-king-jr-challenge, accessed February 15, 2024.

137. King, *The Trumpet of Conscience*, 59.

138. Commentators on 1960s US looting, however, noted that this phenomenon abated by the decade's end: on E. L. Quarantelli and Russell R. Dynes, "Property Norms and Looting: Their Patterns in Community Crisis," *Phylon* 31, no. 2 (1970): 178.

139. "Understand that I am trying only to explain the *reasons* for violence and the threat of violence. Let me say again that by no means and under no circumstances do I condone outbreaks of looting and lawlessness." Martin Luther King Jr., "*Playboy* Interview" [1965], in *A Testament of Hope: The Essential Writings and Speeches of Martin Luther King, Jr.*, ed. James M. Washington (New York: HarperCollins, 1986), 360–361. King's worries have arguably been corroborated by recent research: Omar Wasow, "Agenda Seeking: How 1960s Black Protests Moved Elites, Public Opinion and Voting," *American Political Science Review* 14, no. 3 (2020): 638–59.

140. King, *Where Do We Go from Here?*, 59.

141. Vicky Osterweil, *In Defense of Looting: A Riotous History of Uncivil Action* (New York: Bold Type Books, 2020), 3. On looting as basically anticapitalist, see Joshua Clover, *Riot, Strike, Riot: The New Era of Uprisings* (New York: Verso, 2019).

142. Fogelson, *Violence as Protest*, 12. The author correctly observed that it made no sense to group the US riots and related looting with leftist insurrections in developing countries.

143. MacGinty, "Looting in the Context of Violent Conflict," 861.

144. Nassauer, *Situational Breakdowns*, 78–81.

145. MacGinty, "Looting in the Context of Violent Conflict," 861.

146. Kalyvas, *Logic of Violence in Civil War*, 330–63.

147. Newburn et al., "Shopping for Free," 999.

148. Dynes and Quarantelli, "What Looting in Civil Disturbance Really Means," 13; Fogelson, *Violence as Politics*, 17.

149. Stuart P. Green, "Looting, Law, and Lawlessness," *Tulane Law Review* 81 (2007): 1171.

150. Farah Stockman, "'They Have Lost Control': Why Minneapolis Burned," *New York Times*, July 3, 2020, https://www.nytimes.com/2020/07/03/us/minneapolis-governmenTrt-george -floyd.html, accessed February 13, 2024.

151. Shelby, "Justice, Deviance, and the Dark Ghetto," 151.

152. Shelby, "Justice, Deviance, and the Dark Ghetto," 154.

153. Shelby, "Justice, Deviance, and the Dark Ghetto," 154.

154. Those who view unruly social movements as effective (e.g., Piven and Cloward, *Poor People's Movements*) do not always disaggregate its various types. This impedes them from recognizing how some—for example, looting—can be counterproductive.

155. In 1998, Brazil's MST helped organize the looting of supermarkets and trucks transporting food. Subsequent surveys pointed to decreased public support for the group. Ondetti, *Land, Protest, and Politics*, 161, 167–68.

156. Trump took the quip from former hardline Miami Police Chief Walter Headley, who made the inflammatory comment in 1967 in the context of widespread urban riots.

157. Dumpster diving refers to incidents in which people salvage discarded, often unused items. Its legal status is complicated: even when illegal, police and state officials may opt not to pursue charges. As with squatting, not all cases are existentially motivated: some green activists, for example, engage in it to oppose wasteful, environmentally destructive consumer capitalism.

158. Lynne Taylor, "Food Riots Revisited," *Journal of Social History* 30, no. 2 (1996): 492. Bread and food riots have often involved significant participation from women, who justify their acts with appeals to traditional views of mothers as care givers. Other forms of looting seem disproportionately male-dominated.

159. Irving Bernstein, *The Lean Years* (Boston: Houghton Mifflin, 1960), 422; Roy Rosenzweig, "Organizing the Unemployed: The Early Years of the Great Depression, 1929–1933," in *Workers' Struggles, Past and Present: A Radical America Reader*, ed. James Green (Philadelphia: Temple University Press, 1983), 168–89.

160. On early 1930s Germany: Molly Loberg, "The Fortress Shop: Consumer Culture, Violence, and Security in Weimar Berlin," *Journal of Contemporary History* 49, no. 4 (2014): 675–701.

161. Mauritz A. Hallgren, *Seeds of Revolt: A Study of American Life and the Temper of the American People During the Depression* (New York: Alfred Knopf, 1933), 99.

162. Hallgren, *Seeds of Revolt*, 58.

163. Alexander and Peñalver, *Introduction to Property Theory*, 204.

164. Cited in Alexander and Peñalver, *Introduction to Property Theory*, 86.

165. G. W. F. Hegel, *Elements of the Philosophy of Right*, ed. Allen Wood (New York: Cambridge University Press, 1991 [1821]), 155 (para 127).

166. Frederic Vandenberghe has astutely suggested that my argument relies on some version of the idea of a "moral economy." For a classic statement, see E. P. Thompson, "The Moral Economy of the English Crowd in the Nineteenth Century," *Past & Present* 50, no. 1 (1971): 76–121. However, in diverse, intensely pluralistic societies any shared "moral economy" is likely to be fragile and highly contestable. We therefore need empirically minded, normative political theory, along the lines endeavored here.

167. Green, "Looting, Law, and Lawlessness"; also, Stephanie J. Hamrick, "Is Looting Ever Justified? An Analysis of Looting Laws and the Applicability of the Necessity Defense During Natural Disasters and States of Emergency," *Nevada Law Journal* 7 (2006): 182–211.

168. Hamrick, "Is Looting Ever Justified?," 186.

169. Wright, *Does the Law Morally Bind the Poor?*, 105. On the necessity defense as challenging existing property relations, see Shaun P. Martin, "The Radical Necessity Defense," *Cincinnati Law Review* 73, no. 4 (2005): 1527–1608.

170. Wright, *Does the Law Morally Bind the Poor?*, 105.

171. Wright, *Does the Law Morally Bind the Poor?*, 117.

172. I draw here on Green, "Looting, Law, and Lawlessness," 1165–69. Green, however, favors a codification that would legalize subsistence looting, chiefly in the context of disasters.

173. Green, "Looting, Law, and Lawlessness," 123–24.

174. Unfortunately, the empirical literature often fails to differentiate property damage from violence against persons. But see Dan J. Wang and Alessandro Piazzo, "The Use of Disruptive Tactics in Protest as a Trade-Off: The Role of Social Movement Claims," *Social Forces* 94, no. 4 (2016): 1675–1710.

175. Smith, "Disruptive Democracy," 18.

176. Delmas, *A Duty to Resist*, 49.

177. Smith, "Disruptive Democracy," 19.

Chapter 6

1. Alexander and Peñalver, *Introduction to Property Theory*, 211.

2. Christopher Pierson, *Just Property*, vol. 3, *Property in an Age of Ideologies* (New York: Oxford University Press, 2020).

3. Even Waldron's imposing study rushes over the particularities of modern corporate property (*Right to Private Property*, 57–9). See, in contrast, Max Weber's fine-grained distinctions between and among property's diverse types ("Class, Status, and Power," in *From Max Weber: Essays in Sociology*, ed. Hans Gerth and C. Wright Mills [New York: Oxford University Press, 1946], 182).

4. Radin distinguishes between *personal* and *fungible* property, with the former referring to property that is bound up with the person and seems irreplaceable, and the latter property whose loss could be compensated for by some replacement (Radin, *Reinterpreting Property*, 1–71). Her approach has generated lively debates (Alexander and Peñalver, *Introduction to Property Theory*, 66–69). Whatever its flaws, Radin is right that some types of property seem "wrapped up" with our persons in ways that justify relatively strict protections.

5. Alexander and Peñalver, *Introduction to Property Theory*, 127.

6. Marx and Engels sometimes conflated personal property with property in small-scale economic activities, "the property of the petty artisan and of the small peasant," based on "the fruit of . . . labor." Karl Marx and Friedrich Engels, *Communist Manifesto* (New York: Appleton-Century-Crofts, 1955 [1848]), 24. For reasons to be explored, this conflation makes some sense.

7. On social acceleration, see Hartmut Rosa, *Social Acceleration; A New Theory of Modernity* (New York: Columbia University Press, 2015). On its challenges to property's durability: Hartmut Rosa "Property as the Hidden Form of *Weltbeziehung*," in '*Weltbeziehung*': *The Study of Our Relationship to the World*, ed. Bettina Hollstein, Jörge Rüpke, and Hartmut Rosa (Frankfurt: Campus, 2023), 19–35.

8. On property's dematerialization, see Gunnar Folke Schuppert, "Wandel des Eigentums: Zu seiner Verortung in Dreieck von Struktur-, Funktions- und Auffassungswandel," *Archiv des öffentlichen Rechts* 147 (2022): 475–79. On property in digital capitalism, see Tilman Reitz, Sebastian Sevignani, Marlen van der Ecker, "Eigentum im digitalen Kapitalismus," in *Theorien des*

digitalen Kapitalismus, ed. Tanja Carstensen, Simon Schaup, and S. Sevignani (Berlin: Suhramp, 2023), 264–84.

9. However, there is evidence among younger people that the association of personal property with durable possessions may be less important (Rifkin, *Age of Access*, 13).

10. However, note that small and/or family-owned business may opt to incorporate. In the United States, for example, family-owned businesses frequently take the form of *closely held corporations* in which more than 50 percent of the value of stock is owned by a small number of shareholders, often from the same family. For our limited purposes, I am forced to leave aside some important legal complexities. For-profit corporations, for example, also take a variety of legal and organizational types.

11. Frank Michelman, "Mr. Justice Brennan: A Property Teacher's Appreciation," *Harvard Civil Rights-Civil Liberties Law Review* 15, no. 2 (1980): 306.

12. See my discussion of *robinhoodism* in Chapter 5.

13. Thurman Arnold, *The Folklore of Capitalism* (New Haven: Yale University Press, 1932). Corporate property is a neglected subject among political theorists, but see Scott R. Bowman, *The Modern Corporation and American Political Thought* (University Park: Penn State Press, 1996).

14. Adam Winkler, *We the Corporations: How American Businesses Won Their Civil Rights* (New York: Norton, 2018), xvi. See also David Ciepley, "Neither Persons nor Associations: Against Constitutional Rights for Corporations," *Journal of Law and Courts* 1, no. 2 (2013): 221–45; Susan Kim Ripken, *Corporate Personhood* (New York: Cambridge University Press, 2019).

15. Arnold, *The Folklore of Capitalism*, 233–34. Arnold was referencing the 1936–37 Flint (Michigan) sit-down strikes targeting General Motors.

16. Arnold, *The Folklore of Capitalism*, 191.

17. Adolph A. Berle and Gardiner Means, *The Modern Corporation and Private Property* (New York: MacMillan, 1933).

18. Peter A. Gourevitch and James Shinn, *Political Power and Corporate Control: The New Politics of Corporate Governance* (Princeton: Princeton University Press, 2005).

19. David Ciepley, "Beyond Public and Private: Toward a Political Theory of the Corporation," *American Political Science Review* 107, no. 1 (2013): 148.

20. Kent Greenfield, *Corporations Are People Too* (New Haven: Yale University Press, 2018), 218–20.

21. Judith N. Shklar, "The Liberalism of Fear," in *Political Thought & Political Thinkers*, by Judith N. Shklar, ed. Stanley Hoffmann (Chicago: University of Chicago Press, 1998), 12.

22. Waldron, *The Right to Private Property*, 58.

23. Ciepley, "Beyond Public and Private," 146–48. See also Jean-Philippe Robe, "The Legal Structure of the Firm," *Accounting, Economics, and the Law* 1, no. 1 (2011): 1–89.

24. Ciepley, "Neither Persons nor Associations," 228.

25. Macpherson, *Democratic Theory*, 131.

26. A view suggested, for example, by Cohen, "Civil Disobedience in a Constitutional Democracy," 211–16.

27. Timo Wesche, *Die Rechte der Natur* (Berlin: Suhrkamp, 2023), 43–73.

28. Wesche, *Die Rechte der Natur*, 79, 310–20.

29. Waldron, *The Right to Private Property*, 33–37.

30. Wesche, *Die Rechte der Natur*, 57–83. Wesche describes this a shift from *Sacheigentum* (property in relation to generic "thingness") to *Gütereigentum* (property in goods).

31. Franz L. Neumann, "The Concept of Political Freedom," in *The Rule of Law Under Siege: Selected Essays of Franz L. Neumann and Otto Kirchheimer*, ed. William E. Scheuerman (Berkeley: University of California Press, 1996), 195–230.

32. For an analysis, see Titus Stahl, *Immanent Critique* (London: Rowman & Littlefield, 2021).

33. Immanent critique's role in property disobedience should not surprise us perhaps since "[a] great deal of the critical literature on property" in what Christopher Pierson calls the Latin West "consists of this kind of critique," that is, "subjecting justificatory accounts of political practices to criticism in terms of their own self-professed values." Christopher Pierson, *Just Property*, vol. 1, *A History in the Latin West* (New York: Oxford University Press, 2013), 18.

34. Anarchist and socialist squatters often seek a novel economic order, sometimes based on *common property* envisioned as different from both (existing) state or private property. Even ideologically more mainstream squatters often desire significant reforms to housing and land ownership.

35. Waldron, *The Right to Private Property*, 49.

36. Alexander and Peñalver, *Introduction to Property Theory*, 140.

37. Epstein, *Takings*, 104, 281.

38. Macpherson, *Democratic Theory*, 131. For an earlier influential account of this position, Charles Reich, "The New Property," *Yale Law Journal* 73, no. 5 (1964): 733–87.

39. Macpherson, *Democratic Theory*, 132.

40. For an overview, see Jacob Hacker and Paul Pierson, *American Amnesia: How the War on Government Led Us to Forget What Made America Prosper* (New York: Simon & Schuster, 2016).

41. Quinn Slobodian, *The End of Empire and Birth of Neoliberalism* (Cambridge: Harvard University Press, 2020).

42. Banner, *American Property*, 257–75.

43. While criticizing free trade (and, of course, the free movement of people across borders) and attacking "globalist" elites, right-wing authoritarian populists have not sought a rollback of corporate property rights. Under President Trump, for example, populist anti-globalist rhetoric goes hand in hand with enhanced protections for large banks and corporations, along with a frontal assault on the regulatory state: William E. Scheuerman, "Carl Schmitt Meets Donald Trump," *Philosophy & Social Criticism* 49 (2019): 1170–85.

44. Rifkin, *The Age of Access*. The *New York Times* recently reported that even our brain waves (that is, neural data) have become desirable commodities that large corporations are eagerly trying to acquire: see Jonathan Moens, "Your Brain Waves Are Up for Sale: A New Law Wants to Change That," *New York Times*, April 18, 2024, A1.

45. I reflect on this phenomenon elsewhere: see William E. Scheuerman, "Digital Disobedience and the Law," *New Political Science* 38, no. 3 (2016): 299–314.

46. The legal theorist Lon Fuller, *Morality of Law* (New Have: Yale University Press, 1964), described eight "virtues" that make up legality's "inner morality." Only one of them referenced official *enforcement* of laws and statutes. The reduction of the rule of law to repressive criminal sanctions is transpiring, unfortunately, in many supposedly consolidated democracies: Pichl, *Law statt Order*.

47. Jeremy Waldron, *The Rule of Law and the Measure of Property* (New York: Cambridge University Press, 2012), 72.

48. On tensions between property-centered and more plausible views of the rule of law, see Gowder, *The Rule of Law in the United States*.

49. Raymond Wacks, *The Rule of Law Under Fire?* (Oxford: Hart, 2021).

50. This is not likely to be an easy task, even in the wealthy democracies of the Global North.

51. Macpherson, *Democratic Theory*, 123.

52. Gregory S. Alexander, Eduardo Peñalver, Joseph William Singer, and Laura S. Underkuffler, "A Statement of Progressive Property," *Cornell Law Review* 94, no. 4 (2009): 744; see also Joseph William Singer, "Democratic Estates: Property Law in a Free and Democratic Society," *Cornell Law Review* 94, no. 4 (2009): 1009–62.

53. Alexander et al., "Statement of Progressive Property."

54. Pierson, *Just Property*, vol. 3, *Property in an Age of Ideologies*, 305.

55. Michelman, "Mr. Justice Brennan," 298, 305. See also Frank Michelman, "Property as a Constitutional Right," *Washington and Lee Law Review* 38, no. 4 (1981): 1097–114.

56. Michelman, "Mr. Justice Brennan," 305.

Chapter 7

1. Smith, "Disruptive Democracy," 18.

2. For example, the special issue of *New Political Science* 44, no. 2 (2022), edited by Kevin Duong. Among recent theorists redefining civil disobedience to encompass violent lawbreaking, see Michael Allen, "Civil Disobedience and Terrorism: Testing the Limits of Deliberative Democracy," *Theoria* 56 (2009): 15–39; Brownlee, *Conscience and Conviction*; Robin Celikates, "Rethinking Civil Disobedience as a Practice of Contestation: Beyond the Liberal Paradigm"; Celikates, "Democratizing Civil Disobedience"; Moraro, *Civil Disobedience*; A. John Simmons, "Civil Disobedience and the Duty to Obey the Law," in *A Companion to Applied Ethics*, ed. R. G. Frey and Christopher Wellman (Chichester: Wiley, 2005), 50–61; A. John Simmons, "Disobedience and Its Objects," *Boston University Law Review* 90 (2015): 1805–31. Those defending potentially violent uncivil disobedience or resistance include: Delmas, *A Duty to Resist*; Greenwood-Reeves, *Justifying Violent Protest*; Ten-Herng Lai, "Justifying Uncivil Disobedience," in *Oxford Studies in Political Philosophy* 5 (2019): 90–114; David Lyons, *Confronting Justice: Moral History and Political Theory* (New York: Oxford University Press, 2013). Political realists are also energetically criticizing allegedly "moralistic" commitments to nonviolence: see Robert Jubb, *Unjust Authority: Justice, Liberal Democracy, and Political Rule* (New York: Oxford University Press, 2024).

3. For major statements from this older literature, see Peter Ackerman and Jack Duvall, *A Force More Powerful: A Century of Nonviolent Conflict* (New York: Palgrave, 2000); Richard B. Gregg, *The Power of Nonviolence*, 2nd ed. (New York: Schocken, 1970); Mark Kurlansky, *Non-Violence: The History of a Dangerous Idea* (New York: Modern Library, 2006); Jonathan Schell, *The Unconquerable World: Power, Nonviolence, and the Will of the People* (New York: Henry Holt, 2003).

4. Peter Gelderloos, *How Nonviolence Protects the State* (Olympia, WA: AK Press, 2018), 12, 171–73; see also Mark Bray, *Antifa: The Anti-Fascist Handbook* (Brooklyn: Melville House, 2017).

5. Domenico Losurdo, *Non-Violence: A History Beyond the Myth*, trans. Gregory Elliott (Lanham, MD: Lexington, 2015), 205.

6. Brownlee, *Conscience and Conviction*, 21–22.

7. Brownlee, *Conscience and Conviction*, 198–99.

8. Brownlee, *Conscience and Conviction*, 198.

9. Bufacchi, *Violence and Social Justice*, 40.

10. Contra Reinhold Niebuhr, *Moral Man and Immoral Society* (New York: Charles Scribner's Sons, 1932), 247–8, 251.

11. Gwilym David Blunt, *Global Poverty, Injustice, and Resistance* (New York: Cambridge University Press, 2020); Christopher J. Finlay, *Terrorism and the Right to Resist: A Theory of Just Revolutionary War* (New York: Cambridge University Press, 2015).

12. Scheuerman, "Goodbye to Nonviolence?"

13. Consider, for example, Andreas Malm's defense of ecotage, discussed in Chapter 4.

14. Thus, some epistocratic and realist theories of democracy that eviscerate the notion of political equality conflict with my argument: they have given up on democracy.

15. Benjamin Ginsberg, *The Value of Violence* (Buffalo: Prometheus, 2013).

16. Scheuerman, "Goodbye to Nonviolence?," 1287–89.

17. Delmas, *A Duty to Resist*, 135.

18. Delmas, *A Duty to Resist*, 175.

19. On backsliding, see Fabio Wolkenstein, "What Is Democratic Backsliding?," *Constellations* 30 (2023): 261–75.

20. Brennan, *When All Else Fails*, 26.

21. Brennan, *When All Else Fails*, 3.

22. For a blunt statement, see Peter Gelderloos, *The Failure of Nonviolence* (Seattle: Left Bank Books, 2015). Its elements surface in scholarly analyses as well.

23. Greenwood-Reeves, *Justifying Violent Protest*, 147.

24. Greenwood-Reeves, *Justifying Violent Protest*, 147.

25. Sharon Eriksen Nepstad, *Nonviolent Revolutions: Civil Resistance in the Late Twentieth Century* (New York: Oxford University Press, 2011); Adam Roberts and Timothy Garton Ash, eds., *Civil Resistance and Power Politics: The Experience of Non-violent Action from Gandhi to the Present* (New York: Oxford University Press, 2011); Kurt Schock, *Civil Resistance: Comparative Perspectives on Nonviolent Struggles* (Minneapolis: University of Minnesota Press, 2015).

26. Rawls sensibly insisted that officials' obligations to obey the law were stricter than those of ordinary citizens (*A Theory of Justice*, 112–14); William E. Scheuerman, "Official Rule Departures," in *Routledge Handbook to the Rule of Law*, ed. Michael Sevel (New York: Routledge, 2024), 100–11.

27. Zick, *Managed Dissent*, 55.

28. Zick, *Managed Dissent*, 166.

29. Zick, *Managed Dissent*, 57.

30. Pietro Lombardo, "Rioters Fight Brussels Police, Smash Headquarters of EU Foreign Service," *Politico*, January 23, 2022, https://www.politico.eu/article/protest-against-covid-restriction-police-violent-brussels/, accessed December 9, 2022.

31. Martin Luther King Jr., "An Experiment in Love," in *A Testament of Hope: The Essential Writings and Speeches of Martin Luther King, Jr.*, ed. James M. Washington (New York: HarperCollins, 1986), 18.

32. King, "An Experiment in Love," 18.

33. Milligan, *Civil Disobedience*, 14.

34. Delmas, *A Duty to Resist*, 95–98.

35. In this vein, see Brennan, *When All Else Fails*; Simmons, "Disobedience and Its Objects."

36. Elsa Dorlin, *Self-Defense: A Philosophy of Violence* (New York: Verso, 2022).

37. See, for example, Karuna Mantena, "Showdown for Nonviolence: The Theory and Practice of Nonviolent Politics," in *To Shape a New World: Essays on the Political Philosophy of Martin Luther King, Jr.*, ed. Tommie Shelby and Brandon M. Terry (Cambridge: Harvard University Press, 2018), 84. In the same volume, Martha Nussbaum claims that King acknowledges "a morally legitimate role for nonviolence—self-defense being the general rubric he uses" ("From Anger to Love: Self-Purification and Political Resistance," p. 118). Brandon M. Terry does so as well: King "never denied either the existence of a natural or civil right to self-defense" ("Requiem for a Dream: The Problem-Space of Black Power," p. 296). See also Daniel J. Ott, "Nonviolence and the Nightmare: King and Black Self-Defense," *American Journal of Theology and Philosophy* 39 (2018): 64–73.

38. Martin Luther King, "Nonviolence: The Only Road to Freedom," in *A Testament of Hope: The Essential Writings and Speeches of Martin Luther King, Jr.*, ed. James M. Washington (New York: HarperCollins, 1986), 56.

39. King, "Nonviolence," 56.

40. King, "The Social Organization of Nonviolence," 32.

41. King, "Nonviolence," 57.

42. King, "The Social Organization of Nonviolence," 32.

43. King, "The Social Organization of Nonviolence," 33.

44. Butler, *The Force of Non-Violence*, 8–9.

45. Butler, *The Force of Non-Violence*, 54.

46. Howard Zinn, *Disobedience and Democracy: Nine Fallacies on Law and Order* (Cambridge: South End, 2002 [1968]), 48.

47. King, "Love, Law, and Civil Disobedience," 47.

48. Martin Luther King Jr., "A Gift of Love" (1966), in *A Testament of Hope: The Essential Writings and Speeches of Martin Luther King, Jr.*, ed. James M. Washington (New York: HarperCollins, 1986), 63.

49. William E. Scheuerman, "Political Nonviolence and Self-Defense: Reconsidering Martin Luther King Jr.," in *Political Violence: Historical, Philosophical, and Theological Perspectives*, ed. P.-M. Pöykko, P. Slotte, V. Salo (Oldenbourg: De Gruyter, 2024), 71–90.

50. Celikates, "Rethinking Civil Disobedience as a Practice of Contestation," 41; Milligan, *Civil Disobedience*, p. 14.

51. Delmas, *A Duty to Resist*, 179.

52. Delmas, *A Duty to Resist*, 96.

53. King, "Where Do We Go from Here?" [1967], in *A Testament of Hope: The Essential Writings and Speeches of Martin Luther King, Jr.*, ed. James M. Washington (New York: HarperCollins, 1986), 249.

54. King, Where Do We Go From Here?, 57–58.

55. Amid antiracist BLM-related protests in Kenosha (Wisconsin) on August 22, 2020, Kyle Rittenhouse shot three men, two of whom died, with an AR-15. He later claimed that he had brought his weapon to the protests to protect local businesses from looters. During his trial, he claimed a right to self-defense and was acquitted. Rittenhouse is now a right-wing celebrity.

56. For example, incidents of openly displayed firearms doubled at abortion rights protests between 2021 and 2022 (Zick, *Managed Dissent*, 146).

57. Zick, *Managed Dissent*, 148.

58. Chambers, *Contemporary Democratic Theory*, 3.

59. Andreas Schedler, "Democratic Reciprocity," *Journal of Political Philosophy* 29, no. 2 (2021): 271.

60. On populism, see Dirk Jörke and Veith Selk, *Theorien des Populismus* (Hamburg: Junius, 2017); Jan-Werner Müller, *What Is Populism?* (Philadelphia: University of Pennsylvania Press, 2016); Marco Revelli, *The New Populism: Democracy Stares into the Abyss* (New York: Verso, 2019); Nadia Urbinati, *Me the People: How Populism Transforms Democracy* (Cambridge: Harvard University Press, 2019).

61. Nadia Urbinati, *Democracy Disfigured* (Cambridge: Harvard University Press, 2014), 128–70.

62. Andreas Schedler, *The Politics of Uncertainty: Sustaining and Subverting Electoral Authoritarianism* (New York: Oxford University Press, 2013).

63. Schedler, *The Politics of Uncertainty*, 2.

64. John Keane makes a strong argument that similar trends elsewhere suggest the emergence of a new global despotism. See John Keane, *The New Despotism* (Cambridge: Harvard University Press, 2020); also (on the case of India), Debasish Roy Chowdhury and John Keane, *To Kill a Democracy: India's Passage to Despotism* (New York: Oxford University Press, 2021).

65. Russell Muirhead and Nancy L. Rosenblum, *A Lot of People Are Saying: The New Conspiracism and the Assault on Democracy* (Princeton: Princeton University Press, 2019).

66. Chenoweth, *Civil Resistance*, 233–40; Lee A. Smithey and Lester R. Kurtz, "'Smart' Repression," in *The Paradox of Repression and Nonviolent Movements*, ed. Lester R. Kurtz and Lee A. Smithey (Syracuse: Syracuse University Press, 2018), 185–214.

67. Robert Dahl's "democratic criteria" remain a useful starting point for reflecting on democracy's core traits in *On Democracy* (New Haven: Yale University Press, 1998), 37–43.

68. In this vein, Jubb, "Disaggregating Political Authority."

69. Rawls, *A Theory of Justice*, 364n19.

70. Rawls, *A Theory of Justice*, 366.

71. Andrew Sabl, "Looking Forward to Justice: Rawlsian Civil Disobedience and Its Non-Rawlsian Lessons," *Journal of Political Philosophy* 9, no. 3 (2001): 309.

72. Jennet Kirkpatrick, *Uncivil Disobedience: Studies in Violence and Democratic Politics* (Princeton: Princeton University Press, 2008), 58–60, 114–18.

73. Kirkpatrick, *Uncivil Disobedience*, 6.

74. On populism and digitalization, see Paolo Gerbaudo, *The Digital Party: Political Organization and Online Democracy* (London: Pluto, 2019).

75. A view, I think, consistent with Arendt, *On Violence*.

76. King, *Where Do We Go from Here?*, 196.

INDEX

Abbey, Edward, 93–98
abolitionism, 11, 61, 155. *See also* anti-racism; Black Lives Matter
Adams, Alexander, 66
adverse possession, 122, 130, 147. *See also* squatting
African Americans, 40–44, 54–55, 60–73, 83–84, 134, 137–38, 208n28. *See also* Black Lives Matter; civil rights movement
African National Congress (ANC), 11, 206n100
Alabama, 32, 69
Alcatraz Island, 112–17
Al-Qaeda, 95
American Legal Exchange Council (ALEC), 95
anarchism: philosophical, 171–74; political, 11, 66, 72, 97, 100, 209n45, 218n34. *See also* anarcho-syndicalism
anarcho-syndicalism, 78, 88, 92, 94
Animal Enterprise Terrorism Act, 86, 95
animal rights activism, 11, 85–86
anonymity, 17, 81, 90, 100. *See also* secrecy
Anonymous, 9, 20
anticolonialism, 99. *See also* colonialism; Fanon, Frantz; Gandhi, Mahatma
antinuclear protests, 24, 82
antiracism, 8–9, 21, 55, 60–75, 84, 138, 153. *See also* abolitionism; Black Lives Matter
antisemitism, 1, 11, 133–35, 150, 206n105
antistatism, 96, 172–74. *See also* anarchism
Aquinas, Thomas, 142
Arizona, 132
armed insurgency, 16, 86–87, 96–97, 116, 132. *See also* collective violence
Arnold, Thurman, 151
arson, 7, 9, 42, 82, 86, 93, 139, 154
art works, 57–60, 66–68. *See also* iconoclasm

Asian Americans, 135, 139
assassinations 98, 101
Audi, Robert, 36–37
authoritarian populism, 2, 6, 20, 169–71, 178–83. *See also* authoritarianism; Trump, Donald
authoritarianism, 20–21, 25–26, 76, 96, 104–5, 128, 170–83
autonomous zones, 9, 130–31

backlash, political: against Black Lives Matter, 74–75; King, Martin Luther on, 42, 52, 79, 116, 138–40, 177; and riots, 42, 138–40; and sabotage, 91, 95, 98, 102
Baker, Edwin, 22, 34
Bedau, Hugo, 13
Beijing, China, 20, 25
Belgium, 174
Berle, Adolphe A., 151, 159
Berrigan, Daniel, 7
Bevan, Robert, 63
Biden, Joseph, 1–2
Black Lives Matter (BLM), 82, 174; civil disobedience, 72–75; goals, 19, 196n6; protests, 8–9, 21, 106, 130, 134, 139–40, 168; symbolic disobedience, 5, 21–22, 25–26, 54–55, 60–75, 147, 157–58; in United Kingdom, 10
Black Power Movement, 116, 175
blockades, 33, 80–83, 97, 99, 108, 162
Bolsonaro, Jair, 9–10, 129
Bondurant, Joan V., 31
Boston Tea Party, 2, 53
Bourdieu, Pierre, 200n59
Brazil, 9–10, 86, 120–21, 124, 127, 129
Brennan, Jason, 171–72
Brennan, William, 165–66
Bristol, United Kingdom, 10

Brownlee, Kimberley, 169–70, 192n24
Bufacchi, Vittoria, 30, 33–34, 40
Bundy, Ammon, 131–32
Bundy, Cliven, 131–32
Butler, Judith, 47, 176

Canada, 11, 40, 50, 80
capitalism: corporations, 101, 150–53; and housing market, 122–23; King, Martin Luther, on, 49–50; labor theory of property, 34–35, 90; and looting, 136–38; and material inequality, 51; personal property, 35, 149–50; property law, 150–53; racialized, 138; sabotage, 78, 88–93; squatting, 127; structural violence and, 30, 39. See also corporations; private property
Capitol, United States, 10, 86–87, 168
Carmichael, Stokely, 175
Carter, April, 96–97
Carter, Chelsey, 65–66
Catholic Workers Movement, 7, 85, 96
Catholicism, 7, 11, 85, 96. See also Christianity
Celkates, Robin, 33
Chandhoke, Neera, 195n93
Charlottesville, 1
Chavez, Cesar, 57
Chenoweth, Erica, 15–17
Chicago, 176
China, 8, 20, 25, 180
Christianity, 43–44, 49–50, 128–29, 142, 177. See also Catholicism; Protestantism
civil disobedience, 2–4, 13–14, 19, 156; coercive, 31–32, 80–81; core traits, 13–14, 19, 71, 82–83; deliberative, 80–81; disruptive property disobedience, 80–81, 82–83; legal fidelity, 13, 71, 74–75, 114, 140, 161; liberal view, 13, 17, 45–46, 84, 115, 129, 181; property seizures, 114–15, 129–30; symbolic property disobedience, 55, 72–74; violence, 169–70. See also Rawls, John; sit-ins; uncivil disobedience
Civil Rights Act, 84
civil rights movement, 23, 32, 56, 60, 83–84, 134. See also Black Lives Matter
civility, 71, 82–84. See also civil disobedience
climate activism, 55–60, 79–80, 97–102, 147
Climate Direct Action, 85
climate emergency, 58, 99–100

Coady, C. A. J., 30–32, 36
coercion, 31–32, 50, 81, 170. See also force; violence
collective violence, 14–16, 18, 92, 115–16, 131–32, 170, 175–83. See also armed insurgency
Collins, Randall, 135
colonialism, 9, 15, 18, 73, 106, 110–15. See also anticolonialism; dispossession
Colston, Edward, 10
Columbia, 123
commodification, 12, 130
commons, 22–23, 127, 162, 218n34. See also anarchism; communism
communism, 34, 50
The Communist Manifesto, 149
Confederate States of America, 5, 9, 18, 25, 54–55, 65–75, 78, 106, 147, 157–58
Congress, United States, 10, 86–87
conscientiousness, 13, 82–84, 129
conservationism, 93, 120
conservatism: political, 43, 56, 63, 69, 124, 191n5; theoretical: 12, 30, 34, 111, 159
Constitution, United States, 4, 23, 64, 131–32, 165–66, 175, 177–78. See also Supreme Court, United States
corporate personhood, 151–53. See also corporations
corporations: closely held, 217n10; large for-profit, 5, 12, 22, 34, 101, 108, 117, 150–53, 168, 193n34; and natural persons, 124, 152; and personhood, 151–53; as private property, 124, 150–53; shareholders, 86, 150–53, 217n10. See also capitalism; partnerships; private property; shareholders; sole proprietorships
Corr, Anders, 125
courts. See judiciary; Supreme Court, United States.
COVID-19, 174
criminal law, 4, 8, 38, 104–5, 163, 173, 175
criminal syndicalism, 90–93, 95. See also International Workers of the World

Dakota Access Pipeline, 7–8, 26, 80, 85, 107–14
Degas, Edgar, 58
Delmas, Candice, 13, 17, 170, 174. See also uncivil disobedience

Demandt, Alexander, 67–68
democracy, 20; backsliding, 5–6, 20, 171,
  178–83; and nonviolence, 44–46, 73,
  76–77, 163–65; 170–77, 182–83; political
  equality, 3, 44–45, 73, 76–77, 164–65,
  173–74; and property, 163–66; theories of,
  44, 170–71, 220n14
democratic socialism, 49, 88
democratic underlaboring, 3
Department of Government Efficiency,
  United States, 81
Detroit, 29, 41, 141
Diggers, 117, 129
digitalization, 12, 161
dignity, 40, 43, 50, 115, 145, 158, 164
dispossession, 106, 109–17, 131
disruptive property disobedience, 5, 26,
  78–105; coercive, 80–81; communicative,
  80–81; core traits, 26, 78–87; and nonviolence, 89–95, 98–102; normative preconditions, 102–5; and property theories, 90,
  147; symbolism, 81
Dorlin, Elsa, 175
dumpster diving, 141, 215n157
Dworkin, Ronald, 202n12

Earth Liberation Front, 82, 93
EarthFirst!, 93
eastern Europe: 1989 revolutions, 61
Ebinger, Rebecca Goodgame, 7–8, 10
ecodefense, 93–95
Ecodefense: A Field Guide to Monkeywrenching, 93–94
ecotage, 7–8, 79, 81–82, 85–86, 93–103, 106
eco-terrorism, 86, 92, 95–96, 98, 104–5, 108
electoral authoritarianism, 179
Ende Gelände, 99–100
Energy Transfer Partners, 109, 114
Engels, Friedrich, 149, 216n6
environmental protests, 155, 160; disruptive,
  7–8, 10, 79–80, 85, 93–102, 164; symbolic,
  57–60. See also climate activism; ecotage
Epstein, Richard A., 159, 162
equal respect. See political equality
equality. See political equality
Espionage Act, 91
European Union, 161
expropriation. See takings
external critique, 157–58
extractivism, 108

Failer, Judy, 210n66
Fanon, Frantz, 99–100
feminism. See women's movement
First Amendment, 71. See also free
  expression
Flanagan, Peggy, 73–74
flank violence, 33
Floyd, George, 8. See also Black Lives Matter
Flynn, Elizabeth Gurley, 11, 88
The Folklore of Capitalism, 151–52
food riots, 133, 141–42
force, 28, 30–33, 129, 145, 170. See also
  coercion; violence
Forcia, Mike, 73–74
Foreman, David, 93–95, 98
fossil-fuel capitalism, 59, 98–100. See also
  capitalism; Malm, Andreas
Foucault, Michel, 188n32
Fox, Carl, 70
France, 15, 61, 78, 88, 129
France, Anatole, 123
free expression, 23–28, 71, 156
Freedberg, David, 59
French Revolution, 61
Fuchs, Martin, 121
Fuller, Lon, 218n46

Galtung, Johan, 30–32
Gamboni, Dario, 61–62
Gandhi, Mahatma: civil disobedience, 13,
  31–32, 72–73, 81; nonviolence, 99–101,
  172, 174–77
Garver, Newton, 34
genocide, 117, 133
Georgia, 69–70
German Idealism, 49. See also
  Hegel, G. W. F.; Kant, Immanuel
Germany, 58, 98–99, 104, 133–35, 180
globalization, 161–62
Grant, Ulysses, 61, 86
greens. See climate activism; environmental
  protests
Greensboro, North Carolina, 83–84
Gregory, William C., 70
guerrilla warfare, 93, 95–96. See also armed
  insurgency; collective violence

hacktivism, 9, 19, 22, 26, 85, 162
Hamas, 1, 95
Hargrove, Eugene, 94

Harvard University, 23
Havercroft, Jonathan, 18
Hegel, G. W. F., 35, 37, 49, 142, 170
Hendrix, Burke, 114–16
hidden resistance, 118
Hiroshima, Japan, 37
Hirschman, Albert O., 123
historical injustice, 109–17
Hochschild, Adam, 104
Holmes, Oliver Wendell, 64
Holocaust, 133. *See also* genocide
homelessness, 26, 106, 117–28, 141–43, 164.
    See also squatting
Homes Not Jails, 121
Honderich, Ted, 32–33
Hong Kong, 8, 20–21, 25, 76, 174. *See also*
    China; pro-democracy movements
How to Blow Up a Pipeline, 98–102, 164
Hungary, 178, 180

iconoclasm, 57–61, 66–67
ideal types, 25–27, 107
immanent critique, 157–58
incorporation. *See* corporations
India, 15, 121, 180
indigenous protests, 7, 26; civil disobedi-
    ence, 114–16; disruptive property disobe-
    dience, 80; militant resistance, 114–16;
    property seizures, 106–17; symbolic
    property disobedience, 73–75. *See also*
    Native Americans; repossessions
Indignados, 23
Industrial Workers of the World, 79, 87–98,
    104, 106
intellectual property, 12, 22, 149
internal critique, 157–58
International Monetary Fund, 12, 19, 161
International Workers of the World, 11, 79,
    87–93
intimidation, 1–2, 4, 10, 42, 61, 132, 138,
    168. *See also* violence
Iranian Revolution, 16
Israel-Gaza War, 1

January 6, 2021 protests, 10, 86–87, 168
January 8, 2023 protests, 19–20, 86–87, 168
Jasper, James M., 57
Jefferson, Thomas, 10, 86
Johnson, Kevin, 86
Jubb, Rob, 189n58, 222n68

judaism, 11. *See also* antisemitism; Holocaust
judges. *See* judiciary; rule of law
judiciary: 3–4, 10, 132, 162; civil disobedi-
    ence, 3, 13, 73; disruptive property disobe-
    dience, 7–8, 85; property seizures, 142–43;
    symbolic property disobedience, 73–74.
    See also rule of law; Supreme Court

Kant, Immanuel, 49
Katyal, Sonia K., 21–22, 107
Keane, John, 37, 44, 222n64
King, Martin Luther, 2–4; on capitalism,
    49–50; as Christian, 44, 174; on civil dis-
    obedience, 13, 23, 72; on looting, 41–42,
    137–38; on materialism, 79, 116; on
    nonviolence, 29–31, 40–44; on property,
    48–52, 79, 183; on riots, 40–44, 134–41;
    on self-defense, 115–16, 174–78. *See also*
    Black Lives Matter; civil rights movement;
    sit-ins
King, Rodney, 135
Kirkpatrick, Jennet, 181–82
Klein, Naomi, 97

labor movement, 3, 5, 11, 78–79, 87–93,
    141. *See also* International Workers of the
    World; workplace sabotage
labor theory of property, 34–35, 90, 106,
    119, 124–26, 131, 146
Lai, Ten-Herng, 67
Landless Workers Movement, 120–21, 124,
    127
Latinos, 135, 138
law enforcement. *See* police; rule of law
Lee, Robert E., 56, 60, 68, 70. *See also* Con-
    federate States of America.
legal fidelity, 13, 71, 75, 82–84, 114, 122,
    140, 161, 188n35. *See also* judiciary; rule
    of law
legality. *See* rule of law
Leninism, 102
"Letter From Birmingham City Jail," 32
Levellers, 117
Levinson, Sanford, 53
liberal democracy, 13, 45–46, 90, 104,
    171–72, 179–80
liberalism, 2, 159; on civil disobedience, 13,
    17, 84; on property, 32, 50, 72, 80, 152,
    158–59; on violence, 32. *See also* neoliber-
    alism; Rawls, John; rule of law

libertarianism, 23, 94–96, 109, 159–61, 171–74, 205n70
limited liability, 150–53. *See also* corporations
Livingston, Alexander, 194n72
Locke, John, 34–35, 125, 193n34. *See also* labor theory of property
looting: 8–9, 15, 26, 48, 132–43, 168; of art works, 214n127; King, Martin Luther, on, 41–42, 136–41; by Nazis, 133; and violence, 138–43
Los Angeles, 9, 41, 86, 135
Lost Cause, 60
Luddites, 11, 78
luxury carbon emissions, 101–2

Machiavelli, Niccolo, 172
Macpherson, C. B., 50, 159–61, 165
Malcolm X, 175
Malheur National Wildlife Preserve, 131–32
Malm, Andreas, 60, 98–102
Mandela, Nelson, 11, 206n100
Marx, Karl, 50, 127, 142, 149, 187n20, 216n6
Marxism, 66, 88, 92, 97, 101–2, 154
May, Todd, 40
Means, Gardiner, 151, 159
Michelman, Frank, 165–66
Mill, John Stuart, 127–28
Milligan, Tony, 35
Minneapolis, 8–9, 139–40
mixed economy, 165
The Modern Corporation and Private Property, 151–52
modern state, 172–73
Modi, Narenda, 178, 180
The Monkey Wrench Gang, 93–97
Montoya, Ruby Katherine, 7–8, 10, 26, 85, 96
Moody-Adams, Michele, 63–64, 74
moral holidays, 135, 139, 167. *See also* riots
moral paradoxes, 172
moral shocks, 57
Moraro, Piero, 40
Mumbai (India), 121
Munch, Eduard, 59
museums: protests, 55, 57–60, 75. *See also* climate activism
Musk, Elon, 81

Nagasaki, Japan, 37
National Review, 34, 124

Native Americans, 7, 73, 107–17. *See also* indigenous protests; repossessions
Nazis, 1, 79, 133, 150. *See also* racism; white supremacy
necessity defense, 122, 142–43
neoliberalism, 12–13, 161–63
Netherlands, 128–29
Nevada, 132
New Deal, 4, 151
New York City, 2, 25, 191n86
Newark, 29, 41
Nielsen, Kai, 35
nonviolence: absolute versus strategic, 100; civil disobedience, 3, 13–14, 17, 31–32, 72–73, 82–85, 100–102, 129–30; criticisms of, 168–78; defense of, 44–48, 167–83; and democracy, 44–46, 73, 76–77, 163–65, 170–77, 182–83; and disruptive property disobedience, 86–87, 89–90, 93, 102; King, Martin Luther, on, 13, 40–44; as prefiguration, 47–48; in property seizures, 115–17, 128–30, 141–43; in social movements, 15–17; and symbolic property disobedience, 65–68, 72, 76–77. *See also* pacifism; violence
North Dakota, 109
Norway, 58, 61
Nozick, Robert, 193n34

Oakes, Richard, 112–13
occupancy: and property, 110–14
occupations, 15, 24–26, 83, 99, 108. *See also* repossessions; squatting
Occupy Movement, 23–25
Occupy Our Homes, 119–20
Orban, Viktor, 178, 180

pacifism, 100, 128, 175. *See also* nonviolence
Palestine, 1
Palmer, Michael, 91
Pankhurst, Emmeline, 11
paramilitary orientation, 5, 79, 92–97, 103–5, 116, 128–29, 177–78
partnerships, 5, 22, 150–51. *See also* corporations; sole proprietorships
Pasternak, Ava, 18
Patil, Varun, 121
Patriot Act, 96
Pelosi, Nancy, 10, 86–87
Peñalver, Moises, 21–22, 107

Pence, Mike, 10, 87
personal property, 148–50. *See also* personality theory of property
personality theory of property, 34–35,
48–51, 67, 90, 125–26, 136, 146, 149
personhood: corporate, 151–53; and
property, 34–35, 49, 51, 67, 136, 146, 149;
and violence, 38. *See also* corporations;
personality theory of property
philosophical anarchism, 171–73
pluralism, 3, 21, 64, 114, 126, 131, 146–47,
155, 171. *See also* democracy
police: brutality, 61, 130, 171–74; militarized: 41–43, 172–75; and protests, 8–10,
24, 41, 128; racialized, 19, 21, 25–26,
139, 173; rule of law, 72, 173, 190n65;
violence targeting, 8–10, 26, 67, 139,
175, 182
political equality, 3, 44–46, 64–65, 86,
182–83, 195n86. *See also* democracy;
nonviolence
Portland, Oregon, 9
poverty, 30, 39, 42, 111, 119, 121, 136
prefiguration, 26, 107, 119, 127, 136, 141,
145, 148, 182, 191n88
private property: as bundle of rights,
22–23, 158–60; exclusion from, 23, 123,
126, 153, 159–60; extension theories,
33–35; and inequality, 51–52, 56, 109,
121–24, 126, 137, 158–66, 171; and legal
formality, 154–67; partnerships, 5, 22,
150–51; and personhood, 34, as right to
income, 159–62, 164–65; sole proprietorships, 5, 22, 150–51; theories of, 34–35,
48–52, 125–26, 148–50, 193n34. *See also*
capitalism; corporations; Locke, John;
personality theory of property; personhood; property; public property; small
businesses; takings
pro-democracy movements, 8, 76, 174
propaganda of the deed, 100. *See also* anarchism; Malm, Andreas
property: dematerialization, 149, 161–62; in
natural goods, 155–56; public versus private, 22–24, 153–54; social functions, 22;
theories of, 22–24, 33–35, 48–52, 101–2,
121–27, 158–66; thingness of, 154–55;
types of, 10, 19, 22–23, 117, 146–66. *See
also* capitalism; corporations; Locke, John;
personality theory of property; private

property; property disobedience; public
property
property disobedience: defined, 18–25; and
democratization, 105, 164–66, 183; ideal
types, 4–5, 25–27, 147–48; normative
preconditions, 143–45; political contours,
10, 19, 105; as social critique, 156–58; and
violence, 28–52. *See also* civil disobedience; disruptive property disobedience;
nonviolence; property seizures; symbolic
property disobedience
property harms, 2–6, 9–16, 25, 134,
143, 150–51, 183. *See also* property
disobedience
*Property Outlaws: How Squatters, Pirates,
and Protestors Improve the Law of Ownership,* 21–22
property rights, 12, 22–23, 158–66
property seizures, 5, 26–27, 106–45, 147–48;
core traits, 106–8; disruptive, 107; as
enactments, 106, 136; and nonviolence,
114–17, 128–32, 140; normative preconditions, 144–45; and property theories,
121–28, 135–36, 142–44, 158–60; symbolism, 107–8; types, 5, 107–8. *See also*
looting; repossessions; squatting
proprietization, 12, 162
protest repertoires, 14
Protestantism, 11, 129. *See also* Catholicism;
Christianity
Proudhon, Pierre-Joseph, 110, 142
public housing, 127, 163
public monuments, 60–75. *See also* symbolic
property disobedience
public property, 23–24, 34, 55, 62, 70–72,
75–76, 82, 94, 101, 153–54. *See also*
property
public schools, 153–54

racial capitalism, 138
racism, 9, 19, 54–55, 60–75, 106, 116, 124,
131–32, 138–39. *See also* Nazis; white
supremacy
Radin, Margaret Jane, 34–35, 51, 216n4
Rawls, John: on civil disobedience, 13, 19,
75; on nonviolence, 17, 145–65; militant
resistance, 17
resistance, 17, 45–46, 140, 180–81. *See also*
liberalism
Reagan, Ronald, 65, 159

reclamations. *See* repossessions

Recznick, Jessica, 7–8, 10, 26, 96

Red Power Movement, 112–14. *See also* Native Americans

Red Scare, 79, 90–93, 95

Reflections on Violence, 92

regulatory state, 159–62, 218n43

repossessions, 108–17

repression, 4, 8, 79, 88, 90–93, 128, 163, 177–79, 185n9. *See also* backlash, political

resistance, 17, 45–46, 114–16, 140, 181–84; civil, 15–16; hidden, 118. *See also* collective violence; liberalism

retaliation, 8, 11, 27, 135, 177, 182

retribution. *See* retaliation

Richmond, Virginia, 70, 73

Rifkin, Jeremy, 12

right to assemble, 24–25

right to housing, 130

rights. *See* First Amendment; free expression; property rights; rule of law; Second Amendment; social rights

rights of nature, 59, 155

riots, 4, 17–18, 26, 29, 40–44, 76, 134–38

robinhoodism, 141–43

rule of law, 1–2, 72, 83–84, 104–5, 162–64, 173, 179, 182–83. *See also* judiciary; legal fidelity

Sabl, Andrew, 181

sabotage, 8–9, 11, 14–17, 20, 78–85, 107. *See also* disruptive property disobedience; ecotage

Saint Paul, Minnesota, 73, 139–40

San Francisco, California, 112–14

Santos, Neymar da Silva, 9

Scarry, Elain, 37

Schedler, Andreas, 179

Schulz, Johannes, 64, 68–69

Scott, James, 118

Sea Shepherds, 93

Seattle, Washington, 9, 12, 130

Second Amendment, 177–78

secrecy, 24, 74, 79, 81–83, 85, 90, 93–97, 142. *See also* anonymity

self-defense, 8, 89, 128–29, 182, 221n37, 221n55; individual versus collective, 114–17, 175–78. *See also* collective violence; guerilla warfare

settler colonialism, 109–17, 131. *See also* colonialism

shareholders, 86, 150–53, 217n10. *See also* corporations

sharing economy, 162

Sharp, Gene, 47, 129, 195n98

Shelby, Tommie, 140

Shklar, Judith, 152

Shue, Henry, 101

Singer, Peter, 74–75

sit-ins, 14, 24, 33, 83–84. *See also* civil disobedience

slavery, 11, 60. *See also* Confederate States of America

small businesses, 9, 18, 76, 135, 139, 141, 150–54, 162, 168

Smith, Walker C., 88–89

Smith, William, 144–45, 202n10

social acceleration, 56, 149

social democracy, 9, 159, 161

social rights, 50, 159–62, 165–66

sole proprietorships, 5, 22, 150–51

South Carolina, 59, 60

Spain, 129

squatting, 5, 22, 26, 52, 117–32, 162. *See also* property seizures

Standing Rock Reservation, 109. *See also* Dakota Access Pipeline

statues. *See* public monuments; symbolic property disobedience

Stephan, Maria J., 15–17

stigmatization, 55, 64–65

Stone Mountain, 69

Stop Oil, 58–59

strikes, 32, 88, 151, 192n24, 193n35

structural violence, 30–31, 39, 177. *See also* violence

Supreme Court, United States, 4, 64, 84, 165, 177. *See also* Constitution, United States; judiciary; rule of law

Sweden, 60, 98, 180

symbolic property disobedience, 4–5, 53–77; and civil disobedience, 55, 71–75; core traits, 25–26, 53–60; and nonviolence, 72–77; normative preconditions, 71–77; and private property, 47, 62, 71, 75–77; and public property, 62, 64, 71, 142. *See also* iconoclasm; public monuments

symbolic violence, 200n59

symbolism, political, 53–57

takings, 5, 12, 159, 163, 210n50
Taliban, 58, 98
terrorism, 1, 7–8, 58, 86, 95–96, 101, 105.
    See also eco-terrorism
Thompson, E. P., 211n79, 215n166
Tilly, Charles, 14, 16
Trautmann, William E., 88, 90
Treaty of Fort Laramie, 109, 112, 207n6
tree spiking, 86, 93
Truman, Harry, 84
Trump, Donald, 1–2, 8, 66–68, 130, 141,
    168, 178, 181. See also authoritarian
    populism

Umbrella Movement, 8
uncivil disobedience, 4, 13, 17–18, 67, 171,
    181–82. See also Delmas, Candice
unhoused. See homelessness
United Farm Workers Movement, 57
United Kingdom, 78, 122, 129

Vail, Colorado, 82, 93
Van Gogh, Vincent, 58–60
vandalism. See symbolic property
    disobedience
Vasudevan, Alexander, 130
Vietnam War, 53, 63, 94
vigilantism, 17, 92, 174, 177, 182
Vinthagen, Stellan, 47–48
violence: and civil disobedience, 17, 33,
    169–70; core traits, 16, 28, 30–40; defense
    of, 169–78; minimalist versus maximalist
    views, 30–34, 39–40, 95; and property,

28–52; and vulnerability, 36–39, 55. See
    also armed insurgency; collective vio-
    lence; nonviolence; resistance
Vorobej, Mark, 36

Waldron, Jeremy, 35, 51, 110–14
Walz, Tim, 73–74
Washington, D. C., 10, 58, 63, 130
Watts, California, 41, 138
Weber, Max, 191n87, 211n3
Wesche, Tilo, 154–56
West Virginia, 142
whistleblowing, 9, 17
White Earth Band of Ojibwe, 73–74
white supremacy, 1, 19, 22, 25, 54, 60, 63, 66,
    68, 75, 131–32, 158. See also Nazis; racism
Why Civil Resistance Works: The Strategic
    Logic of Nonviolent Conflict, 15–16
Williams, Robert F., 175
Wilson, Woodrow, 104
Wobblies. See Industrial Workers of the
    World
Wolff, Robert Paul, 33
women's movement, 11, 21, 48
workplace sabotage, 78–79, 88–93. See also
    International Workers of the World
World Trade Organization, 12, 19, 161
Wright, R. George, 143

Xi, Jinping, 180

Zick, Timothy, 24
Zizek, Slavoj, 191n6

ACKNOWLEDGMENTS

I have been extraordinarily fortunate to have received critical feedback from colleagues who patiently tolerated my efforts to formulate early versions of ideas brought together in this volume. Conference, seminar, and workshop participants in Bloomington, Darmstadt, Dublin, Erfurt, Frankfurt, Hamburg, Jena, Madison, Madrid, Mexico City, Paris, Reading, Richmond, Sao Paulo, Schenectady, and Stockholm constructively insisted that I work harder to clarify my claims. I am grateful to everyone who did so, but special thanks to those who were particularly generous with their time: Isabelle Aubert, Purnima Bose, Cigdem Cidam, Maeve Cooke, Jessica Flanigan, Rainer Forst, Dirk Jörke, Rob Jubb, Maria Pia Lara, David Lefkowitz, Agustin Jose Menendez, Darrel Moellendorf, Peter Niesen, Marcos Nobre, Ludwig Norman, Christy Ochoa, Markus Patberg, Hartmut Rosa, Laila Yousef Sandoval, Howard Schweber, and Bianca Tavolari. Colleagues and friends at Indiana University also offered feedback and support, but a few stand out for their words of encouragement: Purnima Bose, Jeffrey Isaac, Michael Morgan, and Susan Williams.

During the summer of 2022, I was a Distinguished Visiting Lecturer at the Mecila Center (Sao Paulo), where I gained from lively exchanges with students and scholars there and at CEBRAP. Marcos Nobre, Bianca Tavolari, Gabriel Brito, Marina Slhessarenko Barreto, Leonardo Barbosa, Joaquim Toledo, Tomaz Amorim, and Roberta Hesse hosted and generously showed me around Sao Paulo. In the spring of 2024, I spent three months at the Max Weber Center for Advanced Studies (Erfurt, Germany). Thanks to the Center's Co-Directors—Bettina Hollstein, Jöerg Rüpke, and Hartmut Rosa—for the invitation. Markus Hoppe and Kathleen Rottleb helped with important everyday matters. Many colleagues in Erfurt generously commented on parts of the volume: Lars Aaberg, Stefan Bargheer, Supriya Chaudhuri, Martin Fuchs, Tom Hamilton, Bettina Hollstein, Gesa Lindemann, Andreas Pettenkofer, Katja Rakow, Hartmut Rosa, and Frederic Vandenberghe.

Elisabeth Maselli at the University of Pennsylvania Press has patiently worked with me on the manuscript since I first laid out a crude version of what I wanted to do. Thanks, of course, to the anonymous readers who provided critical but constructive feedback.

While finishing the manuscript, I learned of the passing of Ingeborg Maus, a German political theorist from whom I have learned so much. I suspect she would have disagreed with some claims here, but I hope her contrarian spirit can be detected in its pages.

As always, my greatest debts are to Julia, Zoe, and Lily.

Some snippets of the book have previously appeared as parts of journal articles in *Annual Review of Law & Ethics, Harvard Review of Philosophy, Journal of International Political Theory, Political Research Quarterly,* and *Populism.* I thank them for permitting me to reprint some previously published remarks.

To my astonishment, I have now spent thirty-five years teaching and writing about political theory. Looking back, I realize that most of my efforts have revolved around trying to reform our crisis-ridden democracies. Given the unsettled political times we face, it would be absurd to declare victory. A quote from Audre Lorde that I first came across far away from home, on a billboard at Goethe University in Frankfurt, nicely captures my efforts in recent decades and their relationship to my country: "Sometimes we are blessed with being able to choose the time, and the arena, and the manner of our revolution. But more usually we must do battle where we are standing."[1]

---

1. Audre Lord, *A Burst of Light and Other Essays* (Mineola, NY: Dover, 2017), 119.

www.ingramcontent.com/pod-product-compliance
Lightning Source LLC
Chambersburg PA
CBHW030303100426
42812CB00002B/549